[redacted]

MW01710966

STUDY GUIDE
with EXERCISES & CASE STUDIES

to accompany

Johns
ORGANIZATIONAL BEHAVIOR
UNDERSTANDING AND MANAGING LIFE AT WORK
Fourth Edition

John M. Usher
Memorial University of Newfoundland

ADDISON-WESLEY

Addison-Wesley is an imprint
of Addison Wesley Longman

[redacted]

STUDY GUIDE with Exercises and Case Studies to accompany Johns, *Organizational Behavior: Understanding and Managing Life at Work*, Fourth Edition.

Reprinted with corrections April, 1997.

Copyright © 1996 Addison Wesley Longman, Inc.

All rights reserved. Printed in the United States of America. No part of this book may be used or reproduced in any manner whatsoever without written permission from the publisher except, testing materials may be copied for classroom use. For information address Addison Wesley Longman, One Jacob Way, Reading, MA 01867-3999.

ISBN: 0-673-98145-2

3 4 5 6 7 8 9 10-DOC-01 00 99 98 97

Table of Contents

TO THE STUDENT OF
ORGANIZATIONAL BEHAVIOR

The purpose of this book is to help you better understand the concepts in the textbook **ORGANIZATIONAL BEHAVIOR**. Using this book should help you to get better grades. Each chapter contains the following sections:

1. Learning objectives
2. Key concepts
3. Chapter summary
4. Pre-testing your understanding of the chapter
5. Post-testing for exams
6. Answer sheet
7. Exercise or Case study

Below is an explanation of the sections of this study guide, with suggestions for use.

LEARNING OBJECTIVES This section provides a clear statement of what you are expected to learn as a result of studying the chapter. Review these objectives and use them as goals as you work through the study guide materials.

KEY CONCEPTS This section draws your attention to important, new terminology and concepts which you will be exposed to in the accompanying text. You will be able to define each of these terms at the end of each study guide chapter if you have fully understood the material presented.

CHAPTER SUMMARY This section reviews the major information presented in the text. It appears in outline form clearly showing all headings for easy reference to the text. The summary is not meant to replace reading the chapter, it is to help reinforce the most important points in the text. Note that the key concepts identified in bold in the text are also identified in bold in this study guide so that you can easily find the key concepts and their definitions.

PRE-TESTING YOUR UNDERSTANDING OF THE CHAPTER This section is designed to test your understanding of the chapter shortly after reading it. The pre-test contains three parts:

1. **Key Concepts Matching**. The key concepts are the most important concepts from the chapter. To help you learn them, all the key terms in the text are defined for you to complete in a matching format. The number varies based on the number of key concepts. After matching the key concepts check your answers against the answer sheet at the end of the chapter. Review any that you got wrong before going on to the next section.

2. **True/False Questions**. Each chapter contains 20 true/false questions. Answer the questions then check your answers against the answer sheet. Review the material in the text for any question you got wrong, or were not sure of the answer, before going on to the next section.

3. **Multiple-Choice Questions**. Each chapter contains 10 multiple-choice questions. Answer the questions then check your answers against the answer sheet. Review the material in the text for any question you got wrong, or were not sure of the answer, before going on to the next section.

POST-TESTING FOR EXAMS This section is designed to help you prepare for exams. Many of the concepts covered in the "pretesting your understanding of the chapter" section are included in this section as well, but phrased differently to be sure you understand them for the exam. It contains four parts:

1. **True/False Questions**. Each chapter contains 10 true/false questions. Answer the questions then check your answers against the answer sheet. Review the material in the text for any question you got wrong, or were not sure of the answer, before going on to the next section.

2. **Multiple-Choice Questions**. Each chapter contains 20 multiple choice questions. Check your answers against the answer sheet, and review any material you got wrong or did not understand before going on to the next section.

3. **Application Situations Exercise**. Each chapter contains 10 matching questions to test your understanding of the key concepts. The exact answers are usually not in the text, you can find them in the answer sheet. Many test questions are based on the key concepts in the text. If you are not sure you understand all the key concepts review the key concept matching section before the exam.

4. **Short Answer Questions**. Each chapter contains 10 short answer questions requiring you to fill-in the missing word(s).

ANSWER SHEET This section contains the answers to all the above section parts. It appears after the short answer questions. Check your answers against it to see how well you did, and to find out what material you need to spend more time on. Follow this procedure for each section before proceeding to the next section.

If you utilize all these different sections and the parts of the sections, and understand the material, you should do well on the objective sections of the exams. If your instructor uses essay questions, understanding the concepts in the text can help you to write the answers.

EXERCISE / CASE STUDY Each chapter contains either an exercise or a case study. This section is designed for in-class use. However, if your instructor elects not to use these materials in class, you can gain knowledge and understanding of the material by completing them on your own. Your course instructor will have suggested solutions for the case studies and for those exercises which call for specific answers. This Study Guide was designed to include cases that focus on the Canadian environment. Seven cases specifically reflect this; those cases are: Regina Medical Systems (p. 62), Striking Oil (p. 78), Claire (p. 94), Canadian Nuclear Industries (p. 131), Boivin Realties Ltd. (p. 147), ADCO Pharmacy (p. 184), Managing the Marketing Department (p. 221).

Good Luck in this course. We hope you will enjoy the study of organizational behavior.

John Usher & Deborah Hurst

CHAPTER 1

ORGANIZATIONAL BEHAVIOR AND MANAGEMENT

- THE GOALS OF THE FIELD.
- CONTRAST THE CLASSICAL VIEWPOINT OF MANAGEMENT WITH THE LEARNING OBJECTIVES.
- DEFINE ORGANIZATIONS AND DESCRIBE THEIR BASIC CHARACTERISTICS.
- EXPLAIN THE CONCEPT OF ORGANIZATIONAL BEHAVIOR AND DESCRIBE WHICH THE HUMAN RELATIONS MOVEMENT ADVOCATED.
- DESCRIBE THE CONTEMPORARY CONTINGENCY APPROACH TO MANAGEMENT.
- EXPLAIN WHAT MANAGERS DO - THEIR ROLES, ACTIVITIES, AGENDAS FOR ACTION, AND THOUGHT PROCESSES.
- DESCRIBE THE SOCIETAL AND GLOBAL TRENDS THAT ARE SHAPING CONTEMPORARY MANAGEMENT CONCERNS.

KEY CONCEPTS

Organizations

Organizational behavior

Management

Classical viewpoint

Scientific management

Bureaucracy

Hawthorne studies

Human relations movement

Contingency approach

Intuition

Total quality management (TQM)

CHAPTER SUMMARY

Key concepts are identified by **bold** *faced type.*

I. What are Organizations?

A. Social Inventions

Organizations are social inventions for accomplishing common goals through group effort. Their essential characteristic is the coordinated presence of people, not necessarily things. Of primary interest in this course are understanding people and managing them to work effectively.

B. Goal Achievement

Individuals are assembled into organizations for a reason. In the private sector, some organizations have goals like selling cars, delivering news, or winning basketball games. In the nonprofit and public sectors, organizations may have such goals as saving souls, promoting the arts, helping the needy, or educating people. Virtually all organizations have *survival* as a goal.

C. Group Effort

To achieve these goals, organizations are staffed with people who operate together in a coordinated fashion. At times, individuals can accomplish much. But by combining greater resources and wealth with effective teamwork, organizations have become the dominant producing agents in the world.

II. What is Organizational Behavior?

Organizational behavior refers to the attitudes and behavior of groups or individuals within organizations. The field of organizational behavior involves the systematic study of these attitudes and behaviors, and should be of interest to all students of management.

III. Why Study Organizational Behavior?

You should be interested in this field because you will find that behavior of people in an organizational setting is a fascinating study. Aside from its being interesting, organizational behavior is also practical since most of us are members of organizations. Knowledge of human behavior will aid us in a variety of roles such as consumers, producers, and managers.

Knowing about organizational behavior will also aid us in understanding how organizations function, from the smallest corporations to the highest levels of government.

IV. Goals of the Field

The main goals of organizational behavior are:
prediction - knowing in advance the behavior of others;
explanation - knowing why events and behavior occur;

management- the art of getting things accomplished in organizations through others.

Although achieving perfection in these goals is impossible, managers do wish to anticipate how workers will react to change. Managers also need to know why production might or might not slow down. Managers also need to know of workers satisfaction or dissatisfaction. Finally, when the practice of management is directed to the influencing of worker behavior, managers need to know how best to apply rewards and other inducements to bring about the desired worker response. Managers acquire, allocate, and utilize physical and human resources to accomplish goals.

To accomplish these goals, managers should use careful analysis before undertaking actions. With adequate analysis managers do have a better chance of dealing with problems and achieving the desired behavior. One goal of this book is to aid in improving the reader's analytic abilities.

V. Early Prescriptions Concerning Management

A. The Classical View and Bureaucracy

During the early 1900's, a number of experienced managers and consultants including Henri Fayol, James D. Mooney, and Lyndall Urwick were the first writers to set down their thoughts on organizing. This **classical viewpoint** tended to advocate high specialization of labor, intensive coordination, and centralized decision making.

Frederick Taylor's approach, called Scientific Management, was focused more on shop floor activities than the administrative prescriptions of the classical view. **Scientific Management** was a system for using research to determine the optimum degree of specialization and standardization of work tasks.

Max Weber, a German academic, described **bureaucracy** as an ideal type of organization that included a strict chain of command, detailed rules, high specialization, centralized power, and selection and promotion based on technical competence.

B. The Human Relations Movement and a Critique of Bureaucracy

The **Hawthorne studies** involved research conducted at the Hawthorne plant of Western Electric in the 1920's and 1930's that illustrated how psychological and social processes affect productivity and work adjustment.

After World War II, researchers and theorists such as Chris Argyris, Alvin Gouldner, and Rensis Likert took up the theme of the Hawthorne studies. This **human relations movement** was a critique of classical management and bureaucracy that advocated management styles that were more participative and oriented toward employee needs.

VI. Contemporary Management - The Contingency Approach

Contemporary scholars and managers recognize the merits of both the classical approach and the human relations movement. This **contingency approach** to management recognizes that there is no one best way to manage, and that an appropriate management style depends on the demands of the situation.

VII. What Do Managers Do?

A. Managerial Roles

Henry Mintzberg conducted an in-depth study of the behavior of managers and found a rather complex set of roles. Interpersonal roles were those which were used to establish and maintain interpersonal relations. These included the figurehead role, leadership role, and liaison role. Informational roles were concerned with various ways the manager receives and transmits information. Roles in this group included the monitor role, disseminator role and spokesperson role. The final set were decisional roles - roles which involved managerial decision making: the entrepreneur role, the disturbance handler role, the resource allocator role and the negotiator role.

B. Managerial Activities

Fred Luthans and colleagues determined that managers engaged in four basic types of activities: routine communications (exchanging information, handling paperwork), traditional management (planning, decision making, controlling), networking (interacting with outsiders, socializing, politicking) and human resource management (managing conflict, motivating/reinforcing, staffing, training and development).

C. Managerial Agendas

John Kotter has also studied the behaviors of successful general managers and found a strong pattern of similarities that he grouped into the categories of agenda setting, networking, and agenda implementation

D. Managerial Minds

Other researchers have examined not how managers act, but how managers think. Herbert Simon and Daniel Isenberg stress the role of intuition in good management. **Intuition** is problem identification and solving based on systematic education and experiences that locate problems within a network of previously acquired information.

E. International Managers

The style with which managers do what they do and the emphasis given to various activities will vary greatly across cultures because of cross-cultural variations in values that affect both managers' and subordinates' expectations about interpersonal interaction. Geert Hofstede has done pioneering work on cross-cultural differences in values.

VIII. Some Contemporary Management Concerns

A. Diversity - Local and Global

Several factors are influencing the demographics of the North American workforce. More women are entering the workforce and visible minorities are growing as a percentage of overall numbers. Diversity of age is also a factor, as are increased legal and social pressures to better integrate previously disenfranchised groups like women, gays, and the disabled.

Multinational expansion, strategic alliances, and joint ventures between global partners are also bringing people into contact with their counterparts in organizations in other cultures as never before.

B. Morale Crisis?

Downsizing, restructuring, and reengineering have had a profound effect on organizations as firms respond to increased global competition and technological change. Surveys show that the consequences of these events have been decreased morale and shifting loyalties among the survivors.
While people remain attached to the work they do, they are much less attached to their employers.

C. A Focus on Quality and Speed

Many organizations have also begun to pursue **total quality management (TQM)**, a systematic attempt to achieve continuous improvement in the quality of an organization's products and/or services.

PRE-TESTING YOUR UNDERSTANDING OF THE CHAPTER

Key Concepts Matching

Match the letter of the key concepts with the appropriate definitions.

A. Bureaucracy
B. Classical viewpoint
C. Contingency approach
D. Hawthorne studies
E. Human relations movement
F. Intuition
G. Management
H. Organizational behavior
I. Organizations
J. Scientific management
K. Total quality management

______1. Social inventions for accomplishing common goals through group effort.

______2. The behavior and attitudes of individuals and groups in organizations.

______3. The art of getting things accomplished in organizations through others.

______4. An early prescription on management that advocated high specialization of labor, intensive coordination, and centralized decision making.

______5. Frederick Taylor's system for using research to determine the optimum degree of specialization and standardization of work tasks.

______6. Max Weber's ideal type of organization that included a strict chain of command, detailed rules, high specialization, centralized power, and selection and promotion based on technical merit.

______7. Research conducted at the Hawthorne plant of Western Electric in the 1920's and 1930's that illustrated how psychological and social processes affect productivity and work adjustment.

______8. A critique of classical management and bureaucracy that advocated management styles that were more participative and oriented toward employee needs.

______9. An approach to management that recognizes that there is no one best way to manage, and that an appropriate management style depends on the demands of the situation.

_____10. Problem identification and solving based on systematic education and experiences that locate problems within a network of previously acquired information.

_____11. A systematic attempt to achieve continuous improvement in the quality of an organization's products and/or services.

True/False Questions

Circle the letter of the correct answer.

T	F	1. Organizational behavior deals with the handling of materials in organizations.
T	F	2. Most of us are not members of organizations.
T	F	3. Predicting the behavior of others is an essential requirement of everyday living.
T	F	4. Prediction and explanation are exactly the same process.
T	F	5. The phrase "It depends" is an example of poor management.
T	F	6. Organizations are often random collections of workers.
T	F	7. Networking is an important managerial activity.
T	F	8. Speedy delivery of products is an aspect of quality.
T	F	9. Much of the work now done in organizations is performed by individuals.
T	F	10. The field of organizational behavior often deals with contingencies.
T	F	11. Many workers cite the size of their employer as an important factor in job choice.
T	F	12. Being able to influence the behavior of workers is a good example of coercion.
T	F	13. Knowing why and how events occur is a good example of explanation.
T	F	14. The disturbance handler role is one of Mintzberg's interpersonal roles.

T F 15. The field of organizational behavior is concerned with how organizations can survive and adapt to change.

T F 16. To help organizations survive, frequent worker turnover is necessary.

T F 17. Organizational behavior is reasonably concerned with creative decision making and problem solving.

T F 18. Organizations need not be concerned with people who operate in a coordinated manner.

T F 19. Worker behavior is really of little importance to successful organizations.

T F 20. All organizations exist to carry out goals.

Multiple-Choice Questions

Select the correct answer.

______1. Predictions might properly be defined as

A. influencing future events.
B. knowing when events will occur.
C. knowing why future events occur.
D. taking action to award negative outcomes.

______2. The early writers who set down the classical viewpoint on management were

A. business school professors.
B. newspaper editors.
C. managers and consultants.
D. trade unionists.

______3. Max Weber saw bureaucracy as an ideal type of organization that included all of the following, *except*

A. decentralized decision making.
B. detailed rules.
C. a strict chain of command.
D. high specialization.

______4. All of the following are described by Mintzberg as decision making roles, *except*

A. entrepreneur role.
B. leadership role.
C. resource allocator role.
D. negotiator role.

______5. Downsizing, restructuring, and reengineering have had a profound effect on organizations. Surveys show that the consequences of these events include

A. renewed loyalties between organizations and individuals.
B. greater levels of motivation among survivors.
C. decreased morale.
D. increased commitment.

______6. Using the phrase, "It depends" is one example of

A. inept management.
B. contingencies.
C. understatement.
D. stalling for time.

______7. The most essential item for an organization's existence is

A. people.
B. resources.
C. location.
D. finances.

______8. Problem identification and solving based on systematic education and experiences that locate problems within a network of previously acquired information is

A. networking.
B. logic.
C. forecasting.
D. intuition.

______9. The study of organizational behavior deals with

A. the operation of companies within a nation.
B. the operation of companies internationally.
C. competition among companies.
D. the attitudes and behavior of people within organizations.

______10. Individuals are collected into organizations to

A. provide jobs for workers.
B. to carry out goals.
C. to assure high profits.
D. to reduce unemployment figure.

POST-TESTING FOR EXAMS

True/False Questions

Circle the letter of the correct answer.

T F 1. Organizations are actually governmental inventions and contrivances.
T F 2. The purpose of any organization is to achieve certain general goals.
T F 3. An implied goal of any organization is its survival.
T F 4. For organizations to succeed, people must operate in a coordinated fashion.
T F 5. Management is the art of getting things accomplished in organizations through others.
T F 6. A good manager can operate effectively without analysis when dealing with problems.
T F 7. The Hawthorne studies were conducted by Nathaniel Hawthorne.
T F 8. Pressure on organizations to cope with cross-cultural issues will decrease in the future.
T F 9. Organizations usually function despite the departure of specific individuals.
T F 10. The human relations movement was started during the social unrest of the 60's.

Multiple-Choice Questions

Select the correct answer.

______1. All of the following are considered goals of organizational behavior except for
A. prediction.
B. management.
C. profitability.
D. explanation.

______2. Events of interest that studying organizational behavior can help us to understand include
A. using toy model rocket engines to blow up trucks.
B. having to bar employees from starting work too early.
C. forming a committee dedicated to fun in the workplace.
D. all of the above.

______3. After World War II, a number of researchers and theorists took up the theme of the Hawthorne studies. This movement was called
A. Friends of Hawthorne.
B. the Group of Seven.
C. the human relations movement.
D. the peace movement.

______4. The general answer to many managerial questions is
A. "It depends."
B. "We can do it."
C. "We need more money."
D. "Blame the government."

______5. Organizations can be described as
A. government bureaucracies.
B. any group of three or more people.
C. social inventions for accomplishing goals.
D. profit seeking companies.

______6. A study of managerial activities found
A. managing information is crucial to career success.
B. handling paperwork is the most often engaged in activity.
C. people who were promoted quickly tended to do more networking.
D. planning was one of the least engaged in activities.

______7. Determining why workers behave as they do is an example of
A. prediction.
B. explanation.
C. controlling.
D. detective work.

______8. In Henry Mintzberg's research, the disseminator role is an example of
A. an interpersonal role.
B. an informational role.
C. a decisional role.
D. a routine communications activity

______9. _________ was intended as a critique of the classical viewpoint and bureaucracy.
A. The contingency approach.
B. Scientific management.
C. The human relations movement.
D. The New Deal.

______10. All of the following are affecting the demographics of the North American workplace <u>except:</u>
A. entry of more women.
B. growth in numbers of visible minorities.
C. large numbers of immigrants from Eastern Europe.
D. an aging population.

______11. Organizations basically require the coordinated presence of ______ to accomplish their goals.
A. things
B. resources
C. people
D. rules and regulations

______12. Individuals are usually assembled into organizations to
A. become rich.
B. accomplish goals.
C. attain status.
D. build relationships.

______13. All of the following are of concern to the field of organizational behavior *except*
A. minimal turnover.
B. minimal levels of absence.
C. reasonable performance.
D. maximum profits.

______14. Organizations achieve their goals with people who operate in some ______ manner.
A. individual.
B. coordinated.
C. creative.
D. rational.

______15. The ability to anticipate future profits is an example of
A. prediction.
B. good accounting methods.
C. intuition.
D. inspiration.

______16. The name most often associated with scientific management is
A. Lord & Taylor
B. Frederick Taylor
C. Frederick's of Hollywood
D. Max Weber

______17. Knowing why and how events occur is an example of
A. prediction.
B. science.
C. wisdom.
D. explanation.

______18. Marriott International, Inc. is a provider of
A. building products.
B. herbicides and hormones.
C. lodging and food service.
D. camera equipment.

______19. Which of the following factors did more workers say was "very important" in deciding to take a job with a current employer:

A. Supervisor.
B. Salary/wage.
C. Advancement opportunity.
D. Open communication.

______20. Chrysler and Ford are beginning to approach the Japanese standard for getting a new car design into the showroom in

A. 6 months.
B. 18 months.
C. 3 years.
D. 5 years.

Application situations Exercise

Match the key concepts with the statements that best describe them.

A. Bureaucracy	G. Management
B. Classical viewpoint	H. Organizational behavior
C. Contingency approach	I. Organizations
D. Hawthorne studies	J. Scientific management
E. Human relations movement	K. Total quality management
F. Intuition	

_____ 1. We wanted to achieve continuous improvement in the quality of our organization's products.

_____ 2. Industrial Engineering suggested that we use research to determine the optimum degree of specialization and standardization of work tasks.

_____ 3. Some of the older guys thought that sounded good, but wanted to add intensive coordination and centralized decision making.

_____ 4. Max said he thought we were on a roll and added a strict chain of command and selection and promotion based on technical competence.

_____ 5. Industrial Relations didn't think much of any of their suggestions! They felt that the solution was a management style that was more participative and oriented to employee needs.

_____ 6. Fortunately, the systematic education and experiences of the boss helped her to realize that she'd heard all of these approaches before.

_____ 7. What we do, she said, really depends on a variety of things.

_____ 8. We've got this big social invention for accomplishing common goals through group effort.

_____ 9. I'm surrounded by people who claim to know the art of getting things accomplished through others.

_____ 10. What is crucial to our success is the ability to understand and influence the attitudes and behavior or individuals and groups in this organization.

Short Answer Questions

Fill-in the missing word(s).

1. The ________ of the behavior of others is an essential requirement of our everyday lives.

2. In the Netherlands, managers are supposed to exhibit modesty and to strive for ________ .

3. Mintzberg's three interpersonal roles are _________, leader role, and liaison role.

4. Saying "it depends" is an example of the ________ approach.

5. Research on managerial activities suggests that successful managers (when measured by unit effectiveness and subordinate satisfaction) tended to do more _______ .

6. _______ organizations might have as their goals, the saving of souls or the caring of the ill.

7. Criteria for selection and promotion based on impersonal technical skills rather than nepotism and favoritism is a characteristic of _________.

8. Almost everyone belongs to a group that is a part of a larger _______ .

9. As a result of a ________ effort, Boeing designed the 747 jumbo jet.

10. The writings of experienced managers and consultants from the early 1900's is termed the ________ .

ANSWER SHEET FOR CHAPTER 1

PRE-TESTING YOUR UNDERSTANDING OF THE CHAPTER

Key Concepts Matching

1. I 2. H 3. G 4. B 5. J 6. A 7. D 8. E 9. C 10. F 11. K

True/False Questions

1. F 2. F 3. T 4. F 5. F 6. F 7. T 8. T 9. F 10. T 11. F 12. F 13. T 14. F 15. T 16. F 17. T 18. F 19. F 20. T

Multiple-Choice Questions

1. B 2. C 3. A 4. B 5. C 6. B 7. A 8. D 9. D 10. B

POST-TESTING FOR EXAMS

True/False Questions

1. F 2. T 3. T 4. T 5. T 6. F 7. F 8. F 9. T 10. F

Multiple-Choice Questions

1. C 2. D 3. C 4. A 5. C 6. C 7. A 8. B 9. C 10. C 11. C 12. B 13. D 14. B 15. A 16. B 17. D 18. C 19. D 20. C

Application Situations Exercise

1. K 2. J 3. B 4. A 5. E 6. F 7. C 8. I 9. G 10. H

Short Answer Questions

1. prediction 2. consensus 3. figurehead 4. contingency
5. human resource management 6. non-profit 7. bureaucracy
8. organization 9. group 10. classical viewpoint

EXERCISE FOR CHAPTER 1

INTRODUCTIONS

Objectives:

1. To get acquainted with some of your classmates.
2. To gain a better understanding of the course coverage.
3. To get to know more about your instructor.

Procedure 1: (1-3 minutes)
Break into groups of four to six, preferably with people you do not know, or know well.

Procedure 2: (8-12 minutes)
Each group member tells the others his or her name and two or three significant things about himself or herself. After all members have finished, ask each other questions to get to know each other better.

Procedure 3: (2-3 minutes)
Can any group member call the others by name? If yes do so, if not each group member should say his or her name. All members should call the others by name. Continue until everyone does so.

Procedure 4: (5-12 minutes)
Elect a spokesperson/recorder for your group. The members select specific questions to ask the instructor under the three categories below. The spokesperson should not identify who asked what questions.

1. Course expectations. What do you hope to learn or gain from this course? What topics do you want to learn about? (The instructor will tell the class if this is a planned part of the course.)
2. Doubts or concerns about this course. Is there anything about the course that you don't understand? Express any doubts or concerns you have.
3. Questions about the instructor. What would you like to know about the instructor to get to know him or her better? List questions to ask him or her.

Procedure 5: (10-20 minutes)
Each spokesperson ask the group's question under one category at a time. When all questions from category 1 are asked and answered, proceed to category 2 then 3. Spokespersons should not repeat questions asked by other groups.

Discussion Questions: For the groups and/or class

1. Is it important to know and call people by name? Why or why not?
2. What can you do to improve your ability to remember people's names when you first meet them, and at later times?

Conclusion:

The instructor may make concluding remarks.

Application: (2-4 minutes)

What have I learned through this exercise? How will I use this knowledge in the future?

Sharing:

Volunteers give their answers to the application section.

Copyright 1985, Robert N. Lussier, used with permission.

CHAPTER 2

FINDING OUT ABOUT ORGANIZATIONAL BEHAVIOR

LEARNING OBJECTIVES:

- EXPLAIN THE DIFFICULTIES OF RELYING TOTALLY ON COMMON SENSE TO UNDERSTAND ORGANIZATIONAL BEHAVIOR.
- EXPLAIN WHAT A HYPOTHESIS IS AND DIFFERENTIATE RELIABILITY FROM VALIDITY.
- UNDERSTAND OBSERVATIONAL RESEARCH AND DISTINGUISH BETWEEN PARTICIPANT AND DIRECT OBSERVATION.
- DESCRIBE CORRELATIONAL RESEARCH AND EXPLAIN WHY CAUSATION CANNOT BE INFERRED FROM CORRELATION.
- EXPLAIN EXPERIMENTAL RESEARCH AND DISTINGUISH BETWEEN INDEPENDENT AND DEPENDENT VARIABLES.
- DISCUSS THE RELATIVE ADVANTAGES AND DISADVANTAGES OF VARIOUS RESEARCH TECHNIQUES.
- EXPLAIN THE HAWTHORNE EFFECT.
- STATE THE BASIC ETHICAL CONCERNS TO WHICH RESEARCHERS MUST ATTEND.

KEY CONCEPTS:

Hypothesis	Correlational research
Reliability	Experimental research
Validity	Independent variable
Observational research	Dependent variable
Participant observation	Control group
Direct observation	Hawthorne effect

CHAPTER SUMMARY

Key concepts are identified by **bold** *faced type.*

I. How Much Do You Know About Organizational Behavior?

Most of our common sense ideas about human behavior are incorrect. People give contradictory answers to questions, and in many cases, they operate with false information.

II. Common Sense and Organizational Behavior

Our common sense comes from direct and indirect experience, and gives us our views and knowledge of the world. Yet many of our common sense notions are false, and as contradictory proverbs show, we need a better method of evaluating organizational behavior.

III. What Creates Inaccurate Opinions?

A. Overgeneralization

We tend to assume that our experience with one small sample is true for all instances. We are also prone to selective perception which is seeing and hearing what we want to see.

B. Practice and Media Attention

Many of our ideas about organizations come from seeing what is actually practiced. We tend to assume that if companies do certain things, that which is done is correct.

We also react to media coverage of people and organizations. Many best sellers and newspapers columns have made the subject seem oversimplified. Moreover media coverage fails to indicate that much knowledge of organizational behavior was obtained slowly, through trial and error.

C. Value Judgments

Our feelings about right and wrong, our values, often keep us from objectivity in dealing with people and organizations. In general, we favor what we perceive as good, and we also assume that linkages exist between valued phenomena.

IV. Research in Organizational Behavior

Trained behavioral scientists carry out research in organizational behavior using their training in sociology, psychology, and applied psychology. Several different techniques may be employed.

A. The Basics of Organizational Behavior Research

All research in organizational behavior begins with a question about work or organizations. Often, research questions are expressed as hypotheses. A **hypothesis** is a formal statement of the expected relationship between two variables.

Good researchers carefully measure the variables they choose. For one thing, a measure should exhibit high reliability. **Reliability** is an index of the consistency of a research subject's responses.

Measures should also exhibit high validity. **Validity** is an index of the extent to which a measure truly reflects what it is supposed to measure.

B. Observational Techniques

The examination of the natural activities of real people in organizational settings is known as **observational research**. The results are usually summarized in a narrative known as a case study.

C. Participant Observation

Often a researcher will become directly involved in the target behavior. In **participant observation** the researcher will become a functioning member of the unit being studied. Thus, an observer who wanted to study football, might actually work out with a team, and even play in scrimmage and practice games. Such research, carried out in organizations, has resulted in findings which could not be learned in any other fashion.

D. Direct Observation

Another research method is **direct observation** which involves observation without participation in the activity being studied. At times, this method can produce valuable knowledge about organizational behavior. But like participant observation it is time consuming and lacks control over the environment being studied.

E. Correlational Techniques

At times, behavioral scientists use **correlational research**, or the use of interviews and questionnaires to obtain data. These research techniques should show reliability or the concept that other observers would see the same thing and that any one observer would report seeing the same thing if it occurred again. Data from these techniques should also exhibit validity which is a true reflection of what was actually observed and that it measures what it was supposed to measure.

Since correlational research investigates the relationship or correlation between variables, a hypothesis or prediction about the ways in which the variables are expected to be connected is employed in the process.

F. Experimental Techniques

At times, researchers will manipulate nature. In **experimental research**, some variable is manipulated under controlled conditions, and the consequence of this manipulation for some other variable is measured.

The variable that the researcher manipulates is called the **independent variable**. The variable that the independent variable is expected to affect is the **dependent variable**.

To assure the validity of most experimental techniques, we also need a **control group** which is a group of research subjects who have not been exposed to the experimental treatment.

G. A Continuum of Research Techniques

No one research technique is best. Methods can be placed on a continuum ranging from rich, broad-based, and loosely controlled (observation) to specific, precise, and rigorous (experimentation). In general, the technique employed should be dictated by the nature of the problem, and the personnel involved.

H. Combining Research Techniques

Research techniques can also complement one another. For example, observational techniques can be used to examine issues of causation between related variables identified by correlation analysis.

I. Issues and Concerns in Organizational Research

Sampling: Large samples might insure that results are representative of the targets being studied, while random samples will insure that all relevant individuals, organizations or groups have an equal probability of being studied.

Hawthorne Effects: When workers are studied by observers, the workers might respond in an unexpected fashion. This is known as the **Hawthorne effect** which can be defined as a favorable response on the part of subjects in an organizational experiment that is due to some factor other than the independent variable being manipulated.

J. Ethics

No matter who employs them, researchers have an obligation to do accurate and impartial research and to be ethical in all of their work. If possible, individuals should be protected from negative consequences. When people are sure of ethical practices, they will cooperate more readily with researchers.

PRE-TESTING YOUR UNDERSTANDING OF THE CHAPTER

Key Concepts Matching

Match the letter of the key concept with the appropriate definitions.

A. Control Group	G. Hypothesis
B. Correlational Research	H. Independent Variable
C. Dependent Variable	I. Observational Research
D. Direct Observation	J. Participant Observations
E. Experimental Research	K. Reliability
F. Hawthorne Effect	L. Validity

______1. Research which manipulates and changes variables under controlled conditions.

______2. Research in which the researcher is a functioning member of the organization unit being studied.

______3. Data which is a true reflection of what was observed and which measures what is supposed to be measured.

______4. A prediction about the way in which variables are supposed to be connected.

______5. Examination by a researcher of the natural activities of real people in an organizational setting.

______6. Research in which the researcher uses interviews and questionnaires as well as existing data.

______7. The variable that the independent variable is expected to affect.

______8. A favorable response by subjects in an organizational experiment that is due to some factor other than the independent variable being manipulated.

______9. Observation without participation in the activity being observed.

_____10. Different observers seeing the same thing and that any one observer would see the same thing if it occurred again tomorrow.

_____11. A group similar to one being tested that is not directly involved in a given experiment.

_____12. The variable that the researcher manipulates or changes.

True/False Questions

Circle the letter of the correct answer.

T F 1. Popular books are usually accurate in describing organizational behavior.
T F 2. Good research is necessary to form accurate pictures of the world.
T F 3. In participant observation the observer becomes part of the unit being studied.
T F 4. Direct observation and participant observation are exactly the same process.
T F 5. According to Mintzberg, managers preferred verbal communications to other activities.
T F 6. Correlational studies involve arguments and negotiation by different observers.
T F 7. A hypothesis is a side of a triangle.
T F 8. Correlation usually implies causation.
T F 9. The variable manipulated in an experiment is called the independent variable.
T F 10. As a rule, the larger the sample the more accurate the research will be.
T F 11. The Hawthorne effect deals with a favorable response by workers that is due to some factor other than the independent variable being manipulated.
T F 12. Researchers should do vigorous research and report their results accurately.
T F 13. Common sense is an excellent method of forming accurate pictures of the world.
T F 14. Satisfied workers are more productive than dissatisfied workers.
T F 15. A valid experiment gives an accurate picture of what was actually observed.
T F 16. When results are reliable, different observers see the same thing.
T F 17. A hypothesis predicts the way in which variables are to be connected.
T F 18. The variable affected by the dependent variable is called the independent variable.
T F 19. So long as results are valid, ethics are not important in organizational research.
T F 20. As a rule, friendly clerks produce more sales.

Multiple-Choice Questions

Select the correct answer.

______1. Which of the following would tend to create inaccurate opinions?
A. valid test results
B. value judgments
C. experimental research
D. correlational research

______2. A hypothesis is
A. the long side of a triangle.
B. a large independent variable.
C. a prediction about the connections of variables.
D. an idea presented by a supervisor.

______3. The independent variable is one that is
A. constantly changing.
B. manipulated by the researcher.
C. always the same.
D. impossible to measure.

______4. A participant observer is one who
A. sits on the sidelines and watches.
B. encourages desired results.
C. correlates the results of others.
D. is actively involved in the experiment.

______5. Which of the following is not involved in organizational research?
A. profitability
B. sampling
C. ethical issues
D. Hawthorne effect

______6. In direct observation the researcher is
A. actively participating in the experiment.
B. not actively participating.
C. correlating the results of others.
D. using unethical practices.

______7. Common sense is acquired through
A. experimental techniques.
B. much research data.
C. direct and indirect experience.
D. value judgments.

______8. Correlational studies involve
A. direct participation.
B. value judgments.
C. interviews and questionnaires.
D. direct observations.

______9. A control group consists of people
A. not directly involved in the experiment.
B. directly affected by the variables.
C. who supervise airplanes and submarines.
D. who supervise all experiments.

______10. The Hawthorne effect is
A. named after a noted American author.
B. a correlation of results.
C. a response that is not due to the independent variable.
D. worker response to criticism by co-workers.

POST-TESTING FOR EXAMS

True/False Questions

Circle the letter of the correct answer.

T F 1. Management by fad is an effective way of running a company.

T F 2. Observational techniques are effective ways of learning about behavior in organizations.

T F 3. Correlation research involves participant observers.

T F 4. A valid result is one that measures what was supposed to be measured.

T F 5. A control group is in charge of most companies.

T F 6. Ethics are not important factors in research.

T F 7. Generalizations and value judgments are valid methods of acquiring knowledge of organizational behavior.

T F 8. In direct observation, researchers do not participate in the activity being observed.

T F 9. A reliable result occurs when different observers see the same thing again and again.

T F 10. The variable that the observer manipulates is known as the dependent variable.

Multiple-Choice Questions

Select the correct answer.

______1. All of the following could cause inaccurate opinions <u>except</u>

A. practice and media attention.
B. over generalizations.
C. careful experimentation.
D. value judgments.

______2. Which of the following is not a recognized observational technique?

A. direct observation
B. peripheral observation
C. participant observation
D. observational research

______3. Which of the following is not a recognized method of organizational research?

A. correlation research
B. observational research
C. experimental research
D. computer-assisted research

______4. Experimental research is research which

A. involves laboratories and prototypes.
B. manipulates and changes variables.
C. manipulates workers and managers.
D. enhances productivity.

______5. Research in which the researchers are actively involved in the unit being studied is
A. direct observation.
B. experimental research.
C. participant observation.
D. observational research.

______6. A group similar to one being tested that is not directly involved in the experiment is
A. a control group.
B. an outside group.
C. an inside group.
D. neutral observers.

______7. Our value judgments are our
A. cost estimates of items.
B. income and outgo estimates.
C. attitudes about other people.
D. feelings about right and wrong.

______8. Workers responding favorably to something other than the variable being tested is
A. a flawed experiment.
B. the Hawthorne effect.
C. a valid result.
D. an unreliable result.

______9. When companies imitate the actions of other companies, we have
A. management by fad.
B. patent infringement.
C. good management.
D. restraint of trade.

______10. All of the following describe organizational research *except*
A. objective.
B. ethical.
C. intuitive.
D. subjective.

______11. A researcher who joins a team to study baseball is practicing
A. organizational research.
B. participant observation.
C. observational research.
D. experimental research.

______12. A researcher who watches the team from the grandstand is practicing
A. experimental research.
B. correlation research.
C. direct observation.
D. participant observation.

______13. A researcher who studies baseball statistics and questions players is practicing
A. organizational research.
B. experimental research.
C. correlation research.
D. scientific research.

______14. The idea that friendly supervisors will produce more work output is
A. a hypothesis.
B. a proven fact.
C. a false assumption.
D. a management myth.

______15. As a rule, ethical research results in
A. more cooperation from subjects.
B. more expenses to management.
C. lower costs to the company.
D. more data to work unit.

______16. Bensman and Gerver discovered "tapping" by using
A. experimentation.
B. participant observation.
C. correlational research.
D. direct observation.

______17. The most effective method of finding out about behavior in organizations would be
A. common sense.
B. value judgments.
C. observational research.
D. the grapevine.

______18. Which of the following is not normally involved with our common sense?
A. overgeneralization
B. systematic observation
C. value judgments
D. media attention

______19. The products of observational research are often called
A. a case study.
B. a company proposal.
C. a research file.
D. a management dossier.

______20. In his study of managers Mintzberg found that _____ of managerial activities lasted less than an hour.
A. 50%
B. 30%
C. 70%
D. 90%

Application Situations Exercise

Match the key concepts with the statements that best describe them.

A. Control Group
B. Correlational Research
C. Dependent Variable
D. Direct Observation
E. Experimental Research
F. Hawthorne Effect
G. Hypothesis
H. Independent Variable
I. Observational Research
J. Participant Observations
K. Reliability
L. Validity

______1. Our managers had always assumed that music in the mail room would speed-up production.

______2. One day they decided to do research in the mail room to test their assumption.

______3. They stationed a psychologist in the mail room for one month to study how music affected the workers.

______4. When results were obtained, management couldn't agree on what they meant.

______5. So the managers had people watching the mail room through one-way mirrors.

______6. Next the managers experimented with different types of music.

______7. When the tempo of the music increased, the production also increased.

______8. The managers decided to test another department to see if the results were valid.

______9. But workers in the department responded more to the extra attention than to the music.

_____10. In desperation the managers had to resort to statistics and questionnaires to learn if the workers had reacted to the music.

Short Answer Questions

Fill-in the missing word(s).

1. Many of our favorite proverbs tend to _________ each other.

2. Seeing what we want to see or expect to see is known as _________.

3. Our feelings about right and wrong are known as _________.

4. Good behavioral science research should be _________.

5. ________ takes place when a researcher actually works in an organization that s/he is studying.

6. Correlation does not always imply _________.

7. _________ mean that results obtained are representative of the groups being studied.

8. The Hawthorne Effect studies were conducted at _________.

9. Researchers have an ethical obligation to report their results _________.

10. Research evidence and practical management experience generally accumulate through _________.

ANSWER SHEET FOR CHAPTER 2

PRE-TESTING YOUR UNDERSTANDING OF THE CHAPTER

Key Concepts Matching

1. E 2. J 3. L 4. G 5. I 6. B 7. C 8. E 9. D 10. J
11. A 12. H

True/False Questions

1. F 2. T 3. T 4. F 5. T 6. F 7. F 8. F 9. T 10. T
11. T 12. T 13. F 14. F 15. T 16. T 17. T 18. F 19. F 20. F

Multiple-Choice Questions

1. B 2. C 3. B 4. D 5. A 6. B 7. C 8. C 9. A 10. C

POST-TESTING FOR EXAMS

True/False Questions

1. F 2. T 3. F 4. T 5. F 6. F 7. F 8. T 9. T 10. F

Multiple-Choice Questions

1. C 2. B 3. D 4. B 5. C 6. A 7. D 8. B 9. A 10. C
11. B 12. C 13. C 14. A 15. A 16. B 17. C 18. B 19. A 20. D

Application Situations Exercise

1. G 2. E 3. J 4. L 5. D 6. H 7. C 8. A 9. F 10. B

Short Answer Questions

1. contradict 2. selective perception 3. values 4. systematic and objective
5. participant observation 6. causation 7. large samples 8. Western Electric Company
9. accurately 10. trial and error

EXERCISE FOR CHAPTER 2

SETTING COURSE GOALS

Advanced Preparation: To be completed before class.
Chapters 1 and 2 give you an introduction and overview of the course. At this point you should better understand what the course is all about. For this exercise, write down in the space below, and on additional paper if needed, at least five goals for this course. Your goals may be related to grades, specific learning, skill development, etc.

In-Class Part of Exercise 2

Objectives:
To develop goal setting ability and goals.

Option A: (7-15 minutes)
The instructor calls on students to state their goals (advanced preparation) to the class. The instructor may or may not ask for volunteers.

Option B: (10-15 minutes)
Break into groups of four to six and share your goals. Discuss and refine your goals. Give one another ideas on how to refine your goals. You may add additional goals based on other's goals.

Option C: (20-30 minutes)
1. Follow option B, with the addition of: select a spokesperson and as a group select about five of the goals that are representative of the group's goals.
2. The spokesperson for each group states the five goals to the entire class. Once again, you may add additional goals based on other's goals.

Conclusion:
The instructor may lead a class discussion and/or make concluding remarks.

Application: (2-4 minutes)
What have I learned through this exercise? How will I use this knowledge in the future?

Sharing:
Volunteers give their answers to the application section.

CHAPTER 3

LEARNING AND PERSONALITY

LEARNING OBJECTIVES

- DEFINE LEARNING AND UNDERSTAND ITS GENERAL ROLE IN INFLUENCING ORGANIZATIONAL BEHAVIOR.
- DIFFERENTIATE BETWEEN POSITIVE AND NEGATIVE REINFORCEMENT AND EXPLAIN HOW TO USE THEM EFFECTIVELY
- EXPLAIN WHEN TO USE IMMEDIATE VERSUS DELAYED REINFORCEMENT, WHEN TO USE CONTINUOUS VERSUS PARTIAL REINFORCEMENT, AND HOW TO SCHEDULE PARTIAL REINFORCEMENT.
- DISCUSS ORGANIZATIONAL BEHAVIOR MODIFICATION.
- EXPLAIN MODELING AND SELF-MANAGEMENT.
- DISTINGUISH BETWEEN EXTINCTION AND PUNISHMENT AND EXPLAIN HOW TO PUNISH EFFECTIVELY.
- DEFINE PERSONALITY AND DISCUSS ITS GENERAL ROLE IN INFLUENCING ORGANIZATIONAL BEHAVIOR.
- DISCUSS THE "BIG FIVE" DIMENSIONS OF PERSONALITY.
- DISCUSS THE ORGANIZATIONAL CONSEQUENCES OF DIFFERENCES IN LOCUS OF CONTROL, SELF-MONITORING, AND SELF-ESTEEM.

KEY CONCEPTS

Learning	Modeling
Reinforcement	Extinction
Positive reinforcement	Punishment
Negative reinforcement	Self-management
Fixed interval schedule	Personality
Variable interval schedule	Locus of control
Fixed ratio schedule	Self-monitoring
Variable ratio schedule	Self-esteem
Organizational behavior modification	

CHAPTER SUMMARY

Key concepts are identified by bold *faced type.*

I. What is Learning?

Learning occurs when practice or experience leads to a relatively permanent change in behavior potential. We assume that learning has occurred when we see a change in our individual behavior or performance.

II. Increasing the Probability of Behavior

One of the best methods of promoting behavior is **reinforcement**, or the process by which stimuli strengthen behaviors. The two main types of reinforcement are positive reinforcement and negative reinforcement.

A. Positive Reinforcement

Positive reinforcement increases or maintains the probability of some behavior by the application or addition of a stimulus to the situation in question. This stimulus is called the positive reinforcer. Although positive reinforcers tend to be pleasant stimuli, this is not always true since the resultant increase or maintenance of behavior determines whether or not a given stimulus was positive.

B. Negative Reinforcement

Negative reinforcement increases or maintains the probability of some behavior by the removal of a stimulus from the situation in question. Although negative reinforcers tend to be unpleasant, they are defined only by what they do and how they work, not by their unpleasantness. A confusing point about negative reinforcers is that they measure the probability of a behavior, since we learn to repeat behaviors that remove or prevent the onset of negative stimuli.

C. Organizational Errors Involving Reinforcement

- Confusing Rewards With Reinforcers:

If rewards, such as pay, promotions, fringe benefits, and the opportunity for overtime are not made contingent on specific behavior, workers might tend to become confused, since they would not know why benefits were given.

- Neglecting Diversity in Preferences for Reinforcers:

At times organizations fail to take individual differences into account when using reinforcers. Thus, what makes one worker happy, like a longer vacation, might not please a workaholic whose only pleasure in life is work.

- Neglecting Important Sources of Reinforcement:

Positive feedback upon the successful completion of a task is often a neglected source of reinforcement. At times, informal methods of reinforcement such as a smile or a pat on the back can be just as effective as more tangible rewards.

D. Reinforcement Strategies and Their Effects

To obtain the fast acquisition of some response, continuous reinforcement, which is applied by the reinforcer whenever the behavior of interest occurs, and immediate reinforcement which is applied by the reinforcer without delay, should be employed.

Behavior tends to be persistent when partial reinforcement and delayed reinforcement are employed. In partial reinforcement, not every instance of the behavior is reinforced during learning, while with delayed reinforcement there is a time lapse between a behavior and its reinforcement.

In general, reinforcement strategies have to be altered over time to achieve the desired results, and these strategies must be altered when the needs of the situation change.

E. Schedules of Partial Reinforcement

Other types of enforcers include internal schedules in which some time period must elapse after a reinforcement response before another reinforcer is available, and ratio schedules under which some number of responses must occur after a reinforced response before another reinforcement is available.

- Fixed Interval:

A **fixed interval schedules** involve the use of a reinforcer at regular and given intervals. A yearly bonus at Christmas might be an example of such a reinforcer.

- Variable Interval:

A **variable interval schedule** involves reinforcers which occur at varied intervals such as unexpected bonuses and rewards.

- Fixed Ratio:

With a **fixed ratio schedule** a certain number of responses must occur after a reinforced response before another reinforcement is available. Thus, a worker who is late three times might be punished. But a worker late only once will not be noticed.

- Variable Ratio:

With a **variable ratio schedule** some variable number of responses is necessary after a reinforcement before another reinforcement is offered.

F. Organizational Behavior Modification

Organizational behavior modification involves the systematic use of learning principles to influence organizational behavior. Some examples follow:

- Reinforcing Attendance:

Organizations have been successful in using modified bonus plans to induce late workers to arrive on time. Some organizations have been successful in using a card system which rewarded a worker with a poker hand at the end of a five-day week. Workers with the highest hand were able to win as much as $20.

- Reinforcing Workplace Safety:

The use of a slide show illustrating safe, versus unsafe practices in one organization resulted in an immediate improvement. When the reinforcers were terminated, however, the percentage of safe practices returned to the old level.

G. Modeling

At times, workers learn to behave in a certain fashion through **modeling** or the process of imitating the behavior of others. Thus, an aspiring executive might seek to dress the way the CEO does, or a junior clerk might even smoke a certain brand of cigar if upper level managers do.

In general, dynamic, successful people are more often used as models than boring, unsuccessful individuals.

III. Reducing the Probability of Behavior

At times we might wish to eliminate behaviors considered to be undesirable. Several methods might be employed.

A. Extinction

Extinction involves doing away with the reinforcer that is maintaining some unwanted behavior. If workers, for example, spend too much time chatting during coffee breaks, limiting such breaks to certain hours or delivering coffee to desks, might help solve the situation.

B. Punishment

Punishment involves following an unwanted behavior with some unpleasant, aversion stimulus. In general, organizations rely too heavily on punishment, and it should be used carefully and only when other methods of reinforcement fail to work.

C. Using Punishment Effectively

In general, when punishment is applied, another activity, desired by the organization, should be employed as a substitute. This will soften the effects of the punishment and indicate to the employee the activities the organization deems positive.

There are several principles that can increase the effectiveness of punishment:

- Make sure the chosen punishment is truly aversive.
- Punish immediately.
- Do not reward unwanted behaviors before or after the punishment.
- Do not inadvertently punish desirable behaviors.

IV. Self-Management

When employees use learning principles to manage their own behavior, they are practicing **self-management**. This process is economical for organizations, and it builds self-trust and confidence among employees.

V. What is Personality?

Personality is the relatively stable set of psychological characteristics that influences the way an individual interacts with his or her environment. It is reflected in the way people react to other people, situations, and problems.

VI. Personality and Organizational Behavior

A few words of caution are appropriate in discussing the role of personality in organizations. First, we should remember that people have a *variety* of personality characteristics. Second, the is no one best personality. Managers need to appreciate the value of diversity and concentrate on achieving the right "fit" between people and positions. Finally, the role of personality in organizational settings is strongest in "weak" situations where there are loosely defined roles and few rules .

A. The "Big Five" Dimensions of Personality

Psychologists have discovered that there are about five basic, but general dimensions that describe personality:

- Extroversion: sociable, talkative vs. withdrawn, shy
- Emotional Stability: stable, confident vs. depressed, anxious
- Agreeableness: tolerant, cooperative vs. cold, rude
- Conscientiousness: dependable, responsible vs. careless, impulsive
- Openness to Experience: curious, original vs. dull, unimaginative

B. Locus of Control

Locus of control is a set of beliefs about whether one's behavior is controlled mainly by internal or external forces. High "externals" see their behaviors controlled by factors like fate, luck and powerful people. High "internals" see stronger effects on their behavior as a consequence of self-initiative, personal actions and free will.

C. Self-Monitoring

Self-monitoring is the extent to which people observe and regulate how they appear and behave in social settings and relationships. Individuals low in self-monitoring are said to "wear their hearts on their sleeves": they act like they feel and say what they think without regard to the situation. Individuals high on self-monitoring behave somewhat like actors, taking great care to observe and control the images that they project. In particular, they tend to show concern for socially appropriate behavior, tune in to social cues, and respond accordingly.

D. Self-Esteem

Self-esteem is the degree to which a person has a positive self-evaluation. Despite a possible downside to excessive esteem, organizations will generally benefit from a workforce with high self-esteem. Such people tend to make more fulfilling career decisions, they exhibit higher job satisfaction, and they are generally more resilient to the strains of everyday work life.

PRE-TESTING YOUR UNDERSTANDING OF THE CHAPTER

Key Concepts Matching

Match the letter of the key concepts with the appropriate definitions.

A. Extinction
B. Fixed interval schedule
C. Fixed ratio schedule
D. Learning
E. Locus of control
F. Modeling
G. Negative reinforcement
H. Organizational behavior modification
I. Personality
J. Positive reinforcement
K. Punishment
L. Reinforcement
M. Self-esteem
N. Self-management
O. Self-monitoring
P. Variable interval schedule
Q. Variable ratio schedule

______1. That which occurs when practice or experience leads to a relatively permanent change in behavior potential.

______2. The degree to which a person has a positive self-evaluation.

______3. The extent to which people observe and regulate how they appear and behave in social settings and relationships.

______4. The process by which stimuli strengthen behaviors.

______5. That which increases or maintains the probability of some behavior by the application or addition of a stimulus to the situation in question.

______6. That which increases or maintains the probability of some behavior by the removal of a stimulus from the situation in question.

______7. A set of beliefs about whether one's behavior is controlled mainly by internal or external forces.

______8. The relatively stable set of psychological characteristics that influences the way an individual interacts with his or her environment..

______9. The systematic use of learning principles to influence organizational behavior.

_____10. The process of imitating the behavior of others.

_____11. Doing away with the reinforcer that is maintaining some unwanted behavior.

_____12. Following an unwanted behavior with some aversive stimulus.

_____13. The process of using learning principles to manage one's own behavior.

_____14. Reinforcement in which a certain number of responses must occur before another reinforcement is taken.

_____15. Reinforcement in which a variable number of responses are necessary before another reinforcement is offered.

_____16. Reinforcement which occurs at regular and given intervals.

_____17. Reinforcement which occurs at variable intervals, such as an unexpected bonus.

True/False Questions

Circle the letter of the correct answer.

T F 1. In general, positive reinforcers tend to be pleasant stimuli.
T F 2. In general, negative reinforcers increase the probability of behavior.
T F 3. Rewards and reinforcers are the same thing.
T F 4. Continuous and immediate reinforcement can slow the learning process.
T F 5. Persistent learning can be facilitated by delayed, partial reinforcement.
T F 6. Modeling refers to workers who pose before their peers.
T F 7. An individual with an internal locus of control would be a better choice to staff a start-up operation than an external .
T F 8. Extinction refers to the firing of an undesirable employee.
T F 9. Punishment is a very effective way of eliminating unwanted behavior.
T F 10. Money and financial rewards are the most effective ways of inducing learning.
T F 11. High self-monitors are said to "wear their hearts on their sleeves".
T F 12. Interval and ratio schedules refer to production quotas.
T F 13. Self-management occurs when workers use learning principles to manage their own behaviors.
T F 14. Practice and experience are important factors in the learning process.
T F 15. Skinner's learning experiments involved rabbits.
T F 16. Reinforcers are usually applied before some behavior occurs.
T F 17. Under certain circumstances nagging could serve as a positive reinforcer.
T F 18. In general, reinforcement should be applied without delay whenever the desired behavior occurs.
T F 19. Imitating a boss's behavior is a good way to advance in an organization.
T F 20. Organizations generally benefit from a workforce with high self-esteem.

Multiple-Choice Questions

Select the correct answer.

______1. Learning by observing the behavior of others is known as
A. operant conditioning.
B. social Learning.
C. modeling.
D. flattery.

______2. Which of the following in NOT an effective use of punishment?
A. rewarding unwanted behavior
B. immediate punishment
C. using evasive methods
D. apologizing for applying punishment

______3. Which of the following is NOT a usual self-management process?
A. observing models
B. collecting self-observation data
C. goal setting
D. asking managerial intervention

______4. Which of the following are usually involved in partial reinforcement?
A. hourly schedules
B. ratio schedules
C. random schedules
E. chaotic schedules

______5. Learning is said to occur when
A. enough punishment is applied.
B. many rewards are given.
C. practice or experience leads to change in behavior potential.
D. extinction is applied.

______6. Which of the following does NOT relate to the "Big Five" of dimensions of personality?
A. emotional stability
B. extroversion
C. openness to experience
D. intelligence

______7. Once in place, reinforcement strategies should
A. be rigidly applied.
B. be ignored.
C. be tailored to the needs of the situation.
D. be dropped after a short time.

______8. In business, good models tend to be
A. vivid and memorable individuals.
B. quiet individuals.
C. "beautiful people."
D. chief executives in companies.

______9. A high self-monitor might be at a disadvantage where an organizational role required
A. negotiation.
B. behavioral flexibility.
C. ingratiation.
D. innovation.

______10. Which of the following is NOT an error involving reinforcement?
A. confirming rewards with reinforcers
B. neglecting source of reinforcement
C. neglecting individual preferences for reinforcers
D. paying some workers more than others

POST-TESTING FOR EXAMS

True/False Questions

Circle the letter of the correct answer.

T F 1. What one learns is not always reflected in one's performance.

T F 2. Reinforcers should be judged by what they do, and how they do it, not by their surface appearance.

T F 3. When negative behavior decreases it is either being extinguished or punished.

T F 4. As a rule, the same reinforcers will be acceptable to all individuals.

T F 5. A reinforcer should follow behavior.

T F 6. Individuals with an internal locus of control tend to perform better in jobs that require initiative and innovation.

T F 7. Rewards and reinforcers are the same things.

T F 8. One's co-workers can also be a source of reinforcement.

T F 9. People with low self-esteem tend to be less susceptible to social influence.

T F 10. In general, managers should ignore modeling and its implications.

Multiple-Choice Questions

Select the correct answer.

______1. Reinforcement is a process by which
A. workers are punished frequently.
B. stimuli strengthen behaviors.
C. managers earn bonuses.
D. supervisors choose favorites.

______2. Under negative reinforcement, a stimulus is
A. removed from a situation.
B. added to a situation.
C. strengthened in a situation.
D. decreased in a situation.

______3. Workers laughing at a co-worker's horseplay might serve as an example of
A. modeling.
B. positive reinforcement.
C. negative reinforcement.
D. operant learning.

______4. Behavior tends to be persistent when it is learned under
A. negative reinforcement.
B. positive reinforcement.
C. operant learning.
D. partial and delayed reinforcement.

______5. Which of the following is NOT a usual reinforcement schedule?
A. variable ratio schedule
B. fixed interval schedule
C. fixed ratio schedule
D. fixed payout schedule

______6. Which of the following might be an example of detrimental behavior?
A. good attendance
B. good performance
C. good grapevine discussions
D. good safety

______7. Punishment usually
A. follows an unwanted behavior with aversive stimuli.
B. precedes an unwanted behavior.
C. removes an unwanted stimulus after behavior.
D. is a poor method of managing workers.

______8. Good managers should
A. constantly monitor worker behavior.
B. provide an acceptable alternative for a punished response.
C. react emotionally to worker behavior.
D. criticize freely and frequently.

______9. The description "dull, unimaginative" might be applied to individuals at one extreme of which dimension of personality?
A. extroversion.
B. innovativeness.
C. openness to experience.
D. fantasy deficiency syndrome.

______10. Which of the following is NOT considered to be involved in learning?
A. reinforcement
B. intuition
C. punishment
D. extinction

______11. Which of the following might be involved in self-management?
A. positive reinforcement
B. immediate reinforcement
C. goal setting
D. negative reinforcement

______12. The purpose of negative reinforcement is to
A. increase the probability of behavior.
B. decrease the probability of behavior.
C. extinguish behavior.
D. none of the above.

______13. Which of the following is apt to be a negative reinforcer?
A. a slap on the back
B. a threat
C. a joke
D. an invitation

______14. Praising a worker for a job well done is an example of
A. immediate reinforcement.
B. negative reinforcement.
C. positive reinforcement.
D. needless flattery.

______15. Assigning overtime work only on the basis of seniority is an example of
A. confusing rewards with reinforcers.
B. positive reinforcement.
C. fixed interval schedules.
D. modeling.

______16. Which of the following is NOT considered a good reinforcer?
A. feedback from the job itself
B. the weekly paycheck
C. feedback from customers
D. feedback from co-workers

______17. As a general rule, reinforcement should be applied
A. after a suitable delay.
B. before a situation occurs.
C. immediately after the behavior of interest occurs.
D. very seldom and sparingly.

______18. An hourly pay scheme is an example of
A. a fixed interval reinforcement schedule.
B. a variable reinforcement schedule.
C. a variable interval schedule.
D. a variable ratio schedule.

______19. The process of extinction involves
A. firing workers.
B. using negative reinforcement.
C. doing away with the reinforcement that is maintaining unwanted behavior.
D. wiping out unions.

______20. An individual with a high external locus of control would NOT believe his/her behavior was determined largely by
A. fate.
B. self-initiative.
C. powerful people.
D. luck.

Application Situations Exercise

Match the key concept with the statements that best describe them.

A. Extinction
B. Fixed interval schedule
C. Fixed ratio schedule
D. Learning
E. Locus of control
F. Modeling
G. Negative reinforcement
H. Organizational behavior modification
I. Personality
J. Positive reinforcement
K. Punishment
L. Reinforcement
M. Self-esteem
N. Self-management
O. Self-monitoring
P. Variable interval schedule
Q. Variable ratio schedule

______1. Our company wanted to use learning theory to get workers to work on time.

______2. At first managers tried a bonus system for punctual workers.

______3. Then managers tried to berate employees who were late.

______4. When that didn't work, managers wanted to cut the salaries of late workers.

______5. Psychologists suggested that workers should learn to control their own behavior.

______6. They wanted workers to imitate the behaviors of successful executives.

______7. Other experts thought that continued criticism would alter the workers' behavior.

______8. But there was concern that such a tactic would have a negative impact on individual's self-evaluations.

______9. Some experts suggested that late workers be criticized only once a week.

_____10. Management finally just gave up and didn't pay any attention to lateness at all. Within two weeks, tardy behavior had almost disappeared!

Short Answer Questions

Fill-in the missing word(s).

1. Psychologist _____________ was a pioneer in the study of operant learning.

2. Benefits such as pay, promotions, and creative work, not contingent upon specific behaviors are known as _____________.

3. Letting people know how well or how badly they are doing is an example of ____________.

4. People who are ____________ do not make good models.

5. The ability, typical of high self-monitors, to adapt to one's clients and contacts would be very useful in a job such as ________________ .

6. If substitute activities are not provided, the message contained in the ____________ might be lost.

7. ____________ can lead to higher response rates because the individual can increase the frequency of reinforcement by responding faster.

8. It is important to remember that personality will have the most impact in __________ situations.

9. When dealing with reinforcers, managers should seek to take ____________ into account.

10. In general, fast learning is facilitated by ____________.

ANSWER SHEET FOR CHAPTER 3

PRE-TESTING YOUR UNDERSTANDING OF THE CHAPTER

Key Concepts Matching

1. D	2. M	3. O	4. L	5. J	6. G	7. E	8. I	9. H	10. F
11. A	12. K	13. N	14. C	15. Q	16. B	17. P			

True/False Questions

1. T	2. T	3. F	4. F	5. T	6. F	7. T	8. F	9. F	10. F
11. F	12. F	13. T	14. T	15. F	16. F	17. T	18. T	19. F	20. T

Multiple-Choice Questions

1. B	2. A	3. D	4. B	5. C	6. D	7. C	8. A	9. D	10. D

POST-TESTING FOR EXAMS

True/False Questions

1. T	2. T	3. T	4. F	5. T	6. T	7. F	8. T	9. F	10. F

Multiple-Choice Questions

1. B	2. A	3. B	4. D	5. D	6. C	7. A	8. B	9. C	10. B
11. C	12. A	13. B	14. C	15. A	16. B	17. C	18. A	19. C	20. B

Application Situations Exercise

1. H	2. J	3. G	4. K	5. N	6. F	7. L	8. M	9. B	10. A

Short Answer Questions

1. B.F. Skinner
2. rewards
3. feedback
4. bores
5. sales, law, public relations or politics
6. punishment
7. ratio schedules
8. weak
9. individual preference
10. continuous, immediate reinforcement

CASE STUDY

MR. P., THE PHILIPPINE MANAGER

Mr. P., a promising young manager in a multinational corporation, was placed in charge of one section of a large Philippine manufacturing plant. His section was one of four identical sections producing the same product; each section had the same physical set-up, used the same work method, and had the same number of workers. All four section managers were informed of the total daily output of each section.

When Mr. P. was first given the position of section manager, he learned that his section output was lower than the output of the other three sections: 360 units per day versus approximately 400 units output in the other three sections. The executive over him encouraged him to "think of something to raise productivity."

Mr. P. (an eager fellow who brims with enthusiasm and good will), had had a management training course when he had been originally hired in the multinational corporation. He had learned about positive reinforcement as a well-substantiated method of motivation to increase production. He considered the kinds of positive reinforcement he could give to the workers. Because of organizational politics, he could not offer raises, promotions, or fringe benefits. The number of workers in his section was too large for him to offer "individual praise." He hit on the idea of offering the workers the privilege of stopping work one minute early each day for seven units of increased group production (over the base figure of 360 units). He figured that if they could look forward to stopping early, he could get them to increase daily output.

First thing the next morning, he assembled his workers and enthusiastically presented his idea. He explained, however, that if they produced more and therefore stopped early, they could not leave the plant because they were getting paid by the hour. However, they could talk and have a soft drink and relax.

To his delight, worker production quickly went up to the point where workers got thirty-three minutes free at the end of the day. This meant that output was up from 360 to 590 units! During that half hour at the end of the day, workers sat around talking and smoking. They were enthusiastic about the new arrangement. They indicated that the boring work was not quite so boring with a goal to look forward to. Besides, they liked getting acquainted.

Over a period of about two months, they gradually improved their speed even more. Finally, they reached a level of efficiency where they earned the right to a full hour off at the end of each day. The hour off had a party atmosphere. Their morale was high. They were pleased with the new rules of the game, they were pleased with the social time, and they were proud of their performance.

Mr. P. was just as pleased and proud. His section was now producing 800 units per day, twice the production output of each of the other units. The managing director of the plant phoned and congratulated him. He announced that he had recommended Mr. P. to be sent to a fast-track corporate management program at the Executive and Environment Center in Switzerland.

Source: Elbing, C. J. (1984, November-December). "'Yes, but....': Hidden criteria for judging managerial innovations." Business Horizons, 10-14. Copyright 1984 by the Foundation for the School of Business at Indiana University. Used with permission.

But before Mr. P. could leave for Switzerland, disaster struck. The managing director decided to take a plant tour. He arrived at the young manager's "super section" one hour before closing time. The workers, having produced their 800 units, had already quit working. They were lounging about, smoking, drinking sodas, and talking and laughing. Mr. P. was immediately called to the managing director's office, where he was confronted with angry indignation. The managing director threatened to fire the young manager on the spot. Why was he allowing the workers to loaf?

Mr. P. explained his ingenious incentive system. The managing director's angry retort was that if the workers could producc 800 units in seven hours, they could produce 900 units if they worked one more hour!

The younger manager explained in vain. The managing director stated, in no uncertain terms, that if Mr. P.'s unit was caught loafing again, he would be fired. The managing director proclaimed that the workers were being paid to work, and work the whole time, and that workers should obey authority. It would be shocking if "anyone" found out that employees at this plant could get away with loafing.

Sadly, Mr. P. informed his workers the next morning that the incentive system was over. The workers went back to working to the very end of the day, and production gradually slipped back to that of the other units.

The managing director of the plant scolded the workers for their fall in production and suggested Mr. P. do the same. But production did not rise, and interestingly enough, Mr. was never reprimanded for that.

1. What was the precise problem that Mr. P. faced when he assumed his job as section manager?

2. In learning theory terms, describe precisely the system that Mr. P. implemented. What reinforcers were used and how were they scheduled?

3. Evaluate the effectiveness of Mr. P.'s system. What were its good points and bad points?

4. Can you think of any alternative solutions to Mr. P.'s problem that would satisfy the managing director?

CHAPTER 4

PERCEPTION, ATTRIBUTION, AND JUDGMENT OF OTHERS

LEARNING OBJECTIVES

- DEFINE PERCEPTION AND DISCUSS SOME OF THE GENERAL FACTORS THAT INFLUENCE PERCEPTION.
- EXPLAIN SOME BASIC BIASES IN PERSONAL PERCEPTION.
- DESCRIBE HOW SOME PEOPLE FORM ATTRIBUTIONS ABOUT THE CAUSES OF BEHAVIOR.
- DISCUSS VARIOUS BIASES IN ATTRIBUTION.
- APPRECIATE THE CONCEPTS OF WORKFORCE DIVERSITY AND VALUING DIVERSITY.
- DISCUSS HOW RACIAL, ETHNIC, GENDER, AND AGE STEREOTYPES AFFECT ORGANIZATIONAL BEHAVIOR.
- DISCUSS HOW PERCEPTION AFFECTS THE OUTCOMES OF SELECTION INTERVIEWS AND PERFORMANCE APPRAISALS.

KEY CONCEPTS

perception	attribution	self-serving bias
perceptual defense	dispositional attributions	workforce diversity
primacy effect	situational attributions	contrast effects
recency effect	consistency cues	leniency
central trait	consensus cues	harshness
implicit personality theory	distinctiveness cues	central tendency
projection	fundamental attribution error	halo
stereotyping	actor-observer effect	similar to me effect

CHAPTER SUMMARY

Key concepts are identified by **bold** *faced type.*

I. What Is Perception?

Perception is the process of interpreting the message of our senses to provide order and meaning to the environment. Among the most important perceptions that influence organizational behavior are the perceptions that organizational members have of each other.

II. Components of Perceptual Events

A. The Perceiver

The perceiver's experience, motives, and emotions can affect his or her perceptions.

1. Experience. One of the most important influences on perception is experience - our past experiences lead us to develop expectations and these affect current perceptions - differences in perception caused by experience can lead to problems within organizations.

2. Motivational State. Differences in our needs at a given moment in our motivational state can also be a source of conflict within organizations, since our motivational states influence our perception and interpretation of events.

3. Emotional State. Emotional state refers to the particular emotions that an individual feels at a given time. Emotions such as anger, happiness, or fear, can and do affect our perceptions. In some cases we employ a **perceptual defense** which occurs when our perceptual system serves to defend us against unpleasant emotions. In general, we tend to "see what we want to see."

B. The Target

Our perceptions are also affects by the target's social status and ambiguity.

1. Ambiguity or lack of information about a target can also blur our perceptions.

2. The target's social status will also affect our perception. People with more prestigious titles are perceived as being of higher social status than people of lower titles. The status of a target also affects our perception of what the target says.

C. The Situation

The control of the situation can greatly affect our perceptions by adding information about the target.

III. A Model Of The Perceptual Process

Psychologist Jerome Bruner has developed a model of perception that deals with how we select cues in our interpretations and we develop perceptual constancy and consistency once we have formed our opinions.

IV. Perceptual Biases In Person Perceptions

A. Primacy and Recency Effect

We form our impressions of others fairly quickly. One reason for this is the **primacy effect** which deals with our tendency to rely on ones we encounter early in the relationship. Another reason is the **recency effect** which gives undue weight to cues encountered most recently.

B. Reliance on Central Traits

We tend to organize our perceptions of others around the presence of certain traits that are of interest to us. This concept called the **central trait** can often have a very powerful influence on our perceptions of others.

C. Implicit Personality Theory

Each of us uses our **implicit personality theory** which assumes connections between differing personality traits. For example, we might assume that hard workers are all honest or that slow workers are not very bright.

D. Projection

The tendency to attribute one's own characteristics and feelings to others is called **projection**. If we are always honest, for example, we often assume that others are too.

E. Stereotyping

The assumption that people have certain characteristics by virtue of the category they fall into is known as **stereotyping**. Thus we might assume that all scientists are bright and that all football players are ignorant. Since most stereotyping is inaccurate, it is best to obtain information about targets before jumping to conclusions.

V. Attribution: Perceiving Causes and Motives

Attribution is the process by which we assign causes and motives to other people's behavior. **Dispositional attributions** suggest that some personality characteristic "inside the person" is responsible for the behavior. **Situational attributions** suggest that the external situations are an environment in which the target exists was responsible for the behavior.

A. Consistency Cues

If a person engages in the same behavior regularly and consistently we have **consistency cues**.

B. Consensus Cues

If most people engage in a behavior, or it is unique to one person, we have **consensus cues**. In general, acts which deviate from social expectations provide us with more information about the actor's motives than conforming behaviors do.

C. Distinctiveness Cues

If a person engages in one behavior in many situations, or if the behavior is distinctive to one situation we have **distinctiveness cues**.

D. Attribution in Action

We often have information at hand about consistency, consensus, and distinctiveness, and we tend to use this information whenever we judge people and their behavior.

E. Biases in Attribution

Despite our best efforts in attributing and interpreting behavior, several errors and biases can occur.

- Fundamental Attribution Error. When judging the behavior of people other than ourselves, we tend to overemphasize dispositional explanations at the expense of situational explanations. This is called the **fundamental attribution error**.

- Actor-Observer Effect. When actors and observers often view the same situations from different perspectives the phenomenon is called the **actor-observer effect**.

- Self-Serving Bias. The tendency to take credit and responsibility for success and to deny blame for failure is called the **self-serving bias**.

VI. Person Perception and Workforce Diversity

Workforce diversity refers to differences among employees or potential recruits in characteristics such as race, gender, age, religion, cultural background, physical ability, and sexual orientation.

A. Racial and Ethnic Stereotypes

Stereotypical views of other races and cultures are pervasive, persistent, frequently negative, and often self-contradictory. Stereotypical views that 'blacks can't handle pressure" or that "Asian Americans are technical whizzes" have interfered with their opportunities for advancement to upper management positions.

B. Gender Stereotypes

Women are severely underrepresented in managerial and administrative jobs merely because of their gender. Since males dominate business, and since many males have a false picture of women's executive capabilities, women have not been able to advance as easily as men to higher management levels.

C. Age Stereotypes

Many older people are perceived as having less capacity for performance than younger people. They are also viewed as being less productive and as lacking potential for development. As a result of these false stereotypes many older people have experienced discrimination, and many have taken their complaints to human rights agencies.

VII. The Accuracy of Person Perception in Organizations

A. Interviewers' Perceptions of Job Applicants

When applicants previously interviewed affect the interviewer's perception of a current candidate, we see **contrast effects**. These effects can help or hinder a current interview, and can create false impressions of a candidate's qualifications.

B. Observers' Perceptions of Job Performance

Organizations need to measure performance for decisions about pay raises, promotions, and training needs.

C. Objective and Subjective Measures

Both objective measures, such as attendance records and sales figures can be used to measure performance. At times, subjective measures such as rating scales and observers' opinions are also used to measure performance.

D. Rater Errors

When subjective performance is measured, several rater errors can occur. **Leniency** refers to the tendency to perceive the performance of one's ratee as especially good. **Harshness** is the tendency to see ratees as especially ineffective. **Central tendency** involves assigning most ratees to a middle performance category.

Other perceptual errors include **halo** which occurs when the observer allows the rating of an individual on one trait or characteristic to color ratings on other traits or characteristics and the **similar-to-me effect** in which the rater tends to give more favorable evaluations to people who are similar to the rater in background and attitudes.

PRE-TESTING YOUR UNDERSTANDING OF THE CHAPTER

Key Concepts Matching

Match the letter of the key concepts with the appropriate definitions.

A. Actor-observer effect
B. Attribution
C. Central tendency
D. Central trait
E. Consensus cues
F. Consistency cues
G. Contrast effects
H. Dispositional attribution
I. Distinctiveness cues
J. Fundamental attribution error
K. Halo
L. Harshness
M. Implicit personality theory
N. Knowledge of predictor bias
O. Leniency
P. Perception
Q. Perceptive defense
R. Primacy effect
S. Projection
T. Recency effect
U. Self-reviewing bias
V. Similar to-me effect
W. Situational attributions
X. Stereotyping

_______1. The process of interpreting the message of our senses to provide order and meaning to the environment.

_______2. The phenomenon in which our perceptual system serves to defend us against unpleasant emotions.

_______3. Reliance on early cues and first impressions.

_______4. Giving undue weight to cues encountered most recently.

_______5. Organizing perceptions around the presence of certain traits or characteristics of interest to the perceiver.

_______6. Assumed connections about which personality traits go together.

_______7. The tendency to attribute one's own characteristics and feelings to others.

_______8. The assumption that people have certain characteristics by virtue of some category they fall into.

_______9. The process by which we assign causes or motives to people's behavior.

______10. The concept that some personality characteristic inside a person is responsible for their behavior.

______11. The concept that the external situation or the environment is responsible for the target's behavior.

______12. Behavior engaged in regularly and consistently.

______13. Behavior engaged in by most people, or unique to the target.

______14. Behavior engaged in many situations, or distinctive to one situation.

______15. The overemphasis or dispositional explanations at the expense of situational explanations when we judge the behavior of other people.

______16. The concept that actors and observers often view the causes for the actor's behavior very differently.

______17. The tendency of people to take credit for success and to deny responsibility for failures.

______18. During interviews, applicants interviewed previously can affect the interviewer's perception of a current applicant.

______19. The tendency to perceive the performance of one's ratees as especially good.

______20. The tendency to perceive the performance of one's ratees as especially ineffective.

______21. The assigning of most ratees to a middle-range performance category.

______22. Allowing the rating of one individual of one trait or characteristic to color ratings or other traits or characteristics.

______23. The tendency of the rater to give more favorable evaluations to people similar to the rater in terms of background or attitudes.

______24. The cases in which the rater gains knowledge of some factor that might predict the success of the ratee and then rates the subordinate to confirm this prediction.

True/False Questions

Circle the letter of the correct answer.

T F 1. Social status has nothing at all to do with our perceptions.
T F 2. As a rule, attractive people are favored in the hiring process.
T F 3. People watching another person's behavior can usually agree on its causes.
T F 4. People tend to take credit for their successes and deny blame for their failures.
T F 5. Objective performance measures are excellent ways of judging workers.
T F 6. Central tendency involves assigning most ratees to a middle- range category.
T F 7. The halo effect occurs when we constantly rate someone in a positive light.
T F 8. Knowing about the rater helps the ratee in knowledge of predictor basis.
T F 9. Sexual and aging stereotypes are no longer problems for most organizations.
T F 10. Using perceptual defense, we tend to see "what we want to see."
T F 11. Cues are tips given to us at racetracks.
T F 12. First impressions often have a lasting effect on perceptions.

T F 13. In general, most stereotypes are inaccurate ways of perceiving others.
T F 14. Today women are no longer underrepresented in managerial and executive jobs.
T F 15. Age discrimination complaints have been increasing in the United States.
T F 16. Behavior performed regularly is an example of distinctiveness cues.
T F 17. Watching stage performances is part of the actor-observer effect.
T F 18. When organizations perform poorly, they tend to blame external factors.
T F 19. Even today, interviews are an imperfect method of judging job applicants.
T F 20. Harshness refers to the needless firing of workers.

Multiple-Choice Questions

Select the correct answer.

______1. Which of the following is NOT usually involved in perceptions?
A. perceiver's motives
B. perceiver's status
C. perceiver's emotions
D. perceiver's experience

______2. Harshness refers to
A. cruel treatment of workers.
B. needless firing of workers.
C. tendency to judge ratees severely.
D. tendency to pay substandard wages.

______3. Giving favorable ratings to people with similar backgrounds is an example of
A. sexual stereotyping.
B. the "old-boy" network.
C. the similar-to-me effect.
D. the halo effect.

______4. Which of the following is NOT considered a perceptual rater error?
A. leniency
B. central tendency
C. harshness
D. sexism

______5. Which of the following is NOT part of the attribution process?
A. consistency cues
B. distinctiveness cues
C. concurrent cues
D. consensus cues

______6. Engaging in the same behavior regularly is an example of
A. consistency cues.
B. inflexibility.
C. inability to learn.
D. consensus cues.

______7. Older workers today are seen positively as having
A. more stable work habits.
B. less potential for development.
C. less capability of performance.
D. less flexibility than younger workers.

______8. Sexual stereotypes today
A. no longer really exist.
B. help women obtain jobs.
C. block women's ascent into managerial jobs.
D. have improved women's learning abilities.

______9. Attributing one's own feelings to others is an example of
A. stereotyping.
B. self-serving bias.
C. implicit personality theory.
D. projection.

______10. Which of the following might NOT be a usual category of stereotyping?
A. occupations
B. food preferences
C. age
D. race

POST-TESTING FOR EXAMS

True/False Questions

Circle the letter of the correct answer.

T F 1. Leniency refers to giving workers many benefits.
T F 2. As a rule, less attractive women have an edge in obtaining management positions.
T F 3. Differences in perception do not usually lead to organizational conflict.
T F 4. Perceptual defense is one method of avoiding unpleasant emotion.
T F 5. Assumed connections about personality characteristics are examples of the actor-observer effect.
T F 6. Deciding that all football players are dumb is an example of projection.
T F 7. Price Waterhouse is one of the country's largest public accounting firms.
T F 8. People involved in illegal business practices tend to blame situational forces.
T F 9. The self-serving bias refers to managers who vote themselves excessively large bonuses.
T F 10. One interview is a generally accurate method of forming accurate impressions of others.

Multiple-Choice Questions

Select the correct answer.

______1. Subjective measures of effectiveness are usually performed by
A. a worker's peers.
B. a worker's direct superiors.
C. top management.
D. outside observers.

______2. Which of the following is NOT considered a perceptual error?
A. the halo effect
B. knowledge of predictor bias
C. the similar-to-me effect
D. stereotyping

______3. Attribution is a process of
A. assigning causes and motives to people's behavior.
B. blaming others for our mistakes.
C. perceiving the target incorrectly.
D. praising others for their efforts.

______4. Belief that certain personality traits go together is an example of
A. attribution.
B. projection.
C. implicit personality theory.
D. the halo effect.

______5. First impressions are examples of the
A. central traits.
B. recency effects.
C. bias.
D. primacy effects.

______6. Arguments for the competitive advantage of a diverse workforce include:
A. cost.
B. system flexibility.
C. creativity.
D. all of the above.

______7. When we blame bad weather for our behavior we are indulging in
A. projection.
B. instinctiveness cues.
C. attributions.
D. perception.

______8. Behavior engaged in by most people is an example of
A. inflexibility.
B. consensus cues.
C. consistency cues.
D. similar-to-me effect.

______9. Overemphasizing dispositional explanations for others' behavior at the expense of situational explanations is an example of
A. fundamental attribution error.
B. stereotyping.
C. projection.
D. perception.

______10. Taking credit for success and avoiding blame for failures is called
A. perception defense.
B. self-serving bias.
C. good business sense.
D. attribution.

______11. Assigning most ratees to a middle-range performance category is known as
A. stereotyping.
B. consensus cues.
C. central tendency.
D. pro-management practices.

______12. Deciding that a latecomer is usually a poor worker is an example of
A. harshness.
B. stereotyping.
C. situational attribution.
D. halo.

______13. According to Bruner's model of perception we are
A. very accurate in perception.
B. receptive to cues provided by the target.
C. using computers to rate others.
D. none of the above.

______14. Which of the following is NOT usually part of a perceptual event?
A. a situation
B. a perceiver
C. a target
D. a motive

______15. When we try not to notice threatening signs, we are indulging in
A. perceptual defense.
B. self-serving bias.
C. fundamental attribution error.
D. projection.

______16. Perceptual constancy refers to the tendency for the target to be
A. seen differently at different times.
B. seen in the same way over time.
C. seen as inherently evil.
D. seen as inherently good.

______17. Organizing perceptions around characteristics of interest is an example of
A. projection.
B. primacy effect.
C. central trait.
D. similar-to-me effect.

______18. Previously interviewed applicants influencing our perceptions is an example of
A. stereotyping.
B. recency effect.
C. consensus cues.
D. contrast effect.

______19. Perceiving the performance of most ratees as especially good is an example of
A. halo.
B. leniency.
C. good management.
D. motivation.

______20. After reading this chapter you should realize that judging others is
A. easily done with computers.
B. no longer necessary today.
C. a difficult and inexact process.
D. a job left to the federal government.

Application Situations Exercise

Match the letter of the key concepts with the appropriate definitions.

A. Actor-observer effect
B. Attribution
C. Central tendency
D. Central trait
E. Consensus cues
F. Consistency cues
G. Contrast effects
H. Dispositional attribution
I. Distinctiveness cues
J. Fundamental attribution error
K. Halo
L. Harshness
M. Implicit personality theory
N. Knowledge of predictor basis
O. Leniency
P. Perception
Q. Perceptive defense
R. Primacy effect
S. Projection
T. Recency effect
U. Self-reviewing bias
V. Similar to-me effect
W. Situational attributions
X. Stereotyping

_______1. We never knew that the company would soon lay us off.

_______2. The boss had always smiled and greeted us pleasantly.

_______3. But the boss had always blamed us when the company failed to show a profit.

_______4. Still, we assumed that our work was probably average.

_______5. Lately, the boss had seemed grouchy and irritable.

_______6. Since we liked the boss, we had assumed that the boss liked us.

_______7. We thought that the boss was acting mean because of trouble at home.

_______8. We couldn't imagine that he/she acted as he/she did because of personality traits.

_______9. Then we remembered that the boss was cruel to flies and mosquitoes.

______10. So we decided that our layoffs were really caused by the boss's cruel streak and had nothing to do with our own performance.

Short Answer Questions

Fill-in the missing word(s).

1. According to the courts, Ann Hopkins' denial of partnership by Price Waterhouse was a clear case of ________.

2. Psychologist ________ has developed an important model of the perceptual process.

3. We often make invalid assumptions about a person's behavior or personality when we know that person's _______.

4. Even today women are severely underrepresented in ________ positions.

5. In general, older people are said to be ________ than younger workers.

6. A performance evaluation technique which attempts to reduce the influence of perceptual errors and biases is the __________ .

7. In general interviewers have a tendency to ________ positive information obtained about an applicant before an interview.

8. Very often in organizations the _________ is more important than the reality itself.

9. One of the most important characteristics of the perceiver that influences his or her impressions of the target is _________.

10. The _________ of the target often affects our perceptions of what the target says.

ANSWER SHEET FOR CHAPTER 4

PRE-TESTING YOUR UNDERSTANDING OF THE CHAPTER

Key Concepts Matching

1. P 2. Q 3. R 4. T 5. D 6. M 7. S 8. X 9. B 10. H 11.W 12. F 13. E 14. I 15. J
16. A 17. U 18. G 19. 0 20. L 21. C 22. K 23. V 24. N

True/False Questions

1. F 2. T 3. F 4. T 5. F 6. T 7. F 8. F 9. F 10. T 11. F 12. T 13. F 14. F 15. T
16. F 17. F 18. T 19. T 20. F

Multiple-Choice Questions

1. B 2. C 3. C 4. D 5. C 6. A 7. A 8. C 9. D 10. B

POST-TESTING FOR EXAMS

True/False Questions

1. F 2. T 3. F 4. T 5. F 6. F 7. T 8. T 9. F 10. F

Multiple-Choice Questions

1. B 2. D 3. A 4. C 5. D 6. B 7. C 8. B 9. A 10. B
11. C 12. D 13. B 14. D 15. A 16. B 17. C 18. D 19. B 20. C

Application Situations Exercise

1. Q 2. F 3. V 4. C 5. I 6. S 7. W 8. H 9. D 10. B

Short Answer Questions

1. sexual stereotyping
2. Jerome Bruner
3. occupation
4. managerial and administrative
5. more stable
6. behaviorally anchored scale
7. underweight (downplay)
8. perception of reality
9. experience
10. status

CASE STUDY

REGINA MEDICAL SYSTEMS

Sharon could not believe the words she was hearing:

> Look, I am sorry I have to do this, but things can`t continue the way they have the last few months. We are going to have to let you go. You can stay for a couple of months to give you time to find something else, but you are finished here!

The fact that Robert Delorme, General Manager of Regina Medical Systems, was giving her time to make personal adjustments did little to ease the shock of her being fired or the unreality of the situation. Sharon had thought that she was indispensable, and while she knew her commitment to RMS had lessened in recent months, she had no idea that her position had deteriorated so severely.

Sharon had risen quickly in the firm in the last three years. She had been hired by RMS to be a customer service representative because of her technical background as a certified X-ray technician. The firm, which offered hospitals and clinics a monitoring process that substantially improved both the quality and cost performance of various radiographic tests, had increased sales revenues by a factor of 10 in a three-year period. Total employment had grown from 8 to 24 employees during this time, and as the sales force grew, Sharon's position had naturally expanded to the point where she effectively was the head of all sales personnel. Her enthusiasm, her aggressiveness, and her buoyant nature had been key elements in her ability to personally capitalize on the firm's rapid growth.

In the early periods of Sharon's employment at Regina Medical Systems she had been extremely satisfied with her job. The growth of the firm, the success of its innovative process, and the autonomy the RMS unit was granted by its conglomerate parent company had created a dynamic work environment with tremendous opportunities for everyone in the firm. The team spirit that developed among all of the employees had made RMS an exciting and fun place to work. It was very satisfying at the end of the month when the sales results were calculated, and the firm would take everyone to a restaurant to celebrate what had been accomplished. Many close relationships had developed among the young staff members.

The relationship between Sharon and her boss, Delorme, had slowly deteriorated over the last year or so. While no one incident had initiated this change, Delorme had criticized Sharon for being too emotional and for not using a more businesslike approach in carrying out her duties. On one occasion, Sharon had predicted that certain competitors would go after some major segments of the market. Delorme would not approve the expenditures to counter these potential entries in the market without facts. "Back up what you are arguing," he had told Sharon. Sharon had been unable to do this, but she knew she was right and subsequent events had proved the accuracy of her intuition.

Things had really deteriorated four months ago when Delorme had announced the decision to appoint a sales manager. Sharon had not been consulted on this move, nor was she consulted on the selection of the individual who was eventually hired.

Source: Case prepared by William D. Taylor and Shara Rosen.

She had felt very awkward when the new sales manager, Richard Martin, had not invited her to his first sales meeting when he arrived at RMS. She had been the one who had built the sales group, and many of the group were her close personal friends.

As she walked back to her office after her meeting with Delorme, Sharon realized that she had been short-tempered, she had snapped responses to those who had requested information, and she had made no real effort to help Martin, whom she regarded as incompetent. With respect to Martin she felt little guilt: her friends in the sales group had kept her informed of his many "goofs" and she, herself, had seen the way he had fumbled the development of a marketing plan for RMS which was eventually written by Delorme.

When she reached her desk, her mood had changed. Sharon began to feel more and more anger towards Delorme and his "buddy" Martin. She resented Delorme's insinuation that she had not learned to work within an organization. In her mind, she knew that she had made a major contribution to RMS's success, and everyone knew it!

1. In retrospect, which factors in the case might have predicted Sharon's firing from RMS?

2. What are some possible explanations for the events described in the case? In other words, what are some possible reasons for Sharon's problem at RMS?

3. In retrospect, could Robert Delorme have behaved more effectively? Could Sharon have behaved more effectively? Could a better understanding of the field of organizational behavior have helped both of them?

CHAPTER 5

VALUES, ATTITUDES, AND JOB SATISFACTION

LEARNING OBJECTIVES

- DEFINE VALUES AND DISCUSS THE IMPLICATIONS OF CROSS-CULTURAL VARIATION IN VALUES FOR ORGANIZATIONAL BEHAVIOR.
- DEFINE ATTITUDES AND EXPLAIN HOW PEOPLE DEVELOP AND CHANGE ATTITUDES.
- EXPLAIN THE CONCEPT OF JOB SATISFACTION AND DISCUSS SOME OF ITS KEY CONTRIBUTORS.
- DISCUSS THE ROLE OF DISCREPANCY, FAIRNESS, AND DISPOSITION IN PROMOTING JOB SATISFACTION.
- OUTLINE THE VARIOUS CONSEQUENCES OF JOB SATISFACTION AND EXPLAIN THE RELATIONSHIP BETWEEN JOB SATISFACTION AND MENTAL HEALTH, ABSENTEEISM, TURNOVER, PERFORMANCE, AND ORGANIZATIONAL CITIZENSHIP BEHAVIOR.

KEY CONCEPTS

values

power distance

uncertainty avoidance

individualistic vs. collective attitude

attitudes

cognitive dissonance

job satisfaction

discrepancy theory

distributive fairness

equity theory

inputs

outcomes

procedural fairness

"satisfaction causes performance"

"performance causes satisfaction"

organizational citizenship behavior

CHAPTER SUMMARY

Key concepts are identified by **bold** *faced type.*

I. What Are Values?

Values can be defined as a "broad tendency to prefer certain states of affairs over others." Not everyone holds the same values; and values may be classified into intellectual, economic, social, aesthetic, and political categories.

A. Occupational Differences in Values

Members of different occupational groups espouse different values. Salespeople rank social values less than the average American, while professors value "equal opportunity for all" more than the average American.

B. Work Values Across Cultures

Cross-cultural differences often contribute to failed business negotiations.

C. Work Centrality

Different cultures value work differently. Thus, Japanese managers tend to work longer hours than their American or British counterparts.

D. Hofstede's Study

Geert Hofstede, a social scientist studied over 116,000 IBM employees in forty countries about their work-related values. His results show that differences occurred in power distance, uncertainty avoidance, masculinity/femininity and individualism/collectiveness.

- **Power distance** is the extent to which an unequal distribution of power is accepted by society members.
- **Uncertainty avoidance** is the extent to which people are uncomfortable with uncertain and ambiguous situations.
- More masculine cultures clearly differentiate gender roles, support the dominance of men, and stress economic performance. More feminine cultures accept fluid gender roles, stress sexual equality, and stress quality of life
- **Individualistic** cultures stress independence, individual initiative and privacy. **Collective** cultures favor interdependence and loyalty to family or clan.

Given these differences, it is important for managers to take care when exporting or importing OB theories. An awareness of cross-cultural differences in values can help managers better appreciate global customers and develop global employees.

II. What Are Attitudes?

An **attitude** is a fairly stable emotional tendency to respond consistently to some specific object, situation, person or category of people.

III. Attitude Formation

A. Beliefs

Beliefs are assumed facts or statements about the nature of the world that do not involve evaluation.

B. Belief + Value = Attitude

Attitudes are the product of a related belief and value. In general, belief + value = attitude which might change behavior. Thus it is important to understand the belief and value systems which influence attitudes.

IV. Changing Attitudes

A. Communicator

The communicator, or person who imparts information, who is perceived as believable will often be effective in changing attitudes. To change attitudes, communicators should also be perceived as unbiased as well as likable.

B. Persuasion Techniques

Techniques used to affect attitude change are know as persuasion techniques. These may take the form of written communications such as posters or newsletters, or face-to-face communications such as conferences or meetings.

C. Cognitive Dissonance Theory

When our cognitions (thoughts or knowledge) that people have about their own beliefs, values, attitudes, and behavior are contradictory or inconsistent with each other, we have the theory of **cognitive dissonance** which explains the tensions such contradictions can produce.
In general, dissonance is an unpleasant feeling and individuals are usually motivated to reduce this feeling.

D. Changing Behavior to Change Attitude

Techniques such as modeling of correct behavior, role-playing of correct behaviors, and social-reinforcement of role-played behaviors are effective in altering behaviors and ultimately in changing attitudes.

V. What Is Job Satisfaction?

Job satisfaction refers to a set of attitudes that workers have about their jobs. Such satisfaction is measured by the Job Descriptive Index (JDI) and the Minnesota Satisfaction Questionnaire (MSQ). Both of these questionnaires can give effective measurements of satisfaction.

VI. What Determines Job Satisfaction?

A. Discrepancy

Discrepancy theory holds that satisfaction is a function of the discrepancy between the job outcomes a person wants and the outcomes that are perceived to be obtained. Thus, a person wanting to be a baseball pitcher might be dissatisfied with the team when placed in an outfield position.

B. Fairness

- **Distributive fairness** occurs when we get from our job what we think we deserve.

- **Equity theory** suggests that the inputs that we perceive ourselves as investing in our job and the outcomes that the job provides for us are compared against the inputs and outcomes of some other relevant person or group.

- **Inputs** consist of anything that individuals consider relevant to their exchange with the organization, such as education, training, hard work, high-quality work, etc.

- **Outcomes** are those factors that the organization distributes in return for the inputs. These might include pay, benefits, promotions, recognition or anything else of value to employees.

In general, people who work harder and are better educated than their peers expect higher rewards. Should these not be attained, the hard workers will be upset and angry over the lack of fair treatment. Fairness, thus, is an important factor in dealing with organizational behavior.

5. **Procedural fairness** (often called procedural justice) occurs when the process used to determine outcomes is seen as fair.

Thus, reasons for decision, consistent procedures, accurate information, two-way communication, and our appeals system will contribute to a perception of fairness and help workers to believe they are getting a "fair shake."

C. A Model of Satisfaction

In general, greater satisfaction will be experienced when workers receive the outcomes they expect and when these workers are treated fairly.

D. Key Contributors to Job Satisfaction

Among the key contributors to job satisfaction are; mentally challenging work, high pay, promotions, and friendly co-workers.

VII. The Consequences of Job Dissatisfaction

A. Mental Health and Off-the-Job Satisfaction

In general, happy workers are psychologically healthier than unhappy workers. Also, people with a sense of accomplishment in their work will usually have a happier home life than those unhappy at work.

B. Absence From Work

Some $46 billion in losses occur yearly in American companies due to excessive absenteeism. Canadian estimates run up to $10 billion. Although there is no strong link between absenteeism and job dissatisfaction, job satisfaction is linked to the frequency of absenteeism. Employees who dislike their jobs will tend to be absent more often than contented employees.

C. Turnover

Turnover is very expensive to employers. In general, dissatisfied workers are more apt to quit than happy workers.

D. Performance

Several hypotheses can explain the relationship between performance and satisfaction.
One hypothesis, the **"satisfaction causes performance** hypothesis" claims that satisfied workers might work harder for an organization. Another hypothesis, the "**performance causes satisfaction** hypothesis" claims that work is its own reward.

Although both of these hypotheses are true in certain instances, research demonstrates that the latter relationship is most often supported. Good performers receive rewards which contribute to higher levels of satisfaction.

E. Organizational Citizenship Behavior

At times, workers will work hard even if there is no reward awaiting them. This organizational citizenship behavior is voluntary, informal behavior that contributes to organizational effectiveness.
Helping another worker, being friendly and cooperative, volunteering for extra work, and conscientious attention to detail are examples of good organizational citizenship behavior.

PRE-TESTING YOUR UNDERSTANDING OF THE CHAPTER

Key Concepts Matching

Match the letter of the key concepts with the appropriate definitions.

A. Attitudes
B. Discrepancy theory
C. Distributive fairness
D. Equity theory
E. Individual vs. collective attitude
F. Inputs
G. Job satisfaction
H. Organizational citizenship behavior
I. Outcomes
J. Performance causes satisfaction
K. Power distance
L. Procedural fairness
M. Satisfaction causes performance
N. Theory of cognitive dissonance
O. Uncertainty avoidance
P. Values

______1. A broad tendency to prefer certain states of affairs over others.

______2. A fairly stable emotional tendency to respond consistently to some specific object, situation, person, or category of people.

______3. Societal preference for independence, initiative and privacy over interdependence and loyalty to family or clan.

______4. The extent to which an unequal distribution of power is accepted by society members.

______5. The extent to which people are uncomfortable with uncertain and ambiguous situations.

______6. A theory which deals with the tensions occurring when our cognitions are contradictory or inconsistent with each other.

______7. A collection of attitudes that workers have about their jobs.

______8. The theory that satisfaction is a function of the discrepancy between job outcomes a person wants and the outcomes that are perceived to be obtained.

______9. The concept that we get from the job what we think we deserve.

_____10. The concept that the inputs that we perceive ourselves as investing in our job and the outcomes that the job provides for us are compared against the inputs and out puts of some other relevant person or group.

_____11. Anything that individuals consider relevant to their exchange with the organization, anything that they give up, offer, or trade to the organization.

_____12. Factors that the organization distributes in return for the inputs.

_____13. The concept that the process used to determine outcomes is seen as fair.

_____14. The belief that satisfied workers are more productive than non-satisfied workers.

_____15. The concept that one's performance on the job, if rewarded, may lead to satisfaction.

_____16. Voluntary, informal behavior that contributes to organizational effectiveness.

True/False Questions

Circle the letter of the correct answer.

T F 1. Members of different occupational groups generally espouse the same values.
T F 2. Power distance refers to the distance between the superpowers.
T F 3. A cultural map shows areas where people read and attend classical concerts.
T F 4. An attitude is a fairly stable emotional tendency to respond consistently to a given situation.
T F 5. Beliefs are statements about the world that involve much evaluation.
T F 6. Believable communications are most effective at inducing attitude change.
T F 7. The job descriptive index tells workers exactly how to perform certain tasks.
T F 8. Equity theory is important in determining job satisfaction.
T F 9. Generally, pay and satisfaction are positively related.
T F 10. Satisfied workers are usually more healthy mentally than unhappy workers.
T F 11. Absenteeism costs the United States about $46 billion per year.
T F 12. Absenteeism in Sweden is caused by poor working conditions.
T F 13. Organizational citizenship behavior refers to aiding charity organizations by corporate executives.
T F 14. Satisfied workers are generally better performers.
T F 15. Values refer to our liking for luxury items.
T F 16. International business failures can occur because of cross- cultural differences.
T F 17. In Japan, managers tend to value courageous actions.
T F 18. Attitudes are the products of a related belief and value.
T F 19. A communicator who wishes to change attitudes must be seen as unbiased.
T F 20. Dissonance refers to a feeling of tension produced by loud noises.

Multiple-Choice Questions

Select the correct answer.

_____1. Which of the following is NOT part of the Goldstein and Soarcher technique for changing behaviors?
A. role-playing of correct behaviors
B. social condemnation of incorrect behaviors
C. modeling of correct behaviors
D. social reinforcement of role-played behaviors

______2. cultural variations in attitudes have implications for all of the following *except* for
A. appreciating global customers
B. importing OB theories
C. developing global employees
D. all of the above

______3. In discrepancy theory, satisfaction is
A. a function of the discrepancy between desired and obtained job outcomes.
B. caused by high salaries.
C. a function of one's salary in relation to those of others.
D. a function of one's relationships to supervisors.

______4. Which of the following would NOT normally be considered an input?
A. education
B. seniority
C. absenteeism
D. training

______5. Procedural fairness occurs when
A. a worker receives a higher salary.
B. a worker receives an unexpected promotion.
C. a worker receives a bonus.
D. the process used to determine outcomes is seen as fair.

______6. All of the following are key contributors to job satisfaction except
A. high pay.
B. mentally challenging work.
C. job status.
D. friendly co-workers.

______7. All of the following are involved with organizational citizenship behavior except that
A. the behavior is voluntary.
B. the behavior is rewarded.
C. the behavior is spontaneous.
D. the behavior helps the organization.

______8. Under dissonance theory attitudes can be changed by having people
A. pressured to alter behavior.
B. exact behaviors incompatible with attitudes.
C. receive bonuses.
D. do volunteer work.

______9. A safety message that tries to convince workers that hard-hats and safety glasses are not uncomfortable to wear would be an example of an attempt to
A. change attitudes by modifying beliefs.
B. change attitudes by modifying values.
C. use cognitive dissonance theory.
D. improve perceptions of distributive fairness.

______10. Which of the following was NOT involved in the Hofstede study?
A. power distance
B. individualism/collectivism
C. uncertainty avoidance
D. reward and punishment

POST-TESTING FOR EXAMS

True/False Questions

Circle the letter of the correct answer.

T F 1. Generally managers given foreign assignments are very successful despite cross-cultural differences.

T F 2. Mentally challenging work will tend to upset most employees.

T F 3. Attitudes and beliefs are the same things.

T F 4. Procedural fairness occurs if the process used to determine outcomes is fair.

T F 5. Distributive fairness occurs when we get large salary increases.

T F 6. Discrepancy theory deals with the differences between a worker's desired job outcomes and what the worker actually receives.

T F 7. Job satisfaction refers to a collection of attitudes that workers have about their jobs.

T F 8. Face-to-face communication is a poor method of changing beliefs.

T F 9. Attitudes are the product of a related belief and value.

T F 10. Experts have developed one system that will be very effective in changing most employee beliefs and attitudes.

Multiple-Choice Questions

Select the correct answer.

______1. All of the following are classifications of values *except*

A. intellectual

B. ecological

C. social

D. political

______2. Positive attitudes towards one's job

A. do not relate to family life.

B. relate mainly to compensation.

C. are associated with positive attitudes towards life in general.

D. are manifested only in the workplace.

______3. Turnover refers to

A. firing numbers of employees.

B. recruiting new employees.

C. voluntary resignation from an organization.

D. forced early retirements.

______4. Cognitive dissonance theory refers to

A. feelings caused by discrepancies between cognitives.

B. too much noise at work.

C. contradictory union demands.

D. contradictory management demands.

______5. Under equity theory we should receive
A. more than other workers.
B. less than other workers.
C. similar outcomes as other workers for similar inputs.
D. none of the above.

______6. All of the following are forms of organizational citizenship behavior *except*
A. helping behavior.
B. courtesy and cooperation.
C. conscientiousness.
D. whistle blowing.

______7. Strong uncertainty avoidance cultures stress
A. the belief that people should enjoy life more.
B. rules and regulations.
C. a broad tolerance for diversity.
D. a tendency to focus on short-term outcomes.

______8. All of the following factors might be involved in perceptions of procedural fairness *except*
A. adequate reasons are given for decisions.
B. the allocator is unbiased.
C. the allocator is biased.
D. the allocator seems arbitrary.

______9. Absenteeism from work is said to cost the United States
A. about $46 billion.
B. about $8 billion.
C. about $60 billion.
D. less than $5 billion.

______10. Broad tendency in values means that they
A. can easily be predicted.
B. are of very general emotional orientation.
C. cut across different areas.
D. interfere with work.

______11. Our beliefs are assumed statements about the nature of the world that
A. involve much evaluation.
B. depend upon our jobs.
C. do not involve evaluation.
D. can get us into trouble.

______12. All of the following concepts are related *except*
A. beliefs.
B. values.
C. attitudes.
D. attributes.

______13. The attitude that women are not cut out for business is an example of
A. good thinking.
B. stereotyping.
C. discrepancy theory.
D. cognitive dissonance.

______14. Our getting the "short end of the stick" involves
A. equity theory.
B. stereotyping.
C. discrepancy theory.
D. poor communicators.

______15. Providing good feedback might be an example of
A. distributive fairness.
B. procedural fairness.
C. equity theory.
D. organizational citizenship behavior.

______16. A high frequency of short-term absences might reflect
A. poor management.
B. cognitive dissonance.
C. an attitude problem.
D. lazy workers.

______17. Helping another worker with a difficult job might be an example of
A. organizational citizenship behavior.
B. satisfaction causes performance hypothesis.
C. procedural fairness.
D. self-seeking.

______18. In small power distance cultures
A. electricity is less expensive.
B. inequality is accepted as natural.
C. superiors are accessible.
D. after hours socializing with colleagues is common.

______19. The most effective method of persuasion changing attitudes is
A. telephone calls.
B. face-to-face persuasion.
C. written notices.
D. orders from executives.

______20. As a result of reading this chapter you should realize that
A. achieving worker satisfaction is a difficult task.
B. using computers can facilitate worker satisfaction.
C. managers know exactly how to satisfy their workers.
D. worker satisfaction is no longer important to management.

Application Situations Exercise

Match the letter of the key concepts with the appropriate definitions.

A. Attitudes
B. Discrepancy theory
C. Distributive fairness
D. Equity theory
E. Individual vs. collective attitude
F. Inputs
G. Job satisfaction
H. Organizational citizenship behavior
I. Outcomes
J. Performance causes satisfaction
K. Power distance
L. Procedural fairness
M. Satisfaction causes performance
N. Theory of cognitive dissonance
O. Uncertainty avoidance
P. Values

_____ 1. It seemed to him that most people he worked with in his new country were out for themselves.

_____ 2. Still, he always volunteered to help other workers.

_____ 3. He noticed that people with equal experiences and education received different salaries.

_____ 4. When he tried to complain about it, though, he found his superiors inaccessible.

_____ 5. He and his co-workers got together and saw the problems with how salaries were allocated.

_____ 6. Management's refusal to deal with the issue tended to sour their attitude toward work.

_____ 7. The pay problem could be traced to supervisors not following the company's salary guidelines.

_____ 8. The problem remained unresolved, so many workers just did less work.

_____ 9. Finally, management agreed to provide additional salary.

_____ 10. Each individual now felt that her/his job expectations were being met.

Short Answer Questions

Fill-in the missing word(s).

1. Research shows that ________ percent of American managers terminate foreign assignments because they cannot adjust to the culture.

2. A Dutch scientist _________ asked over 116,000 IBM employees about work-related values.

3. _______ refers to a society's discomfort with uncertain and ambiguous situations.

4. Cognitive dissonance might be experienced if you spent a great deal of money on a car and it turned out to be a ________.

5. The most popular measure of job satisfaction is __________.

6. In general, pay and _______ are positively related.

7. In the United States, absenteeism cost business an estimated ________ per year.

8. Voluntary resignations from an organization are known as ________.

9. The fact that job satisfaction tends to be fairly stable over time is an argument for the influence of ________.

10. Ben and Jerry probably hold ________ social values than the typical entrepreneur.

ANSWER SHEET FOR CHAPTER 5

PRE-TESTING YOUR UNDERSTANDING OF THE CHAPTER

Key Concepts Matching

1. P 2. A 3. E 4. K 5. O 6. N 7. G 8. B 9. C 10. D 11. F 12. I 13. L 14. M 15. J 16. H

True/False Questions

1. F 2. F 3. F 4. T 5. F 6. T 7. F 8. T 9. T 10. T 11. T 12. F 13. F 14. F 15. F 16. T 17. F 18. T 19. T 20. F

Multiple-Choice Questions

1. B 2. D 3. A 4. C 5. D 6. C 7. B 8. B 9.A 10. D

POST-TESTING FOR EXAMS

True/False Questions

1. F 2. F 3. F 4. T 5. F 6. T 7. T 8. F 9. T 10. F

Multiple-Choice Questions

1. B 2. C 3. C 4. A 5. C 6. D 7. B 8. D 9. A 10. B 11. C 12. D 13. C 14. A 15. B 16. C 17. A 18. C 19. B 20. A

Application Situations Exercise

1. E 2.H 3. D 4. K 5. C 6. G 7.L 8. F 9. I 10. B

Short Answer Questions

1. 16% to 40% 2. Geert Hofstede 3. uncertainty avoidance
4. lemon 5. job descriptive index (JDI) 6. satisfaction
7. $46 billion 8. turnover 9. disposition
10. social

CASE STUDY

STRIKING OIL

Bruce Spiece frowned and stared out the window of his high-rise office. He had a problem. A real problem. In business school at the University of Regina he had learned that the recognition of a problem was the first step in finding its solution. In this case, he wasn't so sure.

Spiece was the personnel director for Petrolin, a medium-size, Calgary-based oil company. The problem Spiece faced involved Petrolin's experienced earth scientists. Earth scientists are the professionals who do the "brain work" involved in discovering and extracting oil and gas from the depths of the earth. They include geologists, geophysicists, and petroleum engineers. Underlining the risky nature of oil exploration, Spiece half-jokingly described their work this way: "Geologists guess where the oil is, geophysicists guess what's between the surface and the oil, and petroleum engineers guess how to get the oil out. If they all guess right, we make profits."

With increased domestic oil exploration following the OPEC embargo of 1973, earth science graduates had become the "bonus babies" of the industry. New B.Sc.s in petroleum engineering were now receiving offers near $30,000, with graduates in geology and geophysics following close behind. Spiece's problem was not connected with the high demand for, and high salaries offered to, new graduates; rather, increasing turnover among Petrolin's experienced earth scientists was troubling him. In the past year, 15 percent of the company's earth scientists had resigned. Most were joining very small independent oil companies. Virtually all of these resignees had been employees with five to fifteen years' experience and constituted the very core of Petrolin's exploration staff.

Spiece knew that this problem was not unique. It had begun several years earlier with the major oil companies the big, publicly traded firms such as Exxon, Amoco, Chevron, and Shell. The practical aspects of oil exploration and extraction are complex, and several years of experience are necessary before new graduates become full-fledged professionals. Thus, the majors, as well as medium-size firms such as Petrolin, provided training for earth scientists in the entire oil industry. Only the intermediate and major companies had the resources necessary to carry out this development. With the increase in domestic drilling following the oil embargo, many small independent oil companies had stepped up activities or entered the field. With no training resources and an immediate need for experienced earth scientists, these firms had resorted to "raiding" the majors and medium-size firms for seasoned personnel. Unfortunately, "veterans" were already in short supply since a slowdown in oil exploration in the 1960s had made the earth sciences relatively unattractive to university students at that time.

Some independents used "headhunting" agencies, and Spiece had heard horror stories of telephone calls echoing up and down the corridors of corporate geology departments as aggressive recruiters contacted one professional after another. Similarly, he knew that some headhunters became regulars at restaurants and bars frequented by earth scientists, hoping to forge an "accidental" contact. As a result of this aggressive recruiting, all oil firms were experiencing an unacceptable level of turnover among experienced earth scientists. Just when the need for them was greatest, the experienced personnel of geology and engineering departments were being depleted, only to be made up with high-priced new graduates. Also, Spiece was convinced that some resignees were taking inside information about drilling prospects to the smaller competitors.

Source: Case prepared by Gary Johns. Some data is based on Alexander Stuart, Manhunt in the Oil Fields, *Fortune*, October 6, 1980, 82-86.

Why would an experienced earth scientist forsake the security, prestige, and large support staff of a major or intermediate oil company to join a small independent? Spiece recalled an exit interview he had conducted a week ago with Virginia Knox, a veteran Petrolin geologist who was moving to a small Calgary independent. Knox had received her geology degree from the University of Alberta and started her career at Shell Oil. She had been at Petrolin for eight years. Spiece began by asking Virginia Knox why she was leaving Petrolin after eight successful years, hoping against hope to hear an answer he hadn't heard before.

"Money," Virginia Knox responded, "money and opportunity. Look, Mr Spiece, after fourteen years in the oil business I'm making $40,000 while you're bringing in bonus babies still wet behind the ears at $30,000. That just isn't right. The company I'm going to is paying me $50,000 and giving me a company car. In addition, I'll get a one percent override on everything I find."

Spiece cringed mentally at the word override. An override was a royalty paid on the gross revenues of any producing well developed by the geologist. Thus, Virginia Knox would receive one percent of the revenues of any oil she discovered for the independent. The independents had been using this incentive in their raiding efforts, and rumor was that some defectors from the larger firms had become millionaires due to overrides.

"I'm also excited by the work I'll be doing at the new company," continued Virginia Knox. "I'll be prospecting my own wells, with a two- or three-person team. Here at Petrolin we have dozens of geologists doing the same work I do, and it takes forever to get approval to drill."

Spiece understood Knox's point. The majors and intermediates tended to concentrate on the larger and more remote oil fields. Because drilling in such locations required substantial investment, several levels of management scrutinized drilling proposals very cautiously. The independents generally tended to stick to better-known territory, and geologists frequently took their proposals straight to the company president (usually a "shirt-sleeves" type) for consideration.

Spiece tried his best to discourage Virginia Knox's resignation.

"Look, Ms. Knox, I can understand some of the attraction you see in going to a small independent. But I think you should be aware of what you're in for. There's no support staff there, and you'll find yourself having to do routine work that you haven't done in years, the stuff our bonus babies do for you here. Also, in that environment you're going to stagnate professionally. Here, we've got a large staff with varied backgrounds, and people are coming in from the universities all the time. This keeps you fresh and current. And don't forget the pressure-cooker atmosphere at the independents. You're on call all the time, you're responsible for the prospects, and you can't take a vacation in the middle of a project. Here, you have others to rely on. And finally, don't expect any regular pay raises at the independent. They're generous up front, but stingy afterwards except for the override. And, personally, I think the value of overrides is rated too highly. You know as well as I do that only 10 percent of all prospects yield oil, and the independents are working smaller fields than we are here."

Virginia Knox had thanked Spiece for his advice and emphasized that she had nothing but the highest regard for Petrolin. But she insisted that her resignation was final.

Bruce Spiece continued to stare out his office window, wondering how turnover among the experienced Petrolin earth scientists could be reduced. Salary increases were not out of the question, but it was generally agreed that other employees would react negatively to such a move. Middle managers, marketing personnel, and employees who negotiated oil field leases were already incredulous of the salaries accorded to the bonus babies. For larger firms such as Petrolin, overrides

were difficult to consider. Because such firms concentrated on bigger, more complex oil prospects, large teams of earth scientists worked together on exploration projects. With such teams, it was hard to decide exactly who deserved how much of a royalty on any given oil strike. Perhaps company cars or large cash bonuses based on exceptional individual performance would help to retain the experienced personnel. Spiece just wasn't sure.

1. Describe Virginia Knox's attitudes toward her job at the time of her resignation. Be specific as to job satisfaction facets.

2. Use discrepancy theory and equity theory to explain Virginia Knox's attitudes toward her job at the time of her resignation.

3. Not everyone who experiences job dissatisfaction actually quits his or her job. What factors contributed to Virginia's conversion of dissatisfaction into actual turnover?

4. How might the turnover problem at Petrolin have been prevented if the company had acted earlier?

5. Use your understanding of attitude change to explain why it would have been very difficult for Spiece to change Knox's mind during the exit interview.

6. What should Bruce Spiece do now?

CHAPTER 6

THEORIES OF WORK MOTIVATION

LEARNING OBJECTIVES

- DEFINE MOTIVATION, DISCUSS ITS BASIC PROPERTIES, AND DISTINGUISH IT FROM PERFORMANCE.
- COMPARE AND CONTRAST INTRINSIC AND EXTRINSIC MOTIVATION.
- EXPLAIN AND DISCUSS THE MANAGERIAL IMPLICATIONS OF NEED THEORIES OF MOTIVATION.
- EXPLAIN AND DISCUSS THE MANAGERIAL IMPLICATIONS OF EQUITY THEORY.
- DISCUSS THE CROSS-CULTURAL LIMITATIONS OF THEORIES OF MOTIVATION.
- USE THE PORTER-LAWLER MODEL TO SUMMARIZE THE RELATIONSHIP AMONG THE VARIOUS THEORIES OF MOTIVATION, PERFORMANCE, AND JOB SATISFACTION.

KEY CONCEPTS

Motivation

Intrinsic motivation

Extrinsic motivation

Performance

Need theories

Maslow's hierarchy of needs

ERG theory

McClelland's theory of needs

Need for achievement

Need for affiliation

Need for power

Process theories

Expectancy theory

Outcomes

Instrumentality

Valence

Expectancy

Force

Equity theory

CHAPTER SUMMARY

Key concepts are identified by **bold** *faced type.*

I. What is Motivation?

Motivation means that a person "works hard," "keeps at" his or her work, and directs his or her behavior toward appropriate outcomes. **Motivation** is the extent to which persistent effort is directed toward a goal.

A. Basic Characteristics of Motivation

The three basic components of motivation are: effort, which refers to the strength of a person's work-related behavior; persistence, which refers to the persistence that individuals exhibit in applying effort to their work tasks; and direction, which refers to the quality of a person's work related behavior.

B. Extrinsic and Intrinsic Motivation

Intrinsic motivation stems from the direct relationship between the worker and the task and is usually self-applied.

Extrinsic motivation stems from the work environment external to the task and is usually applied by someone other than the person being motivated.

C. Motivation and Performance

Performance can be defined as the extent to which an organizational member contributes to achieving the objectives of the organization.

Although there is a positive relationship between motivation and performance, the relationship isn't one to one because other factors can intervene.

II. Need Theories of Work Motivation

Need theories attempt to specify the kinds of needs people have and the conditions under which they will be motivated to satisfy their needs in an organizationally useful manner.

A. Maslow's Hierarchy of Needs

Psychologist Abraham Maslow developed a theory based on our satisfying certain needs. These needs range from physiological needs, at the lowest level to self-actualization needs at the highest level.

According to **Maslow's hierarchy of needs**, the lowest level unsatisfied need category has the best motivating potential.

These individuals are motivated to satisfy their physiological needs before they show interest in their self-esteem or safety needs. Maslow's hierarchy also implies that a satisfied need is no longer an effective motivator.

B. Alderfer's ERG Theory

Another need theory was developed by Clayton Alderfer. This theory, the **ERG theory**, argues that we have three basic needs: existence, relatedness, and growth needs.

Alderfer's theory differs from Maslow's theory in that there is no rigid hierarchy of needs and that if higher-level needs are ungratified, individuals will increase their desire for the gratification of lower-level needs.

C. McCelland's Theory of Needs

Psychologist David **McClelland** has developed a **need theory** based not on a hierarchy of needs, but on the specific behavioral consequences of needs.

According to this theory, individuals have needs for achievement, affiliation, and power.

People high in the **need for achievement** have a special desire to perform challenging tasks well.

People high in the **need for affiliation** have a special desire to establish and maintain friendly, compatible interpersonal relationships.

People high in the **need for power** desire to have a strong influence over others.

D. Research Support for Need Theories

Research results show that all these need theories are valid under certain circumstances. In general, McClelland's theory has proven to be a better predictor of motivation than those of Maslow or Alderfer.

III. Process Theories of Work Motivation

Need theories of motivation concentrate on what motivates individuals, while **process theories** deal with how motivation occurs. The two most important process theories are expectancy theory and equity theory.

A. Expectancy Theory

The basic idea underlying **expectancy theory** is the belief that motivation is determined by the outcomes people expect as a result of their actions on the job.

According to psychologist Victor Vroom, **outcomes** are the consequences that may follow certain work behaviors. First-level outcomes are of interest to the organization. Second-level outcomes are consequences of first-level outcomes.

Instrumentality is the probability that a particular first-level outcome (such as high productivity) will be followed by a particular second-level outcome (such as pay).

Valence is the expected value of outcomes, the extent to which they are attractive or unattractive to the individual.

Expectancy is the probability that a worker can actually achieve a particular first-level outcome.
Force is the effort directed toward a first-level outcome and is the end product of the other components of the theory. We expect that an individual's effort will be directed toward the first-level outcome that has the highest force product (force = first-level valence x expectancy).

The main concepts of expectancy theory are that people will be motivated to engage in those work activities that they find attractive and that they feel they can accomplish. The attractiveness of various work activities depends upon the extent to which they lead to favorable personal consequences.

B. Equity Theory

Equity theory claims that workers compare the inputs that they invest in their jobs and the outcomes that they receive against the inputs and outcomes of some other relevant person or group. Individuals that perceive inequity may be motivated to engage in a number of tactics to regain equity:

- perceptually distort one's own inputs or outcomes
- perceptually distort the inputs or outcomes of the comparison other or group
- choose another comparison person or group
- alter one's inputs or alter one's outputs
- leave the exchange relationship

In general, research shows that underpayment inequity leads to resignation, and that workers will lower their production levels to match their perceptions of inequity when paid on an hourly basis, or raise them when paid on a piece rate basis.

IV. Do Motivation Theories Translate Across Cultures?

In general, motivational theories which explain the behavior of workers in North American companies do not always apply to workers elsewhere.

In more collective societies, self-actualization is not the motivator that it is in the United States. In collective cultures, there is a tendency to favor reward allocation based on equality rather than equity.

Although expectancy theory works well when considered cross-culturally, managers should always be aware of cultural differences when dealing with worker motivation.

V. Putting it all Together: The Porter-Lawler Model

The Porter-Lawler model is a depiction of the various theories of motivation and of the relationship between motivation and performance. This model depicts the different theories as well as the concepts of feedback, equity, satisfaction, and reward probability.

VI. A Footnote: Do Extrinsic Rewards Decrease Intrinsic Motivation?

The extrinsic/intrinsic motivation relationship suggests that if intrinsic outcomes and extrinsic outcomes are both highly valence, they should contribute to motivation in an additive fashion.

In general, research has shown that both extrinsic and intrinsic rewards are necessary to enhance motivation in actual work settings.

PRE-TESTING YOUR UNDERSTANDING OF THE CHAPTER

Key Concepts Matching

Match the letter of the key concepts with the appropriate definitions.

A. Equity Theory
B. ERG Theory
C. Expectancy
D. Expectancy Theory
E. Extrinsic Motivation
F. Force
G. Instrumentality
H. Intrinsic Motivation
I. Maslow's hierarchy of needs
J. McClelland's theory of needs
K. Motivation
L. Need for achievement
M. Need for affiliation
N. Need for power
O. Need Theories
P. Outcomes
Q. Performance
R. Process Theories
S. Valence

______1. The extent to which persistent effort is directed toward a goal.

______2. Motivation which stems from the direct relationship between the worker and the task and is usually self-applied.

______3. Motivation which stems from the work environment external to the task and is usually applied by someone other than the person being motivated.

______4. The extent to which an organizational member contributes to achieving the objectives of the organization.

______5. Theories which attempt to specify the kinds of needs people have and the conditions under which they will be motivated to satisfy their needs in our organizationally useful manner.

______6. A premise which states that the lowest-level unsatisfied need has the greatest motivating potential.

______7. A need system using three categories - existence, relatedness, and growth needs.

______8. People high in this need have a special desire to perform challenging tasks well.

______9. People who are high in this need have a special desire to establish and maintain friendly, compatible interpersonal relationships.

_____10. People who are high in this need desire to have a strong influence over others.

_____11. Theories which concentrate upon how motivation occurs.

_____12. The belief that motivation is determined by the outcomes that people expect to occur as a result of their actions on the job.

_____13. The probability that a particular first-level outcome (such as high productivity) will be followed by a particular second-level outcome (such as pay).

_____14. The expected value of outcomes, the extent to which they are attractive or unattractive to the individual.

_____15. The probability that the worker can actually achieve a particular first-level outcome.

_____16. The theory that workers compare the inputs that they invest in their jobs and the outcomes that they receive against the inputs and outcomes of some other relevant person or groups.

_____17. A non-hierarchical need theory of motivation that outlines the conditions under which certain needs result in particular patterns of motivation.

_____18. The consequences that may follow certain work behaviors.

_____19. The relative degree of effort that will be directed toward first-level outcomes in expectancy theory.

True/False Questions

Circle the letter of the correct answer.

T F 1. Downsizing has been found to increase motivation.
T F 2. Extrinsic motivation is self-motivation.
T F 3. Abraham Maslow developed a theory of human compensation.
T F 4. In general, moonlighting does not damage work performance.
T F 5. Clayton Alderfer is a pioneer in the study of need-based theories.
T F 6. Individuals with high need achievements have a strong desire for performance feedback.
T F 7. Expectancy theories claim that workers produce more when they expect a visit from the boss.
T F 8. When workers are underpaid on an hourly basis, they tend to lower their inputs by producing less work.
T F 9. Perceived underpayment will generally cause workers to work harder.
T F 10. In general, people are more concerned about their health, family life, and standard of living than they are about their jobs.
T F 11. Highly motivated people generally are good performers.
T F 12. Our physiological needs are very important in Maslow's formulation.
T F 13. According to Maslow, a satisfied need usually is no longer an effective motivator.
T F 14. McClelland argues that there is a one-to-one correspondence between our needs and our behavior.
T F 15. Expectancy theory is based on the perceptions of the individual worker.
T F 16. Inequities in compensation cause workers to produce more.

T F 17. Workers generally tend to compare their compensation and other outcomes with those of their peers.

T F 18. Motivational theories relevant in the United States are usually affected by cultural differences in other nations.

T F 19. The Porter-Lawler model deals with production processes.

T F 20. Psychologists have recently devised a universally applicable system of motivating all workers.

Multiple-Choice Questions

Select the correct answer.

______1. Self-applied motivation is known as
A. extrinsic motivation.
B. intrinsic motivation.
C. primary motivation.
D. secondary motivation.

______2. Of the following, who was not a pioneer in the study of motivation?
A. McClelland
B. Alderfer
C. Maslow
D. Waterman

______3. A model that summarizes relationships among motivational theories is
A. the Alderfer model.
B. the Maslow hierarchy.
C. the Porter-Lawler model.
D. the Valence model.

______4. Inequities in the work place are
A. unpleasant and tension producing.
B. excellent work motivators.
C. a deliberate management tool.
D. a result of union activities.

______5. Valence refers to
A. the attractiveness of other workers.
B. the expected value of outcomes.
C. our like or dislike of the boss.
D. the rewards we receive from work.

______6. People with a high need for affiliation tend to
A. seek executive positions.
B. perform challenging tasks.
C. establish friendly relationships.
D. seek conflict and challenge.

______7. Which of the following is NOT part of Alderfer's need-based theory?
A. existence needs
B. self-actualization needs
C. growth needs
D. relatedness needs

______8. Which of the following is NOT part of Maslow's hierarchy of needs?
A. esteem needs
B. relatedness needs
C. physiological needs
D. safety needs

______9. All of the following are basic characteristics of motivation *except*
A. ecology.
B. direction.
C. persistence.
D. effort.

10. According to McClelland, all of the following are important needs *except*
A. need for power.
B. need for assimilation.
C. need for achievement.
D. need for affiliation.

POST-TESTING FOR EXAMS

True/False Questions

Circle the letter of the correct answer.

T F 1. Need theories and process theories are the same things.
T F 2. According to Maslow our best motivators are our esteem needs.
T F 3. The ERG theory deals with valences and attractions.
T F 4. McClelland feels that people should be motivated to seek out and perform well in jobs that match their needs.
T F 5. Instrumentality deals with our musical abilities.
T F 6. Equity theory compares inputs and outcomes of different workers.
T F 7. Different office assignments can cause elevated or depressed worker motivation.
T F 8. According to equity theory, workers tend to be happy with two-tier wage contracts.
T F 9. Process theories attempt to explain how motivation occurs rather than what factors are motivational.
T F 10. In general, what motivates American workers will also motivate workers in other countries.

Multiple-Choice Questions

Select the correct answer.

______1. A person who constantly seeks executive positions is said to have
A. strong power needs.
B. strong growth needs.
C. strong esteem needs.
D. strong achievement needs.

______2. Victor Vroom is a pioneer in the study of
A. ERG theory.
B. equity theory.
C. hierarchy of needs.
D. expectancy theory.

______3. Survivors of a corporate downsizing
A. are grateful for being spared.
B. are often less motivated.
C. are often more motivated.
D. have neutral feelings about their work.

______4. All of the following dealt with need theories *except*
A. Maslow.
B. Alderfer.
C. Vroom.
D. McClelland.

______5. All of the following are components of expectancy theory *except*
A. valence.
B. input.
C. outcomes.
D. force.

______6. An equation that describes needs theories is
A. needs inputs outcomes.
B. motivation inputs rewards.
C. needs behavior incentives and goals.
D. force inputs outcomes.

______7. All of the following are components of McClelland's theory of needs *except* the
A. need for achievement.
B. need for power.
C. need for affiliation.
D. need for recognition.

______8. Expectancy is the probability that a worker can
A. achieve a particular first-level outcome.
B. achieve a desirable second-level outcome.
C. be promoted in a short time.
D. anticipate a layoff in hard economic times.

______9. From a motivational standpoint a "superjob" is one that
A. pays high salary for little work.
B. provides for rapid promotions.
C. is especially high in both intrinsic and extrinsic motivations.
D. provides many fringe benefits.

______10. A person working harder because of a bonus system is reacting to
A. intrinsic motivation.
B. extrinsic motivation.
C. valence.
D. achievement needs.

______11. Our needs for food, clothing, and shelter are examples of
A. safety needs.
B. survival needs.
C. physiological needs.
D. basic human needs.

______12. Alderfer's relatedness needs correspond closely to Maslow's
A. safety needs.
B. esteem needs.
C. belongingness needs.
D. growth needs.

______13. All of the following relate to people with needs for achievement *except* that
A. they desire performance feedback.
B. they desire tangible rewards.
C. they like personal responsibility for outcomes.
D. they tend to set moderately difficult goals with calculated risks.

______14. Instrumentality is the probability that a particular first-level outcome will
A. result in a particular second-level outcome.
B. disappoint a worker.
C. please one's biases.
D. result in rapid promotion.

______15. All of the following are involved in expectancy theory *except*
A. valence.
B. instrumentality.
C. needs.
D. force.

______16. An example of an expectancy theory is found in the works of
A. Maslow.
B. Alderfer.
C. Vroom.
D. McClelland.

______17. All of the following are examples of low expectancies *except*
A. arbitrary evaluations.
B. poor feedback.
C. poor equipment.
D. poor environmental practices.

______18. To achieve equity one can do all of the following *except*
A. choose another companion or group.
B. choose new bosses.
C. leave the exchange relationship.
D. alter one's inputs or outcomes.

______19. In general, perceived underpayment in an organization will result in
A. harder work efforts.
B. higher motivation.
C. lower productivity.
D. less absenteeism.

______20. As a result of reading this chapter you should realize that motivating workers is
A. easily done with computers.
B. a difficult task at best.
C. of no real importance.
D. easily achieved by raising salaries.

Application Situations exercise

Match the key concepts with the statements that best describe them.

A. Equity Theory
B. ERG Theory
C. Expectancy
D. Expectancy Theory
E. Extrinsic Motivation
F. Force
G. Instrumentality
H. Intrinsic Motivation
I. Maslow's hierarchy of needs
J. McClelland's theory of needs
K. Motivation
L. Need for achievement
M. Need for affiliation
N. Need for power
O. Need Theories
P. Outcomes
Q. Performance
R. Process Theories
S. Valence

_____ 1. Our boss never thought he was being treated fairly by our top executives.

_____ 2. They thought he wanted to be a top executive himself, so he could have a big impact.

_____ 3. But he calculated that being in upper management would be a real challenge and he wanted to do well.

_____ 4. He was also willing to work very hard to achieve his goals.

_____ 5. He was also willing to do his best to help the company achieve its objectives.

_____ 6. He did have certain needs of his own, though.

_____ 7. He had always expected that he would be rewarded adequately for his dedicated efforts.

_____ 8. He was really self-motivated and didn't need outside pressures to get him to work.

_____ 9. Though he wanted a top job, he never was concerned much about compatible relationships with his colleagues.

_____ 10. He was offered money rewards, but he never regarded them as important as the title to which he aspired.

Short Answer Questions

Fill-in the missing word(s).

1. The developer of a non-hierarchical theory of needs was ___________.

2. The three characteristics of motivation are effort, persistence and ___________.

3. The most basic needs, according of Maslow's theory, are ____________.

4. Clayton Alderfer was a pioneer in the development of the ____________.

5. If __________ is low, workers will not seek to enhance organizational goals.

6. Individuals at work should generally be motivated to maintain an ________ exchange relationship.

7. Perceived _____________ will have a variety of negative emotional consequences for most organizations.

8. In collective cultures there is a tendency to favor reward allocation based on _________ rather than equity.

9. According to the Porter-Lawler Model, the relationship between _________ and performance can be affected by an individual's abilities and traits.

10. _________ attempt to explain how motivation occurs rather than what specific factors are motivational.

ANSWER SHEET FOR CHAPTER 6

PRE-TESTING YOUR UNDERSTANDING OF THE CHAPTER

Key Concepts Matching

1. K 2. H 3. E 4. Q 5. O 6. I 7. B 8. L 9. M 10. N 11. R 12. D 13. G
14. S 15. C 16. A 17. J 18. P 19. F

True/False Questions

1. F 2. F 3. F 4. T 5. T 6. T 7. F 8. T 9. F 10. T 11. F 12. T 13. T
14. F 15. T 16. F 17. 18. T 19. F 20. F

Multiple-Choice Questions

1. B 2. D 3. C 4. A 5. B 6. C 7. B 8. B 9. A 10. B

POST-TESTING FOR EXAMS

True/False Questions

1. F 2. F 3. F 4. T 5. F 6. T 7. T 8. F 9. T 10. F

Multiple-Choice Questions

1. A 2. D 3. B 4. C 5. B 6. C 7. D 8. A 9. C 10. B 11. C 12. C 13. B
14. A 15. C 16. C 17. D 18. B 19. C 20. B

Application Situations Exercises

1. A 2. N 3. L 4. K 5. Q 6. O 7. D 8. H 9. M 10. S

Short Answer Questions

1. McClelland 2. direction 3. physiological needs 4. ERG theory
5. expectancy 6. equitable 7. underpayment 8. equality
9. effort 10. process theories

CASE STUDY

CLAIRE

Claire entered the Accounts Payable department at a large automotive plant in Ontario right after her seventeen and a half week maternity leave in October of 1993. She did not return to her previous position, but was placed in a comparable job with exactly the same pay and level of responsibility as when she had left. Claire was renewed and ready to get back to work. She valued good and competent work and was not afraid to work extra hours or even through break periods to make sure that the job was done correctly and completely. Claire also planned to continue with her part time university study. She had completed the equivalent of two years full time study toward an honors degree. None of her co-workers had progressed past high school.

Claire's first impression of her new work group was that the other members did not appear to work very diligently. She overheard Andy, one of her male colleagues, selling real estate and answering calls on various properties instead of performing his accounts work. Brenda, a female colleague appeared to spend a lot of time talking to her friends on the telephone while she slowly flipped through her bills to be paid. Bob, spent most of his time chatting or flirting with Donna, yet another female colleague. Donna watched all members of the work group intently and apparently saw it as her role to keep everyone informed of everyone else's business. Her list of confidants included the supervisor and it was clear that she viewed the term "reporting relationship" in a way not thought of by organization designers.

Although Claire was aware of these dynamics, she decided to ignore them. She was glad to be back to work and although she missed her new baby, she was confident that she could be a better mother if she was happy and working. She thought that the insights and experience she could gain in this new department would be useful in a management role later on. As far as the behavior of her colleagues was concerned, Claire was confident that their lack of commitment would eventually catch up with them. The incentive package offered by the firm included a performance pay merit pool and promotion for outstanding employees. In her mind, Claire saw no point in joining in with those gossiping about other staff members. Claire believed that her hard work and commitment to improving herself would be noticed and she would be justly rewarded.

When the time came to do performance reviews, however, Claire was greatly surprised. All employees in the group received the same rating of good/competent. The signal from management was apparently that there was no difference in the level of performance of the various employees. That meant that all employees would share equally in the merit pool. Upon finding out this information from the office "grapevine", Claire immediately went in to talk to her supervisor about her feeling that she was being unfairly treated. As she tried to explain her situation, she soon found herself in a box, however. She didn't really feel that her performance was substantially greater than good/competent. Although she had been putting in extra effort, she still felt that she was "learning the ropes". In fact, she felt good about her rating and the additional merit pay it meant; at least as long as she only thought about what her expectations were for her job. What was really upsetting her, she decided, was that her co-workers had also uniformly received identical rewards. In her discussion with her supervisor, however, she did not want to use examples, or put other group members down. Her level of performance had been remarkably different from theirs, but she was reluctant to point the finger at their relatively poorer efforts. As she left her supervisor's office, he was wondering what all the fuss was about.

Source: Case prepared by Deborah Hurst, Memorial University of Newfoundland.

Claire's meeting with the supervisor and her questioning of the situation soon became public knowledge in the work group. Donna had listened in on the first part of Claire's conversation and assumed that she had gone on to "rat" on her colleagues. Donna then dutifully informed all group members about Claire's alleged behavior. The group became somewhat hostile toward Claire after that and refused to interact with her. Andy was the first to comment. He asked Claire why she, as a woman, would expect special treatment. Claire was aghast! She certainly wasn't asking for special treatment as a woman, she merely wanted to have her hard work and efforts recognized. Andy then went on to say that he only made $40,000 a year and, as a divorced father, had heavy support payments and wasn't about to let some woman cause him any trouble. She was "on notice" he said, and then turned back to the real estate listings book that was never out of reach on his desk. Now Claire was really puzzled. Not only was he under performing <u>and</u> had received the same performance rating as she had for doing it, but now it was clear that he was being paid $10,000 more than she was as well!

Claire continued to work diligently, but remained disappointed with the outcome of the performance review. A few weeks later, Claire was called in to meet again with her supervisor. He said he wanted to offer her the opportunity to add some challenging new responsibilities to her job. She was the only bilingual individual in the group and Andy was having a lot of difficulty with his Quebec contact. The individual in Quebec had just called the supervisor and complained again about the lack of service he had been receiving. The supervisor informed Claire that he would like her to take over this file. He explained that Andy really was at a disadvantage because he couldn't speak French and it would be great if Claire could step in and help out. Claire returned to her desk frustrated. "..challenging new responsibilities..." she thought. It seemed pretty clear to her that her ability to speak French, which she had always valued, had only landed her with more work. The fact that it was Andy's work (giving him more time to continue selling real estate!) only made things worse.

As time went by, Claire began to dread going to work and missed her new baby increasingly. She found, in fact, that it was becoming more and more difficult to even get out of bed in the morning. None of her Accounts Payable colleagues would talk to Claire beyond answering her questions curtly. With no one else to talk to, she, like Brenda, began to spend more and more time on the phone with her friends while she sorted her bills for payment. She couldn't leave the company yet as she had her own bills to pay, but found that talking to her friends during her bill sorting helped. Eventually, Claire did leave the company and returned to university full time.

1. How would you analyze Claire's motivation using the need theories in this chapter?

2. How have equity considerations influenced Claire's actions?

3. Use expectancy theory to explain how motivated you think Claire will be to take the new assignment she is being offered.

4. As her supervisor, what would you have done to retain Claire in the company?

CHAPTER 7

MOTIVATION IN PRACTICE

LEARNING OBJECTIVES

- DISCUSS HOW TO TIE PAY TO PERFORMANCE ON PRODUCTION JOBS AND THE DIFFICULTIES OF WAGE INCENTIVE PLANS.
- EXPLAIN HOW TO TIE PAY TO PERFORMANCE ON WHITE-COLLAR JOBS AND THE DIFFICULTIES OF MERIT PAY PLANS.
- UNDERSTAND HOW TO USE PAY TO MOTIVATE TEAMWORK.
- DESCRIBE THE DETAILS OF THE JOB CHARACTERISTIC MODEL.
- DISCUSS THE MOTIVATIONAL PROPERTIES OF JOB ENRICHMENT.
- UNDERSTAND THE CONNECTION BETWEEN GOAL SETTING AND MANAGEMENT BY OBJECTIVES.
- EXPLAIN HOW ALTERNATIVE WORK SCHEDULES RESPECT EMPLOYEE DIVERSITY.
- REVIEW THE MOTIVATIONAL ASPECTS OF TOTAL QUALITY MANAGEMENT.

KEY CONCEPTS

Piecerate	Feedback
Wage incentive plans	Growth need strength
Restriction of productivity	Job enrichment
Merit pay plans	Goal setting
Lump sum bonus	Management by Objectives (MBO)
Profit sharing	Flex-time
Gainsharing	Compressed workweek

Skill based pay

Skill variety

Autonomy

Task significance

Task identity

Job sharing

Total Quality Management (TQM)

Benchmarking

Empowerment

CHAPTER SUMMARY

Key concepts are identified by **bold** *faced type.*

I. Money as a Motivator

The money that employees receive is usually made up of pay and various other fringe benefits that have dollar values.

In general, motivation theories agree that money can be a motivator, but money alone is not the answer to the complicated tasks of job motivation.

Although money is obviously an important motivator, the quality of work life which deals with techniques which make the work experience more rewarding and fulfilling while avoiding stress and negative consequences, is also important in motivation.

A. Linking Pay to Performance on Production Jobs

Under the **piecerate** system, workers are paid a certain sum of money for each completed unit of production. There are other schemes, linking pay to performance known as **wage incentive plans** which often offer a bonus for production over a minimum quota. These wage incentives have often resulted in an increase of production.

B. Potential Problems With Wage Incentives

Wage incentives have some potential problems when they are not managed with care:

- Lowered Quality: While adequate systems can usually be put in place to monitor and maintain quality in manufacturing operations, wage incentives that increase "through-put" in service contexts are more difficult to control.

- Differential Opportunity: Sometimes access to raw materials or the quality of production equipment can privilege some workers over others in their opportunity to earn incentives.

- Reduced Cooperation: Wage incentives can also cause workers to hoard materials intended for common use or neglect common tasks like house-keeping that do not contribute directly to production quotas.

- Incompatible Job Design: It is very difficult to identify individual productivity in such contexts as assembly line work or where teams are large.

- Restriction of Production: In some instances, workers might practice **restrictions of productivity** by coming to an informal agreement about what constitutes a fair day's work and artificially limiting their output.

C. Linking Pay to Performance on White-Collar Jobs

Compared with production jobs, evaluating white-collar performance is more difficult. Attempts to link pay to performance on white-collar jobs are often called **merit pay plans**. Most companies employ these plans, although their implementation is often ineffective since many individuals do not perceive a link between their job performance and their pay.

D. Potential Problems with Merit Pay Plans

- Low Discrimination: A major flaw with merit pay plans is that managers often can't or won't discriminate between good and bad performance.

- Small Increases: Merit increases are often simply too small to act as effective motivators, especially if they are spread out over an entire year and combined with other things like cost of living allowances. To overcome this problem, some companies pay a **lump sum bonus**: merit pay that is awarded in a single payment and not built into base pay.

- Pay Secrecy: Since most companies consider salary information as confidential, employees that receive merit pay have no ability to assess the relative value of what they receive which reduces its motivation potential. Further, research has shown that, in the absence of accurate information, employees tend to *overestimate* the salaries of peers and subordinates, while *underestimating* the salaries of superiors.

E. Using Pay to Motivate Teamwork

- Profit Sharing: One of the most commonly used group oriented incentive systems is **profit sharing**: the return of some company profit to employees in the form of a cash bonus or retirement supplement. However, it is unlikely that profit sharing is highly motivational. Too many factors beyond the control of individual employees can intervene in the determination of profit. It is also difficult to see the impact of one's efforts on overall outcomes.

- Gainsharing Plans: **Gainsharing** plans are group incentive plans based on improved productivity or performance over which the work force has some control. Such plans have the side benefit of building trust and commitment. The most common of these plans is the Scanlon Plan.

- Skill Based Pay: Also called "pay for knowledge", **skill based pay** is a system in which people are paid according to the number of job skills they have acquired. Skill based pay can provide incentives for a more flexible work force, but training costs are high.

II. Job Design as a Motivator

A. Traditional Views of Job Design

In the 1920's, Frederick Winslow Taylor, developed the system of Scientific Management which used careful study to determine the degree of specialization and standardization. He also suggested written instructions to define work procedures as well as standardized movements and rest pauses for maximum efficiency.

While responsible for initial gains in both workplace productivity and employee standard of living, in recent years, behavioral scientists have begun to question the impact of job simplification on performance, customer satisfaction, and the quality of working life.

B. Job Scope and Motivation

Jobs that are both broad and deep are generally most satisfying to workers. Breadth refers to the number of different activities on the job, while depth refers to the degree of control over how the job is performed.

C. The Job Characteristics Model

- Core Job Characteristics: There are five important job characteristics that affect worker morale. The motivating potential of a job measures how well a given job scores in motivating workers.

a. **Skill variety** deals with the degree to which a job requires a variety of different activities in carrying out the work.

b. **Autonomy** is the degree to which the job provides substantial freedom, independence, and discretion to the individual in carrying out the job.

c. **Task significance** relates to the degree to which the job has a substantial impact on the lives of other people.

d: **Task identity** deals with the degree to which a job requires completion of a "whole" and identifiable piece of work.

e. **Feedback** relates to the degree in which carrying out work activities provides the individual with direct and clear information about the effectiveness of his or her performance.

- Critical Psychological States: The Job Characteristics Model argues that work will be intrinsically motivating when it is perceived as *meaningful*, when the worker feels *responsible* for the outcomes of the work, and when the worker has *knowledge* about his or her work progress.

- Outcomes: The outcomes of the model critical psychological states include: high internal work motivation, high "growth" satisfaction, high general job satisfaction, and high work effectiveness.

- Moderators: Jobs that are high in motivating potential do not always lead to favorable outcomes. **Growth need strength** refers to the extent to which workers desire to achieve higher-order need satisfaction by performing on their jobs. Generally, workers with high growth needs will be most responsive to challenging work. Workers unhappy with the context factors, such as pay, supervision, and company policy will be less responsive to challenging work than more satisfied workers.

D. Job Enrichment

Job enrichment is the attempt to design jobs to enhance intrinsic motivation and the quality of working life.

Among common enrichment methods are: combining tasks, establishing external client relationships, establishing internal client relationships, reducing supervision or reliance on others, forming work teams, and making feedback more direct.

E. Job Enrichment at AT&T Enhances Quality

AT&T has established extensive programs of job enrichment. In particular, the job of shareholder correspondent was enriched by combining tasks, increasing teamwork, reducing supervision, and indirectly enhancing the external client relationship. Compared with control groups, job satisfaction increased, while absence and turnover decreased.

F. Potential Problems with Job Enrichment

- Poor Diagnosis: A lack of careful diagnosis can bring about errors like increasing job breadth without changing any other critical job characteristics. The result is simply *more*, boring work. Also, jobs may be enriched that are already seen as too rich by those working in them.

- Lack of Desire or Skill: Some workers do not desire the added responsibility that an enriched job often entails. Alternatively, they may lack the skills and competence necessary to perform enriched jobs effectively.

- Demand for Rewards: The development of new skills and greater responsibility that accompany job enrichment often encourage workers to seek additional extrinsic rewards like extra pay.

- Union Resistance: Traditionally, North American unions have not been enthusiastic about job enrichment. Unions have tended to equate narrow job specialization with the preservation of jobs and resist the combination of tasks and team approaches.

- Supervisory Resistance: Often the autonomy that workers obtain through job enrichment is seen by their supervisors as "disenriching" their own jobs. Supervisors must adjust to be being facilitators or resource obtainers which can be a blow to some individuals.

III. Goal Setting as a Motivator

Goal setting deals with the establishment of definite and recognized company objectives such as production quotas, accident reduction plans, or sales quotas.

A. What Kinds of Goals Are Motivational?

Goals are most motivating when they are *specific*, *challenging*, and *accepted* by organizational members. In addition, *feedback* about progress toward goal attainment should be provided.

- Goal Specificity: Specific goals specify an exact level of achievement for people to accomplish in a particular time frame.

- Goal Challenge: Goals should be difficult but attainable.

- Goal Acceptance: Goals aren't really goals at all until they have been consciously accepted.

- Goal Feedback: Information about an individual's progress on a schedule of tasks is one way of facilitating their ongoing evaluation of movement toward goal accomplishment.

B. Enhancing Goal Acceptance

Some of the factors that might affect the acceptance of challenging, specific goals include *participation*, *rewards* and *management support*.

- Participation: Research results are mixed, but participation can often increase acceptance when a climate of mistrust exists between supervisor and subordinate. Also participation can increase performance when competition or team spirit increase the difficulty of goals an employee is willing to attempt to reach.

- Rewards: While there is little doubt that extrinsic rewards like money will increase acceptance, there is also ample evidence that simply being challenged to do the job "right" can produce goal acceptance.

- Supportiveness: There is considerable agreement that a punitive, coercive approach to goal setting on the part of supervisors will *reduce* the acceptance of goals.

C. Management by Objectives

Management by Objectives (MBO) is an elaborate, systematic, ongoing management program designed to facilitate goal establishment, goal accomplishment, and employee development.

IV. Alternate Working Schedules as Motivators

Although most workers in North America work a forty-hour, five-day week, several alternatives are now being tried. They include *flex-time*, the *compressed workweek*, and *job sharing*. These more flexible approaches to attendance in the workplace are especially well-suited to the needs of today's more diverse workforce.

A. Flex-time

Flex-time is an alternative work schedule in which arrival and quitting times are flexible. Employees are expected to still put in 8 hours each day and to be in attendance during "core hours". Flex-time has generally been limited to white-collar personnel whose jobs are not highly interdependent.

B. Compressed Workweek

The **compressed workweek** is an alternative work schedule in which employees work fewer than the normal five days a week but still put in a normal number of hours per week. The most common approach is the 4-40 system in which employees put in four ten-hour days. Firms or departments may then either choose to operate four days a week or institute a system of rotation to cover more days.

C. Job Sharing

Job sharing is an alternative work schedule in which two part-time employees divide the work of a full-time job. Job sharing is particularly attractive to people who want to send more time with small children or elders than a conventional work routine allows. From a practical standpoint, coordination is extremely important and performance evaluation can be a problem.

V. Total Quality Management and Motivation

Total quality management (TQM) is a systematic attempt to achieve continuous improvement in the quality of an organization's products and/or services. A number of characteristics typical of TQM are relevant to the topic of motivation: *an obsession with customer satisfaction*, *a concern for good relations with suppliers*, *the search for continuous improvement of processes*, *the prevention (not just detection) of quality errors*, *frequent measurement and assessment*, *extensive training*, and *high employee involvement and teamwork.*

A. TQM and Goal Setting

Everything about TQM places a high premium on specific goal setting. Many firms use a process called benchmarking to develop quality goals. **Benchmarking** is a systematic process for examining the products, services, and work processes of firms that are recognized as illustrating the best practices for organizational improvement. Quality-oriented firms often include quality goals as part of the performance appraisal process and use goal setting to motivate quality performances from their suppliers.

B. TQM and Job Design

TQM has a tendency to streamline and simplify processes, but it compensates for the negative impact of simplification on job design by encouraging empowerment of the workforce. **Empowerment** entails giving people the authority, opportunity, and motivation to take initiative and solve organizational problems. Typically, job enrichment results from such initiatives as workers increase feedback by inspecting their own work or increase autonomy by taking independent action to solve customer service problems.

C. TQM and Money

Successful quality-oriented firms go to a lot of trouble to balance individual rewards with team-oriented rewards. Gainsharing may be used to reward teamwork. At the individual level, pay may be based on quality achieved as well as volume of production and skill-based pay schemes are a natural fit with the emphasis of TQM on training. Nonmonetary recognition is also an important component of the TQM approach as the communication of important improvements helps to spread learning throughout the organization.

D. TQM and Alternative Working Schedules

There is often a tension between most alternative work arrangement schemes and TQM's emphasis on customer satisfaction. Customers may be dismayed to find that service reps "haven't shown up yet" or have the day off or only work half of the week. Alternative work schedules can also be problematic for team cohesiveness. Possibilities for dealing with these conflicts include cross-training to improve coverage and placing responsibility for scheduling within the team.

PRE-TESTING YOUR UNDERSTANDING OF THE CHAPTER

Key Concepts Matching

Match the letter of the key concepts with the appropriate definitions.

A. Autonomy
B. Benchmarking
C. Compressed workweek
D. Empowerment
E. Feedback
F. Flex-time
G. Gainsharing
H. Goal setting
I. Growth need strength
J. Job enrichment
K. Job sharing
L. Lump sum bonus
M. Management by Objectives (MBO)
N. Merit pay plans
O. Piecerate
P. Profit sharing
Q. Restriction of productivity
R. Skill based pay
S. Skill variety
T. Task identity
U. Task significance
V. Total Quality Management (TQM)
W. Wage incentive plans

______1. Merit pay that is awarded in a single payment and not built into base pay.

______2. A system in which workers are paid a certain sum of money for each unit of production completed.

______3. Schemes to link pay to performance on production jobs.

______4. An informal agreement by workers to determine what constitutes a full day's pay and artificially limit their output accordingly.

______5. The opportunity to do a variety of job activities using various skills and talents.

______6. The degree to which the job provides, substantial freedom, independence, and discretion to the individual in scheduling the work and in determining the procedures to be used in carrying it out.

______7. The degree to which the job has a substantial impact on other people, whether those people are in the immediate organization or in the world at large.

______8. The degree to which a job requires completion of a "whole" and identifiable piece of work; that is doing a job from beginning to end with a visible outcome.

______9. The degree to which carrying out the work activities provided by the job provides the individual with direct and clear information about the effectiveness of his or her performance.

_____10. The return of some company profit to employees in the form of a cash bonus or a retirement supplement.

_____11. Group incentive plans based on measurable cost reductions under the control of the work force.

_____12. Attempts to link pay to performance on white-collar jobs.

_____13. A system in which people are paid according to the number of job skills they have acquired.

_____14. The extent to which workers desire to achieve higher-order need satisfaction by performing their jobs.

_____15. An alternative work schedule in which two part-time employees divide the work of a full-time job.

_____16. The attempt to design jobs to enhance intrinsic motivation and the quality of working life.

_____17. The establishing of recognized and definite company objectives.

_____18. An elaborate, systematic, ongoing management program that is designed to facilitate goal establishment, goal accomplishment, and employee development.

_____19. A system in which workers report for work on each working day and work a given number of hours, with timing left up to the worker.

_____20. A system which compresses the hours worked each week into fewer days.

_____21. A systematic attempt to achieve continuous improvement in the quality of an organization's products and/or services.

_____22. A systematic process for examining the products, services, and work processes of firms that are recognized as illustrating the best practices for organizational improvement.

_____23. Giving people the authority, opportunity, and motivation to take initiative and solve organizational problems.

True/False Questions

Circle the letter of the correct answer.

T	F	1. For goals setting to work properly supervisors should use coercion and threats.
T	F	2. Job sharing usually requires only minimal coordination between the sharers.
T	F	3. Under gain-sharing plans, workers are paid more when company profits increase.
T	F	4. Benchmarking is usually frowned upon as vandalism.
T	F	5. Job enrichment refers mostly to higher bonuses for workers.
T	F	6. The objectives in MBO are simply another label for goals.
T	F	7. Flextime was first introduced on a large scale in Japan.
T	F	8. Merit pay plans link pay with performance on white-collar jobs.

T F 9. In general, wages incentives produce increases in productivity.
T F 10. Job breadth refers to the number of different activities performed on the job.
T F 11. Under wage incentive systems workers will often restrict productivity.
T F 12. Management jobs are considered to be low-scope jobs.
T F 13. Most workers look forward to job enrichment plans.
T F 14. Flextime has generally been limited to white-collar personnel.
T F 15. In general top executives in Europe receive the same pay and bonuses as American chief executives.
T F 16. Core-job characteristics refer to wages and fringe benefits.
T F 17. In TQM, quality is defined to include timely delivery and value-for-money.
T F 18. Unions in America generally favor job enrichment plans.
T F 19. Challenging, accepted goals can often serve as effective motivators.
T F 20. The traditional assembly-line job is an example of a low-scope job.

Multiple-Choice Questions

Select the correct answer.

______1. Linking pay to performance on production jobs is an example of
A. job enrichment.
B. wage incentive plans.
C. bonuses.
D. management by objectives (MBO).

______2. All of the following are examples of job-core characteristics except
A. skill variety.
B. job feedback.
C. compensation.
D. task significance.

______3. The following are involved in job enrichment plans except
A. making feedback more desired.
B. forming work teams.
C. combining tasks.
D. enriching bonuses and fringe benefits.

______4. Flextime usually involves
A. cutting the work hours.
B. allowing workers to choose when to arrive and when to leave.
C. cutting the work week to four days.
D. allowing workers to decide how many hours they care to work.

______5. Goal setting can be an effective motivator *except* when goals are
A. specific.
B. challenging.
C. acceptable to workers.
D. handed down by bosses.

______6. The most widely used gain-sharing plan is
A. scientific management.
B. the Scanlon plan.
C. management by objectives.
D. job enrichment.

______7. Attempts to link pay to performance on white-collar jobs are often called
A. wage incentive plans.
B. gain-sharing plans.
C. merit pay plans.
D. job enrichment plans.

______8. TQM includes all of the following *except*
A. a search for the lowest possible costs.
B. frequent measurement and assessment.
C. extensive training.
D. a concern for good relations with suppliers.

______9. All of the following jobs contain tasks that have high significance *except* that of
A. college professor.
B. intensive care nurse.
C. sweeper in a hospital.
D. high school teacher.

______10. All of the following jobs are high-scope jobs *except* those of
A. college professors.
B. managers.
C. assembly line workers.
D. chief executives.

POST-TESTING FOR EXAMS

True/False Questions

Circle the letter of the correct answer.

T F 1. As team size increases, the relationship between an individual's productivity and his or her pay decreases.
T F 2. Under gain-sharing plans, workers receive bonuses when cost reductions take place.
T F 3. Job scope refers to the number of units a work team produces.
T F 4. In general, workers are more motivated when jobs are perceived as meaningful.
T F 5. Making workers more responsible for results can cause a deterioration in the quality of output.
T F 6. Job enrichment schemes usually result in larger bonuses for top executives.
T F 7. Empowerment involves giving employees more resources to do their jobs better.
T F 8. Task significance refers to the degree in which the job impacts other people.
T F 9. Goal setting has led to increased performance on a wide variety of tasks.
T F 10. Generally, flextime and a four-day week have been successful motivating tools.

Multiple-Choice Questions

Select the correct answer.

______1. Allowing workers to operate independently is an example of
A. autonomy.
B. poor management.
C. job enrichment.
D. scientific management.

______2. Providing people with data about their performance effectiveness is an example of
A. MBO.
B. job enrichment.
C. feedback.
D. motivating potential.

______3. A merit pay plan would best be used with
A. an assembly-line worker.
B. a middle manager.
C. a pastor.
D. a furniture maker.

______4. All of the following are context factors *except*
A. pay.
B. supervisors.
C. company policy.
D. job enrichment.

______5. At AT&T, all of the following enrichment plans were adopted *except*

A. increasing teamwork.
B. allowing workers to determine merit pay.
C. enhancing the external client relationship.
D. continuing tasks.

______6. All of the following are examples of wage incentive plans *except*

A. piece rate systems.
B. bonus systems.
C. merit pay plans.
D. group wage incentives.

______7. Most gain-sharing plans include all members of the work unit *except*

A. production people.
B. purchasing agents.
C. managers.
D. support staff.

______8. The difference between competitive benchmarking and generic benchmarking is

A. generic benchmarking applies to the "no-name" brand segment.
B. competitive benchmarking occurs when two firms in the same industry are searching for benchmarks at the same time.
C. generic benchmarking looks for the best practices, regardless of industry.
D. nonexistent. Both terms apply to the same practice.

______9. Most organizations

A. fail to differentiate between merit pay and cost-of-living increases.
B. tell workers about executive salaries.
C. usually allow workers to vote on executive salaries.
D. none of the above.

______10. All of the following would be useful adjustments to rewards under TQM *except*

A. gainsharing.
B. piecerate pay.
C. recognition awards for improvement ideas.
D. skill-based pay.

______11. All of the following are involved in appraising job design using the Job Characteristics Model *except*

A. skill variety.
B. bonus measurements.
C. task identity.
D. task significance.

______12. In general, goal setting has led to performance increases

A. after bonuses were increased.

B. after more feedback was introduced.

C. without the use of monetary incentives.

D. after coercion by management.

______13. MBO is ____________ plan designed to facilitate goal establishment, goal accomplishment, and employee development.

A. a costly, temporary

B. a crisis induced plan

C. an inexpensive, easily devised

D. an elaborate, systematic, ongoing

______14. All of the following are MBO practices *except*

A. objectives are left as vague as possible.

B. objectives are modified if new needs or problems are identified.

C. periodic meetings are held.

D. time frames are established.

______15. Flextime is most likely to work well in

A. hospitals.

B. colleges.

C. office environments.

D. schools.

______16. Documented effects from the use of flextime in the workplace include all of the following *except*

A. decreased absenteeism and tardiness.

B. work attitudes generally become more negative.

C. a positive reception by first-line supervisors and managers.

D. slight productivity gains.

______17. To be effective, motivational systems must NOT be

A. well managed.

B. properly implemented.

C. ignored by management.

D. properly financed.

______18. Once established, a motivational system should be

A. monitored over time for adaptation effects.

B. left in place with no changes.

C. changed very frequently.

D. altered by worker elections.

______19. The best "fit" of a motivator with TQM principles is

A. TQM and money.

B. TQM and job design.

C. TQM and alternative working schedules.

D. TQM and goal setting.

______20. In a piecerate system workers are paid
A. a certain amount of money for each unit of production.
B. a sum for each completed product.
C. so much per hour of work.
D. whatever the union negotiates.

Application Situations Exercise

Match the key concepts with the statements that best describe them.

A. Autonomy
B. Benchmarking
C. Compressed workweek
D. Empowerment
E. Feedback
F. Flex-time
G. Gainsharing
H. Goal setting
I. Growth need strength
J. Job enrichment
K. Job sharing
L. Lump sum bonus
M. Management by Objectives (MBO)
N. Merit pay plans
O. Piecerate
P. Profit sharing
Q. Restriction of productivity
R. Skill based pay
S. Skill variety
T. Task identity
U. Task significance
V. Total Quality Management (TQM)
W. Wage incentive plans

______1. My cousin thought her job as a teacher was very important because she helped many people.

______2. She would have liked to have her pay linked to her performance, though.

______3. She was upset when her school tried to reduce costs by watching how teachers used supplies and paying bonuses after the reductions took place.

______4. It never seemed that what they were doing was good enough. She was always getting memos about how some other school was the best at something or other.

______5. Her morale was so low, she requested a performance evaluation from her principal.

______6. The principal told her she should take the initiative and try to solve the organization's problems.

______7. She and her colleagues decided that they would try to get 95% of the eligible students promoted by the end of the year no matter how hard they had to work.

______8. Not everyone was in agreement, however, and some teachers quietly left the school each day as early as they could.

______9. The trouble seemed to be that some of her colleagues had no desire for additional job enrichment.

______10. But my cousin and her colleagues pressured the school committee to enhance the intrinsic motivations and quality of work available at the school for the benefit of everyone else.

Short Answer Questions

Fill-in the missing word(s).

1. The most popular gain-sharing plan in use today is the ____________________ .

2. Merit pay plans are usually applicable only to ____________________ .

3. A worker in a furniture factory who operates a lathe solely to make table legs would be a good example of low ____________________ .

4. Contingency variables that intervene between job characteristics and outcomes are known as ____________________ .

5. ____________________ involves assigning tasks that might be performed by different workers to a single individual.

6. Goal setting can lead to performance increases without the introduction of ____________________ incentives for goal achievement.

7. Most North Americans work a five-day, ____________________ week.

8. Flextime has been generally limited to ____________________ .

9. The tendency of TQM to ____________________ jobs has been counteracted by an emphasis on empowerment in the workplace.

10. Flextime and compressed workweeks have actually had ____________________ effect on productivity.

ANSWER SHEET FOR CHAPTER 7

PRE-TESTING YOUR UNDERSTANDING OF THE CHAPTER

Key Concepts Matching

1. L	2. O	3. W	4. Q	5. S	6. A	7. U	8. T	9.E	10. P
11. G	12. N	13. R	14. I	15. K	16. J	17. H	18. M	19. F	20. C

True/False Questions

1. F	2. F	3. F	4. T	5. F	6. T	7. F	8. T	9. F	10. T
11. T	12. F	13. F	14. T	15. F	16. F	17. F	18. F	19. T	20. T

Multiple-Choice Questions

1. B	2. C	3. D	4. B	5. D	6. B	7. C	8. A	9. C	10. C

POST-TESTING FOR EXAMS

True/False Questions

1. T	2. T	3. F	4. F	5. F	6. F	7. F	8. T	9. T	10. T

Multiple-Choice Questions

1. A	2. C	3. B	4. D	5. B	6. C	7. B	8. C	9. A	10. B
11. B	12. C	13. D	14. A	15. C	16. B	17. D	18. A	19. D	20. A

Application Situation Exercises

1. U	2. N	3. G	4. B	5. E	6. D	7. H	8. Q	9. I	10. J

Short Answer Questions

1. Scanlon plan	2. white-collar workers	3. task identity
4. moderators	5. combining tasks	6. monetary
7. forty-hour	8. white-collar personnel	9. simplify
10. little		

EXERCISE FOR CHAPTER 7

*IMPROVING THE QUALITY OF STUDENT LIFE**

Objective:
To experience a session designed to increasing the quality of student life at your college / university.

Procedure 1: (8-12 minutes)
Break into groups of five or six members. Select a spokesperson. Your group is to come up with a list of the three to five most needed improvements in your "job" as a student. Rank them in order of priority 1- most important, 5- least important. When you are finished, or the time is up, the spokesperson or instructor writes the ranking on the board. Do not discuss ways to improve the quality at this time.

Procedure 2: (3-10 minutes)
The instructor, or the class by consensus, determines the class's top three to five priorities for improvement.

Procedure 3: (8-12 minutes)
Each group selects a new spokesperson. The group develops solutions that will improve the quality of student life for the class's three to five priority areas.

Procedure 4: (5-20 minutes)
For the first priority item, each spokesperson states the group's recommendation for improving the quality of student life. The class votes, or comes to a consensus on the best way to solve the problem. Proceed to priority items two through five until you finish or time is up.

Discussion Questions: For the groups and/or the class
1. Are survey questionnaires and quality of work life programs effective ways to improve the quality of student life on your campus?
2. Did the class consider that quality of work life is a balance between educational institutions, students, and society? Are your solutions going to benefit the college/university and society as well as the students?

Conclusion:
The instructor may make concluding remarks.

Application: (2-4 minutes)
What did I learn from this experience? How will I use this knowledge in the future?

Sharing:
Volunteers give their answers to the application section.

*Note: This exercise is a simulation of what may take place during an actual quality-of-life program. However, in actual programs, top management of the organization should be involved and open to implementing the recommendations of the participants.

Copyright 1988, Robert N. Lussier, used with permission

CHAPTER 8

GROUPS AND TEAMWORK

LEARNING OBJECTIVES

- DEFINE GROUPS, DISTINGUISH BETWEEN FORMAL AND INFORMAL GROUPS, AND DISCUSS THE FACTORS THAT LEAD TO GROUP FORMATION.
- DISCUSS GROUP DEVELOPMENT.
- EXPLAIN HOW GROUP SIZE AND MEMBER DIVERSITY INFLUENCE WHAT OCCURS IN GROUPS.
- REVIEW HOW NORMS, ROLES, AND SOCIAL STATUS AFFECT GROUP INTERACTION.
- DISCUSS THE CAUSES AND CONSEQUENCES OF GROUP COHESIVENESS.
- EXPLAIN THE DYNAMICS OF SOCIAL LOAFING.
- DISCUSS HOW TO DESIGN AND SUPPORT SELF-MANAGED TEAMS.
- EXPLAIN THE LOGIC BEHIND CROSS-FUNCTIONAL TEAMS AND DESCRIBE HOW THEY CAN OPERATE EFFECTIVELY.

KEY CONCEPTS

Group

Formal workgroups

Informal groups

Punctuated equilibrium model

Additive tasks

Disjunctive tasks

Process losses

Conjunctive tasks

Norms

Roles

Role ambiguity

Role conflict

Intrasender conflict

Intersender conflict

Interrole conflict

Person-role conflict

Status

Group cohesiveness

Social loafing

Self-managed work teams

Cross-functional teams

Superordinate goals

CHAPTER SUMMARY

Key concepts are identified by **bold** *faced type.*

I. What is a Group?

A **group** consists of two or more people interacting interdependently to achieve a common goal. Groups exert tremendous influence on us. We can also influence others through groups.

Formal workgroups are those established by the organization to facilitate the achievement of organizational goals. The most common formal group consists of a superior and those subordinates who report to that superior.

Informal groups are groups that emerge naturally in response to the common interests of organizational members.

II. Group Formation

The formation of both types of groups is affected by opportunity for interaction, potential for goal accomplishment, and the personal characteristics of group members.

III. Group Development

A. Typical Stages of Group Development

Leaders and trainers have observed that many groups develop through a series of stages over time. These stages are forming, storming, performing, and adjourning. They correspond to the tendencies of groups to first orient themselves, sort out roles and responsibilities, develop social consensus, undertake task accomplishment, and eventually disband.

B. Punctuated Equilibrium Model

When groups have a specific deadline by which to complete some problem-solving task, we often observe a different stage model than the one above. The **punctuated equilibrium model** is a model of group development that describes how groups with deadlines are affected by their first meetings and crucial midpoint transitions.

IV. Group Structure and Its Consequences

A. Group Size

Although the smallest possible group would consist of two people, most work groups, including task forces and committees usually have between three and twenty members.

- Size and Satisfaction

In general, members of larger groups report less satisfaction with group membership than those who find themselves in smaller groups. Increased potential for conflict, reduced opportunity for participation, inhibition, and inability to identify contributions to the group are among the reasons for this phenomenon.

- Size and Performance

Different types of tasks are performed by groups where performance could depend upon the type of task and the number of individuals involved.

For some tasks, like moving a heavy rock, the potential performance of the group increases with group size. These are **additive tasks** in which group performance is dependent upon the sum of the performance of individual group members.

Other tasks, like searching for a single error in a complicated computer program, also may show performance gains as group size increases, but that is because the chance of including a crucial problem solver are greater. These **disjunctive tasks** are those in which the group depends upon the performance of the best group members.

But as groups get larger, performance may also decrease as a function of **process losses**. These are group performance difficulties stemming from the difficulty of motivating and coordinating larger groups.

Finally, the performance of some tasks assumed by groups, like assembly line work, potentially decreases as group size goes up. That is because these **conjunctive tasks** are those in which the performance of the group is limited by its *poorest performer*.

B. Diversity of Group Membership

Research suggests that heterogeneous or diverse groups have a more difficult time communicating and becoming cohesive, so group development takes longer. Once developed, diversity has little impact on performance except where tasks require creativity and problem solving.

C. Group Norms

Social **norms** are collective expectations that members of social units have regarding the behavior of others. All of us are influenced by norms which regulate many of our daily activities.

- Norm Development

Norms develop to provide regularity and consistency to behavior. They develop from the shared attitudes of supporters. Individuals comply with these norms because the norms often correspond to privately held attitudes.

- Some Typical Norms

There are different types of norms which regulate almost all of our daily activities. Some of these are: loyalty norms, dress norms, reward allocation norms, and performance norms.

D. Roles

Roles are positions in groups that have attached to them a set of expected behaviors. In organizations, we have designated roles which deal with "who can tell others what to do," and assigned roles which indicate "who does what."

- Role Ambiguity

Role ambiguity exists when the goals of one's job or the methods of performing it are unclear. Elements like organizational factors, the role sender, or the focal person can often cause such ambiguity.

- Role Conflict

Role conflict exists when an individual is faced with incompatible role expectations. There are several different types of role conflict:

Intrasender role conflict occurs when a single role sender provides incompatible role expectations to the role occupant.

Intersender role conflict occurs if two or more role senders provide a role occupant with incompatible expectations.

Interrole conflict occurs when several roles held by a role occupant involve incompatible expectations.

Person-role conflict occurs when role demands call for behavior that is incompatible with the personality and skills of the role occupant.

Generally, role conflicts result in job dissatisfaction, stress reactions, lowered organizational commitment, and turnover intentions.

E. Status

Status is the rank, or social position, or prestige accorded to group members.

- Formal Status Systems

Status symbols are tangible indicators of status. All organizations seek to show those people who have more status than others. Symbols like large desks, private secretaries, soft carpets, special telephones are examples of status symbols.

Status judgments of the public at large are influenced by the skill, training, and education of the people being judged. Thus, various occupations are accorded status with college professors and physicians at the highest level and garbage collectors at the lowest.

- Informal Status Systems

At times, job performance is the basis for gaining informal status. So a good hitter, or a good performer will be accorded status, although status symbols might be lacking.

3. Consequences of Status Differences

Status affects the ways in which we communicate with each other. People with lower status are more polite when addressing those with higher status. Higher status people do more talking and have more influence. Also higher status people tend to have more self-confidence and assertiveness than people of lesser status.

4. Reducing Status Barriers

Although powerful motivators for some, status differences also tend to inhibit communication and can make it more difficult to foster a culture of teamwork and cooperation. Many organizations as a result are doing away with executive dining rooms, reserved parking and informal dress codes that signal status differences.

The use of e-mail has also been found to level status barriers, thus facilitating communication between people at all levels of the organization.

IV. Group Cohesiveness

A. Factors Influencing Cohesiveness

There are several important factors which might make one group more cohesive than others. **Group cohesiveness** is the degree to which a groups is especially attractive to its members.

- Threat and competition can force members to work together when group goals are in danger. External threats to survive have often resulted in greater cohesiveness.

- Success can also increase cohesiveness. When a group accomplishes a goal, members feel pride and tend to become more cooperative with each other.

- Member diversity is important in the attainment of cohesiveness since conflict may be increased. At times though, task accomplishment will be a more important factor than membership similarities.

- Size is important because larger groups have a more difficult time in communicating and remaining cohesive. One exception to this rule would be a large group of workers threatening to strike. Size here might promote cohesiveness because it enhances changes for success.

- Toughness of initiation is also a factor of cohesiveness because groups that seen as more exclusive and harder to enter tend to remain more cohesive than others.

B. Consequences of Cohesiveness

Among the consequences of cohesiveness are: more participation in group affairs, more conformity, more success. In general, cohesive groups tend to be successful in accomplishing what they wish to accomplish. In a good labor relations climate, group cohesiveness should foster high productivity. In a disagreeable climate, however, cohesive groups might pursue goals that result in lowered productivity.

V. Social Loafing

Social loafing is the tendency to withhold physical or intellectual effort when performing a group task. It is one of the reasons for process losses in large groups and takes two forms: In the *free rider effect*, people lower their effort to get a free ride at the expense of other group members. This is the phenomenon of others not pulling their weight on a group project. In the *sucker effect*, people lower their effort because of the feeling that others are free riding.

Some ways to counteract social loafing:

- Make individual performance more visible.
- Make sure that the work is interesting.
- Increase feelings of indispensability.
- Increase performance feedback.
- Reward group performance.

VI. Designing Effective Work Groups

Self-managed work teams generally provide their members with the opportunity to do challenging work under reduced supervision. According to J. Richard Hackman, a work group is effective when (1) its physical or intellectual output is acceptable to management and other parts of the organization, (2) group members' needs are satisfied by the group, and (3) the group experience enables members to *continue* to work together.

A. Tasks for Self-Managed Teams

Tasks for self-managed teams should be complex and challenging requiring high interdependence among team members for accomplishment.

Organizations such as Kodak, General Mills, Federal Express, Aetna Life Casualty and others have used these self-managed teams with varying rates of success. The trend toward these teams is likely to continue.

B. The Composition of Self-Managed Teams

A fast answer to how organizations should assemble effective self-managed teams is that they should be stable, small and smart. Group membership should be stable. The team should be as small as is feasible. Team members should have a high level of expertise about the task at hand. And yet the team needs enough diversity to bring a variety of skills to the task at hand.

C. Supporting Self-Managed Teams

- Training: To insure the effectiveness of self-managed teams, companies need to foster adequate training in technical skills, social skills, language skills, and business training.

- Rewards: Tie rewards to team accomplishment rather than individual accomplishment, while still providing team members with some individual performance feedback.

- Management: A study found that the most effective managers in a self-management environment encouraged groups to observe, evaluate, and reinforce their own task behavior.

D. Cross-Functional Teams

Another type of workgroup that organizations are using with increasing frequency is the **cross-functional team**. These workgroups bring people with different functional specialties together to better invent, design, or deliver a product or service. The general goals of cross-functional teams include some coordination of innovation, speed and quality that come from early coordination among the various specialties.

Principles for Effectiveness: Several factors contribute to effectiveness in cross-functional teams:

- Composition: All relevant players must be part of the team, including labor representatives or suppliers where appropriate.
- Superordinate goals: Conflict may sometimes arise from the colliding cultures of different functions. **Superordinate goals** are attractive outcomes that can only be achieved by collaboration. They help to override potential functional level conflicts.
- Physical proximity: Team members must be located close to one another for maximum benefit.
- Autonomy: Individual functional specialists need the ability to provide inputs on behalf of their department without constant reporting and the team itself must have a mandate for meaningful independent action.
- Rules and procedures: Some basic decision procedures must be laid down to prevent anarchy.
- Leadership: Because of the potential for conflict, cross-functional team leaders need especially strong people skills in addition to task expertise.

PRE-TESTING YOUR UNDERSTANDING OF THE CHAPTER

Key Concepts Matching

Match the letter of the key concepts with the appropriate definitions.

A.	Additive tasks	L.	Norms
B.	Conjunctive tasks	M.	Person-role conflict
C.	Cross-functional teams	N.	Process losses
D.	Disjunctive tasks	O.	Punctuated equilibrium model
E.	Formal workgroups	P.	Role ambiguity
F.	Group	Q.	Role conflict
G.	Group cohesiveness	R.	Roles
H.	Informal groups	S.	Self-managed work teams
I.	Interrole conflict	T.	Social loafing
J.	Intersender conflict	U.	Status
K.	Intrasender conflict	V.	Superordinate goals

______1. Two or more people interacting interdependently to achieve a common goal.

______2. Groups established by the organization to facilitate the achievement of organizational goals.

______3. Groups that emerge naturally in response to the common interests of organizational members.

______4. Tasks in which the potential performance can be predicted by adding the performances of individual group members together.

______5. Tasks in which the potential performance of the group depends on the performance of its best member.

______6. Tasks in which the performance of the group is limited by its poorest performer.

______7. Expectations that members of social units have regarding the behavior of others.

______8. Positions in a group that have attached to them a set of expected behaviors.

______9. When the goals of one's job or the methods of performing it are unclear.

_____10. When an individual is faced with incompatible role expectations.

_____11. Conflict which occurs when a single role sender provides incompatible role expectations to the role occupant.

_____12. Conflict occurring when two or more role senders differ in their expectations for a role occupant.

_____13. Conflict occurring when expectations inherent in the roles members play are incompatible.

_____14. Conflict occurring when role demands are incompatible with the personality or skills of the role occupant.

_____15. The rank, or social position, or prestige accorded to group members.

_____16. Workgroups that bring people with different functional specialties together to better invent, design, or deliver a product or service.

_____17. The quality that makes groups especially attractive to their members.

_____18. Groups which provide their members with the opportunity to do challenging work under reduced supervision.

_____19. Group performance difficulties stemming from the problems of motivating and coordinating larger groups.

_____20. A model of group development that describes how groups with deadlines to meet are affected by their first meetings and crucial mid-point transitions.

_____21. The tendency to withhold physical or intellectual effort when performing a group task.

_____22. Attractive outcomes that can only be achieved by collaboration.

True/False Questions

Circle the letter of the correct answer.

T F 1. Group members must meet face-to-face and interact verbally.
T F 2. Informal groups might help or hurt an organization.
T F 3. Most work groups have between three and twenty members.
T F 4. Additive tasks are extra burdens imposed by management.
T F 5. Many of our daily habits are the result of social norms.
T F 6. Roles are parts in a dramatic production.
T F 7. Role ambiguity exists when everyone clearly understands his or her expectations.
T F 8. Role conflict exists when an individual is faced with compatible role expectations.
T F 9. Having a private company bathroom might be an example of high status.
T F 10. All organizations have both informal and formal status systems.
T F 11. In most hospitals, doctors have more prestige than nurses.

T F 12. Despite good performance, blacks and women are often given low status.

T F 13. To be effective, a group must have a common goal.

T F 14. Tasks forces and committees are examples of informal work groups.

T F 15. As group size increases, the time available for verbal participation by each member decreases.

T F 16. In additive tasks, the potential performance of each group increases with group size.

T F 17. The focal person is the person expected to carry out a given role.

T F 18. Informal status systems refer to sloppy dressing and dirty offices.

T F 19. A successful group is usually more cohesive than an unsuccessful group.

T F 20. Groups that are tough to get into are less attractive to outsiders than groups that are easy to join.

Multiple-Choice Questions

Select the correct answer.

______1. All of the following are members of formal groups except

A. board members.
B. company discussion groups.
C. task forces.
D. committees.

______2. Which of the following is NOT a factor in group formation?

A. opportunity for interaction
B. personal characteristics
C. potential for goal accomplishment
D. desire for esteem needs

______3. The following relate to group tasks *except*

A. additive tasks.
B. disjunctive tasks.
C. constructive tasks.
D. conjunctive tasks.

______4. Brushing our teeth daily is an example of

A. social norms.
B. company norms.
C. family norms.
D. good sanitation habits.

______5. All of the following are involved in reward allocation *except*

A. equity.
B. reciprocity.
C. equality.
D. equanimity.

______6. All of the following are typical norms *except*
A. loyalty norms.
B. environmental norms.
C. dress norms.
D. performance norms.

______7. All of the following might lead to role ambiguity *except*
A. the role sender.
B. group cohesiveness.
C. the focal person.
D. organizational factors.

______8. All of the following can result from role ambiguity *except*
A. job satisfaction.
B. anxiety.
C. tension.
D. turnover.

______9. The following are recognized types of role conflict *except*
A. intra-sender conflict.
B. inter-role conflict.
C. person-role conflict.
D. person-company conflict.

_____10. Which of the following is NOT true of status?
A. It is imaginary.
B. We can obtain status by dealing with those who have more.
C. We can easily perceive status differences.
D. Group members agree on who does or doesn't have status.

POST-TESTING FOR EXAMS

True/False Questions

Circle the letter of the correct answer.

T F 1. A successful sports team is a poor model of an effective work group.
T F 2. Self-managed teams should be as large as is feasible.
T F 3. Coaching groups to be independent can decrease their effectiveness.
T F 4. Higher status members are addressed more formally than lower status.
T F 5. Threats contribute greatly to group disintegration.
T F 6. Self-managed groups work best with widely diverse membership.
T F 7. Role ambiguity results in greater job satisfaction and performance.
T F 8. In general, role conflict is good for organizational morale.
T F 9. People can obtain status from a connection with those who have more.
T F 10. In general, bigger groups have a more difficult time in obtaining cohesiveness than smaller groups.

Multiple-Choice Questions

Select the correct answer.

______1. All of the following are ways to counteract social loafing *except*
A. reward group performance.
B. increase feelings of indispensability.
C. make sure work is interesting.
D. make individual performance less visible.

______2. Those with the highest status in a hospital would be
A. doctors.
B. janitors.
C. nurses.
D. phone operators.

______3. As a rule communication moves
A. down the status hierarchy.
B. across the status hierarchy.
C. up the status hierarchy.
D. despite the status hierarchy.

______4. All of the following are factors in forming group cohesiveness *except*
A. threat and competition.
B. success.
C. similarity of members.
D. diversity of members.

______5. All of the following are some results of cohesiveness *except*
A. more conflict.
B. more success.
C. more conformity.
D. more participation.

______6. A work group is effective except when
A. its output is acceptable to management.
B. its members are satisfied.
C. its members are very dissatisfied.
D. its members wish to work together.

______7. All of the following terms apply to self-managed work teams *except*
A. autonomous.
B. autocratic.
C. self-regulated.
D. superteams.

______8. All of the following are characteristics of self-managed work teams *except*
A. they are stable.
B. they have expertise.
C. they encourage conflict.
D. they are fairly small.

______9. In disjunctive tasks the potential performance of the group depends on the performance of
A. the weakest member.
B. all members working together.
C. the best member.
D. the company boss.

_____10. Norms usually develop from the shared _________ of group members.
A. problems
B. pleasures
C. rewards
D. attitudes

_____11. Police officers refusing to squeal on other officers are following
A. performance norms.
B. social norms.
C. loyalty norms.
D. status norms.

_____12. In general, most of us
A. fill only one role at a time.
B. fill several roles simultaneously.
C. ignore roles altogether.
D. can avoid all role conflict.

_____13. All of the following relate to formal status differences in organizations *except*
A. the skill of the person.
B. the education of the person.
C. the training of the person.
D. the affability of the person.

_____14. All of the following terms relate to informal status individuals *except*
A. "power hitters."
B. "cool heads."
C. "hot heads."
D. "fast trackers."

_____15. Principles for effectiveness of cross-functional teams include the following *except*
A. task identity.
B. superordinate goals.
C. physical proximity.
D. autonomy.

_____16. In highly cohesive groups, the productivity of individual members
A. has a relationship to that of other members.
B. is fairly similar to that of other members.
C. has no relationship to that of other members.
D. depends upon instructions from the leader.

_____17. The most basic aspect of all groups is
A. interaction.
B. cohesiveness.
C. attractiveness.
D. belonging.

_____18. All of the following relate to group structure *except*
A. size.
B. norms.
C. status.
D. satisfaction.

_____19. As groups increase in size individual members tend to
A. become less efficient.
B. become more efficient.
C. become more aggressive.
D. become less aggressive.

_____20. The punctuated equilibrium model of group development is useful for understanding
A. self-managed groups.
B. groups with deadlines.
C. forming, storming and norming behavior .
D. cross functional teams.

Application Situations Exercise

Match the key concepts with the statements that best describe them.

A.	Additive tasks	L.	Norms
B.	Conjunctive tasks	M.	Person-role conflict
C.	Cross-functional teams	N.	Process losses
D.	Disjunctive tasks	O.	Punctuated equilibrium model
E.	Formal workgroups	P.	Role ambiguity
F.	Group	Q.	Role conflict
G.	Group cohesiveness	R.	Roles
H.	Informal groups	S.	Self-managed work teams
I.	Interrole conflict	T.	Social loafing
J.	Intersender conflict	U.	Status
K.	Intrasender conflict	V.	Superordinate goals

______1. I really wasn't sure how I should behave as a store manager.

______2. We got the neighborhood people together to clean out drug dealers.

______3. We worked together without any help from the police or other authorities.

______4. We were expected to nurture our children and yet be harsh with them if we caught them using drugs.

______5. Some neighborhood people greatly respected the dealers because of their affluence.

______6. As more of us joined the anti-drug crusade, the cleanup became easier.

______7. We did expect full cooperation and effort once our campaign got started.

______8. Unfortunately, some people wanted the clean-up, but didn't want to help.

______9. Our leaders were obviously expected to lead us in these efforts.

_____10. But several of the leaders were inadequate, and our cleanup effort fell short of its goals.

Short Answer Questions

Fill-in the missing word(s).

1. In practice most work groups have between three and ______________ members.

2. The stages of group development are forming, storming, ______________, performing and adjourning.

3. ______________ are those that develop naturally to meet the social emotional needs of group members.

4. A crucial point in group development according to punctuated equilibrium theory is ____________.

5. In social loafing, the effect of free rider behavior on other group members is called ____________.

6. A fast answer to how organizations should assemble effective self-managed teams: They should be _______, _______ and ________.

7. If the goal is the speed, innovation, and quality that comes from the early coordination of specialties, what's needed is a ______________.

8. Most people wish to communicate with people who are ____________ them in the status hierarchy.

9. An informal agreement among the members of a group of production workers to restrict productivity under a piece rate pay system is an example of a ___________ norm. .

10. As groups get bigger, they usually provide less opportunity for ____________.

ANSWER SHEET FOR CHAPTER 8

PRE-TESTING YOUR UNDERSTANDING OF THE CHAPTER

Key Concepts Matching

1. F	2. E	3. H	4. A	5. D	6. B	7. L	8. R	9. P	10. Q
11. K	12. J	13. I	14. M	15. U	16. C	17. G	18. S	19. N	20. O
21. T	22. V								

True/False Questions

1. F	2. T	3. T	4. F	5. T	6. F	7. F	8. F	9. T	10. T
11. T	12. T	13. T	14. F	15. T	16. T	17. T	18. F	19. T	20. F

Multiple-Choice Questions

1. B	2. D	3. C	4. A	5. D	6. B	7. B	8. A	9. D	10. A

POST-TESTING FOR EXAMS

True/False Questions

1. F	2. F	3. F	4. T	5. F	6. F	7. F	8. F	9. T	10. T

Multiple-Choice Questions

1. D	2. A	3. C	4. D	5. A	6. D	7. B	8. C	9. C	10. D
11. C	12. B	13. D	14. C	15. A	16. B	17. A	18. D	19. A	20. B

Application Situations Exercise

1. P	2. F	3. S	4. Q	5. U	6. A	7. L	8. T	9. R	10. B

Short Answer Questions

1. twenty	2. norming	3. emergent roles	4. mid-point transition
5. sucker effect	6. stable, small, smart	7. cross-functional team	8. above
9. performance	10. member satisfaction		

CASE STUDY FOR CHAPTER 8

CANADIAN NUCLEAR INDUSTRIES

Sue Dittmer and Eve Polanski had been employed by Canadian Nuclear Industries for almost two years. Both had Master's degrees in nuclear engineering and had been hired upon graduation when CNI had obtained a lucrative contract to design a series of nuclear power plants for an emerging third world nation. They had become part of the twelve-member Monitoring and Containment Task Force, which was concerned with part of the design of the safety systems for the nuclear reactor. This involved the arrangement and installation of certain monitoring devices and emergency systems, and, most important, the design of part of the hydraulic cooling system for the reactor core.

The task force was a cohesive group, and this generally provided a pleasant working environment with little dissension or tension. The team was elite and success-oriented, and team members could be relied upon to help each other out when necessary. However, there was some price to be paid for this cohesiveness. Because they had been hired at almost the same time, Sue and Eve had learned the ropes at CNI together. Since there was no formal training or orientation, this learning was basically an informal process, but it was nevertheless very potent. Quickly, both had learned that rookie members of the design team were expected to follow the party line and defer to more experienced team members in design matters. Signals to this effect were subtle but effective. Doing an assigned task quickly and accurately was praised by other members of the staff, but innovative ideas or questions about design parameters were met with responses of detached amusement by more experienced team members. This certainly wasn't the kind of collaborative atmosphere that the women had been led to expect from their university training!

Although this situation was frustrating, both engineers were aware that it was surely temporary. During the two years they had been there, they had observed that team members who conformed to the group's expectations gradually got the autonomy to suggest design features and develop initial plans.

Most recently, Sue and Eve had been involved with a series of computer simulations used to test the effectiveness of the cooling system design.

Although they were unaware of each other's thoughts, both had perceived a disturbing trend to these tests. The first had indicated a clear meltdown of the reactor core, showing that the cooling system wasn't properly designed. After several minor design features were changed, simulations were again run. Each time, as the data indicated that a meltdown was imminent, Max Schmidt, the head of the task force, ordered the test to be terminated. Finally, by reprogramming the simulation to involve an extremely unlikely emergency scenario, they had managed to get a clean run indicating that the safety system would work.

The next day, Sue and Eve had lunch together. After some strained small talk, Eve got to the point.

"Sue, those simulations were dummied up. That cooling system doesn't work worth a damn."

Source: Case prepared by Gary Johns

Sue responded, "Eve, I'm glad you feel this way too. I was beginning to think those tests were my personal fantasy or nightmare. But what can we do? Tomorrow at the group meeting Max is sure to push for the approval of the design. The brass is on him to act fast, and I can't see anyone arguing with him."

"Neither can I," said Ever. "Once they make a decision, the experienced people stick together."

The next day, the group meeting began as expected. Max argued for the approval of the safety design that included the suspect cooling system. When he asked for comments, all were vaguely supportive. Finally, Bob Daniels spoke up. Daniels, an older man, was highly respected as the best engineer on the task force.

"Look, people," said Daniels quietly, "the emperor has no clothes. That cooling system wouldn't chill by beer, let alone prevent a meltdown. Let's stop kidding ourselves."

Quickly, the tide turned as other group members expressed some doubts about the design and the tests. Soon, the group had generated some new design ideas and decided who would work on what. It was agreed that the brass would just have to wait for a good design.

Sue and Eve exchanged smiles and looked relieved.

1. What does this case say about the pros and cons of group cohesiveness?

2. Account for Sue and Eve's reluctance to blow the whistle on the test results.

3. Account for Bob Daniel's ability to protest the problems with the design.

4. How can a group remain cohesive while supporting norms that favor reasonable dissent?

CHAPTER 9

SOCIAL INFLUENCE, SOCIALIZATION, AND CULTURE

LEARNING OBJECTIVES

- UNDERSTAND THE DIFFERENCE BETWEEN INFORMATION DEPENDENCE AND EFFECT DEPENDENCE.
- DIFFERENTIATE COMPLIANCE, IDENTIFICATION, AND INTERNALIZATION AS MOTIVES FOR SOCIAL CONFORMITY.
- DESCRIBE THE FACTORS THAT INFLUENCE CONFORMITY TO SOCIAL NORMS.
- DESCRIBE THE STAGES OF ORGANIZATIONAL SOCIALIZATION AND SOME METHODS OF SOCIALIZATION.
- DIFFERENTIATE AFFECTIVE, CONTINUANCE, AND NORMATIVE COMMITMENT AND EXPLAIN HOW ORGANIZATIONS CAN FOSTER COMMITMENT.
- DEFINE ORGANIZATIONAL CULTURE AND DISCUSS THE CONTRIBUTORS TO A CULTURE.
- DISCUSS THE ASSETS AND LIABILITIES OF STRONG ORGANIZATIONAL CULTURES.
- REVIEW HOW WE CAN DIAGNOSE AN ORGANIZATIONAL CULTURE.

KEY CONCEPTS

Information dependence

Effect dependence

Compliance

Identification

Internalization

Idiosyncrasy credits

Socialization

Debasement

Realistic job previews

Organizational commitment

Affective commitment

Continuance commitment

Normative commitment

Organizational culture

Subcultures

Strong culture

CHAPTER SUMMARY

Key concepts are identified by **bold** *faced type.*

I. Social Influence in Organizations

A. Information Dependence

All of us need information from others, and in most organizations our peers are often the preferred sources of this information. **Information dependence** gives others the opportunity to influence our thoughts, feelings, and actions via the signals they send to us.

B. Effect Dependence

In most organizations both formal and informal methods are used to keep individual members "under the influence". Cooperative behavior is usually rewarded, while lack of cooperation can result in punishment and penalties. This **effect dependence** is the reliance on others due to their capacity to provide rewards and punishment. It occurs because the group has a vested interest in how individual members think and act, and the member desires the approval of the group.

II. Social Influence in Action

A. Motives for Social Conformity

Conformity is the tendency for group members to conform to the norms that have been established by the group. Members might do so because of **compliance** which is the simplest, most direct motive for conformity to group norms. It occurs because a member wishes to acquire rewards from the group and avoid punishment. Other possible motives for conformity include **identification** or an initiation process in which established members serve as models for the behavior of others, and **internalization** which occurs when individuals have truly and wholly accepted the beliefs, values, and attitudes that underlie the norms.

B. Experiments in Social Influence

In the Asch study, subjects were led to believe they were participating in an experiment on visual perception. They were exposed to lines of type of different lengths and asked to judge which was equal to the standard line. Even though inaccurate answers were given at first, other subjects agreed with the answer while knowing that it wasn't correct.

In the Sherif study, subjects were shown a stationary point of light in a darkened room and asked to judge its movement. Subjects invariably reported motion although the light was stationary.

In the Asch study, people relied on each other for information and developed a compromise norm. In the Sherif study, a compromise norm was also reached, although the processes used were different.

C. Factors Influencing Conformity to Norms

With greater *publicity* of behaviors, effect dependence is reduced and conformity is affected. Generally people will tend to conform when they know the group is watching and deviate when there are fewer chances of being detected.

Any tendency to "go along with the crowd" is also enhanced when the "crowd" is it bigger" because the *size of the opposition* is relevant to the number of sources of reward and punishment.
When there is *dissension*, an individual tendency to conform is also reduced because dissenters provide alternate sources of information to the group consensus and change potential reward and punishment patterns.

The *issue at hand* is also relevant. In general, difficult, ambiguous issues increase the tendency to conform to group norms, while issues that are directly relevant to a group's goal accomplishments are also more like to promote high conformity.

Both high and low *status* individuals are not always strict conformers. High status individuals often have **idiosyncrasy credits** which are social credits earned from regular conformity to group norms that allow occasional deviance from the norms. Low-status individuals have little to gain by conformity since they have already rejected the group as a source of information and they are suffering from doing so.

D. The Subtle Power of Compliance

In some cases, individuals conform to norms which they do not support. Much of this occurs because of social pressures and the desire to please others. But compliance often sets the stage for the more complete involvement with organizational norms and roles implicit in the stages of identification and internalization.

III. Socialization: Getting (Some) Conformity from Members

Socialization is the process by which people learn the norms and roles that are necessary to function in a group or organization.

A. Stages of Socialization

A considerable amount of socialization occurs even before a person joins an organization. This process is called *anticipatory socialization*. In the *accommodation* stage, the new recruit encounters the day-to-day reality of organizational life. Later on, the member's attention shifts to fine-tuning and actively managing his or her role in the organization. This stage is referred to as *role management*.

B. The Naive New Member

Although people have expectations about their jobs in organizations many such expectations held by entering members are inaccurate and often unrealistically high. At times, the media is responsible. At other times corporate recruiters or even college classes have contributed to there false expectations.

C. The Dilemmas of Socialization

A serious problem in socialization is that individuals wish to maintain their independence even while working, yet the organization needs support for its norms and goals. Balancing the needs of the individual against those of the organization is tricky, and organizations attempt to solve their socialization dilemma by tailoring socialization practices to their particular needs.

D. Methods of Socialization

The strategy of *reliance on external agents* is often used by organizations to help socialize their members. Thus, hospitals rely on medical schools to socialize doctors, while business firms rely on business schools to produce trained and socialized workers.

Some organizations use a *collective* strategy, as in army host camps, to socialize entire groups of new members. In other organizations new members are likely to take on the particular characteristics and style of their socializers. Under this *individual* socialization, uniformity is less likely. In general, after collective socialization, individual socialization occurs when the individual joins his or her work unit.

Often the commitment of new members will be tested or faulty anticipatory socialization corrected through **debasement**, a series of socialization experiences designed to humble new members and strip away some of their initial self-confidence. These experiences most commonly occur in entry-level jobs. An extreme example of these practices would be the Marine Corps boot camps.

The extent of socialization appropriate to individual organizations varies, but in general, most organizations will try to exact the degree of conformity that is needed to regulate behavior while allowing necessary innovation by individuals.

E. Realistic Job Previews

Realistic job previews provide a balanced, realistic picture of the positive and negative aspects of the job to job applicants. When used properly, these previews can overcome false expectations on the part of new organizational members and reduce costly turnover.

F. Gaining Organizational Commitment

In an era of layoffs, downsizing, restructuring, and reengineering, there is evidence that employees are losing commitment to their organizations. **Organizational commitment** is an attitude that reflects the strength of the linkage between an employee and an organization. Understanding this phenomenon requires that we examine the types, causes and consequences of commitment.

Researchers John Meyer and Natalie Allen have identified *three types of organizational commitment*:

- **Affective commitment** is based on identification and involvement with an organization.
- **Continuance commitment** is based on the costs that would be incurred in leaving an organization.
- **Normative commitment** is based on ideology or a feeling of obligation to an organization

Causes of commitment tend to vary across the three types. Interesting, satisfying work, role clarity, and having one's expectations met after hiring are good predictors of affective commitment. Continuance commitment increases with the length of time an employee spends in an organization and is affected by the prospects of alternate employment. Normative commitment is strongest where a sense of obligation or loyalty to the organization can be fostered.

There are a number of *consequences of commitment*. Turnover may be reduced, but very high levels of commitment can also cause conflicts between work and family life, unethical and illegal behavior, and resistance to change. Organizations should also be careful which type of commitment is being reinforced. Affective commitment is positively related to performance, but continuance commitment is negatively related to performance.

IV. Organizational Culture

A. What is Organizational Culture?

By definition **organizational culture** consists of the shared beliefs, values, and assumptions that exist in an organization. The term "shared" means that all members have had a uniform exposure to these elements and have some minimum common understanding of them. Organizational members often take the influence of culture for granted. Culture tends to be stable, providing social continuity and may influence behaviors both inside and outside the organization. Culture has a strong impact on both organizational performance and member satisfaction.

Subcultures are smaller cultures that develop within a larger organizational culture that are based on differences in training, occupation, or departmental goals.

B. The "Strong Culture" Concept

In a **strong culture**, the beliefs, values and assumptions that make up the culture are both intense and pervasive across the organization. The majority of the firm's members support the culture which provides great consensus concerning what the organization stands for.

C. Assets and Liabilities of Strong Cultures

Organizations with strong cultures have several potential advantages:

- The overarching values and assumptions facilitate the *coordination* of different parts of the organization.
- Sharing core values can also facilitate *conflict resolution*.
- Strong cultures contribute to *financial success* when the culture supports the mission, strategy and goals of the organization.

Strong cultures can also be a liability under some circumstances:

- The same strong consensus about common values and appropriate behavior that gives an organization a strong culture can also make it *resistant to change*.
- Strong cultures pushed together in a joint venture or merger can result in a *culture clash*.
- Some cultures are based on beliefs, values, and assumptions that support a *pathology* of infighting, secrecy, and paranoia that leaves little time to do business.

D. Contributors to the Culture

Many strong cultures reflect the impact on values of *the founder's role*. Walt Disney of the Disney Company, Sam Walton of Wal-Mart, Ray Kroc of McDonald's, Bill Gates of Microsoft, and T. J. Watson of IBM are all examples of the imprint of founders on a company's culture.

The precise nature of the *socialization* process in a given company is also a key contributor to culture because socialization is the means by which the culture's beliefs, values, and assumptions are learned. Research shows that organizations with strong cultures expose employees to a careful step-by-step socialization process:

- Step 1 - Selecting employees
- Step 2 - Debasement and hazing
- Step 3 - Training "in the trenches"
- Step 4 - Reward and promotion
- Step 5 - Exposure to core culture
- Step 6 - Organizational folklore
- Step 7 - Role models

E. Diagnosing a Culture

One way of learning about a culture is to examine the symbols, rituals, and stories that characterize the organization's way of life.

Symbols such as a corporate motto or mascot provide common meaning and an identification focus for employees. Rituals such as parties and gatherings are expressive events that define and build the culture. Stories and anecdotes, both pleasant and unpleasant, are told repeatedly across generations of employees to communicate informally "how things work". Researchers have identified several common themes that appear to underline many such stories.

F. AT&T - A Culture in Transition

In 1984, as a result of federal action, AT&T was required to divest itself of its local telephone company operations.

Aside from financial changes, the culture of the company was greatly altered as its entire mission and goals were transformed. This cultural change is still occurring, and the results so far seem mixed. Some employees are pleased, others are anxious about the new way of life that the changes in culture are fostering.

Although the company is doing all it can to reinforce the cultural change, strong cultures are resistant to change, and it may be some time before a completely successful cultural transformation is effected.

PRE-TESTING YOUR UNDERSTANDING OF THE CHAPTER

Key Concepts Matching

Match the letter of the key concept with the appropriate definitions.

A.	Affective commitment	I.	Internalization
B.	Compliance	J.	Normative commitment
C	Continuance commitment	K.	Organizational commitment
D.	Debasement	L.	Organizational culture
E.	Effect dependence	M.	Realistic job previews
F.	Identification	N.	Socialization
G.	Idiosyncrasy credits	O.	Strong culture
H.	Information dependence	P.	Subcultures

______1. That which gives others the opportunity to influence our thoughts, feelings, and actions via the signals they send to us.

______2. That which involves the group's vested interest in how individual members think and act and the member's desire for group approval.

______3. The simplest, most direct motive for conformity to group norms mainly to receive rewards and avoid punishment.

______4. A motivation for conformity often revealed by an imitation process in which established members serve as models for the behavior of others.

______5. Conformity which occurs because individuals have truly and wholly accepted the beliefs, values, and attitudes of the norms.

______6. The tendency of high-status members to deviate without fear of censure because of their previous history of conformity.

______7. Smaller cultures that develop within a larger organizational culture that are based on differences in training, occupation, or departmental goals.

______8. The process by which people learn the norms and roles that are necessary to function in a group or organization.

______9. The process of putting new members through a series of experiences that are designed to humble them and strip away some of their initial self-confidence.

_____10. Previews which provide a balanced, realistic picture of the positive and negative aspects of the job to job applicants.

_____11. The shared beliefs, values and assumptions that exist in an organization.

_____12. That which occurs when the beliefs, values, and assumptions that make up the culture are both intense and pervasive across the organization.

_____13. An attitude that reflects the strength of the linkage between an employee and an organization.

_____14. Commitment based on identification and involvement with an organization.

_____15. Commitment based on the costs that would be incurred in leaving an organization.

_____16. Commitment based on ideology or a feeling of obligation to an organization.

True/False Questions

Circle the letter of the correct answer.

T F 1. Peers are often a preferred source of work information.
T F 2. Compliance is a very complicated motive for conformity to group norms.
T F 3. The Asch study dealt with the behavior of convicts in a state prison.
T F 4. People often tend to "go along with the crowd" when the "crowd" is bigger.
T F 5. High and low status members are more apt to be nonconformists than other group members.
T F 6. Idiosyncrasy credits refers to rewards members receive for their nonconformity.
T F 7. Continuance commitment should be encouraged by management.
T F 8. Simple compliance can set the stage for more complete involvement with organizational norms and roles.
T F 9. Most expectations held by entering organizational members are very accurate.
T F 10. Anticipatory socialization can occur through watching movies and television shows.
T F 11. Hospitals can now develop their cardiologists from scratch.
T F 12. Uniformity of behavior is important in armies and on airplanes.
T F 13. Debasement is a method of building individual self-confidence.
T F 14. Realistic job previews are effective methods of preventing job turnover.
T F 15. People with a high normative commitment stay with an firm because they *want* to.
T F 16. Only big organizations can have a strong culture.
T F 17. Strong cultures usually result in blind conformity.
T F 18. Some organizations contain subcultures.
T F 19. Many strong cultures represent the influence of the organization's founder.
T F 20. The organization's symbols, rituals, and stories usually have no relationship to its culture.

Multiple-Choice Questions

Select the correct answer.

______1. Which of the following are considered to be preferred sources of information?
A. peers
B. bosses
C. subordinates
D. parents

______2. All of the following are motives for conformity *except*
A. compliance.
B. identification.
C. coercion.
D. interrogation.

______3. All of the following are factors which influence conformity *except*
A. dissension.
B. publicity.
C. status.
D. economics.

______4. People with idiosyncrasy credits are often allowed to
A. attack people who won't conform.
B. deviate without fear of censure.
C. behave without conformity.
D. ignore all rules.

______5. All of the following are stages of socialization except
A. role management.
B. role playing.
C. accommodation.
D. anticipatory socialization.

______6. All of the following are usual methods of socialization *except*
A. debasement and hazing.
B. reliance on external agents.
C. collective socialization strategy.
D. bribery and inducements.

______7. All of the following topics might be covered in a job preview *except*
A. compensation.
B. customers.
C. capitalization.
D. career opportunities.

______8. Organizational cultures consists of

A. shared beliefs, values, and assumptions in an organization.

B. literary and musical societies in a company.

C. lectures and programs in an organization.

D. theater and operas presented by organizations.

______9. All of the following may be consequences of high employee commitment *except*

A. resistance to change.

B. harmonious work and family relations.

C. reduced turnover intentions.

D. unethical and illegal behavior.

______10. Lack of cooperation with an organizational group might result in all of the following *except*

A. harassment.

B. name calling.

C. social isolation.

D. promotion.

POST-TESTING FOR EXAMS

True/False Questions

Circle the letter of the correct answer.

T	F	1. Stories about past organizational events are a common aspect of organizational culture.
T	F	2. As a result of government action, AT&T has undergone a radical change in its culture.
T	F	3. Effect dependence relates to what outsiders tell employees about an organization.
T	F	4. Identification as a motive for conformity is often revealed by an imitation process.
T	F	5. In the Sherif study, participants were asked to estimate the lengths of two lines.
T	F	6. Dissenters often provide alternative sources of information to the group consensus.
T	F	7. In general, difficult, ambiguous issues decrease the tendency for conformity to group norms.
T	F	8. At times people conform to group norms simply to avoid trouble or obtain rewards.
T	F	9. Normative commitment increases with the time that an employee spends with a company.
T	F	10. The Marine Corps relies on voluntary compliance to obtain its group socialization.

Multiple-Choice Questions

Select the correct answer.

______1. ________ is the simplest, most direct motive for conformity to social norms.
A. compliments
B. coercion
C. curiosity
D. compliance

______2. With internalization, conformity occurs because it
A. is seen as right.
B. achieves rewards.
C. avoids punishment.
D. pleases others.

______3. In the Sherif study, students were asked to
A. judge pennies in a jar.
B. judge line lengths.
C. judge moving rings.
D. estimate the movement of a point of light.

______4. In the Asch study, students were asked to
A. judge dimes in a pile.
B. judge and compare line lengths.
C. judge circle sizes.
D. judge peoples' weights.

______5. The tendency to "go along with the crowd" is enhanced when the crowd is
A. smaller.
B. hostile.
C. friendly.
D. bigger.

______6. All of the following are causes of commitment *except*
A. enriched jobs.
B. high pay.
C. rapid promotion.
D. special training.

______7. An especially bad combination for organizational performance is
A. low continuance commitment + high normative commitment.
B. low normative commitment + low affective commitment.
C. high continuance commitment + low affective commitment.
D. high affective commitment + low continuance commitment.

______8. All of the following are stages of accommodation *except*
A. orientation programs.
B. training sessions.
C. salary adjustment.
D. rotation through different jobs.

______9. To socialize potential doctors in the role requirements of being physicians, hospitals depend upon
A. medical schools.
B. lectures.
C. films.
D. television.

______10. All of the following are examples of collective socialization strategy *except*
A. Army boot camps.
B. fraternity pledge classes.
C. training classes for salespeople.
D. one-on-one orientation services.

______11. The purpose of hazing is to
A. strengthen member confidence.
B. weaken self-confidence.
C. foster more obedience.
D. foster group conflict.

______12. Which of the following are most likely to rely on radical socialization?
A. charities
B. religious orders
C. universities
D. volunteer groups

______13. To inform new workers of the realities of given jobs, companies might employ
A. realistic job previews.
B. hazing.
C. group previews.
D. social events.

______14. Once a culture is established in an organization, it is
A. persistent and hard to change.
B. easily altered.
C. controlled by management.
D. controlled by unions.

_____15. All of the following are common to excellent organizations *except*
A. care for the customer.
B. hands-on value drives.
C. simple form, lean staff.
D. strong profitability.

______16. All of the following might be part of a culture *except*
A. salary schedules.
B. symbols.
C. rituals.
D. stories.

______17. In 1984, _______ divested itself of local telephone company operations.
A. Pacific Telephone
B. Sprint
C. New England Telephone
D. AT&T

______18. All of the following might be used in socialization *except*
A. debasement and hazing.
B. use of reward and punishment.
C. use of parties and social events.
D. exposure of member to organizational folklore.

______19. The lighting of the torch at the Olympics is an example of (a)
A. ritual.
B. symbol.
C. folklore.
D. hazing.

______20. All of the following are examples of companies with strong cultures *except*
A. General Electric.
B. Sears.
C. Southwest Airlines.
D. 3M.

Application Situations Exercise

Match the key concepts with the statements that best describe them.

A.	Affective commitment	I.	Internalization
B.	Compliance	J.	Normative commitment
C	Continuance commitment	K.	Organizational commitment
D.	Debasement	L.	Organizational culture
E.	Effect dependence	M.	Realistic job previews
F.	Identification	N.	Socialization
G.	Idiosyncrasy credits	O.	Strong culture
H.	Information dependence	P.	Subcultures

______1. Before taking the job, she was told all about the positive and negative aspects of the work she would be doing.

______2. She was warned about the experiences designed to humble her and make her more compliant.

______3. She already knew that the organization had shared beliefs and values.

______4. She didn't know how intense and pervasive these beliefs, values, and assumptions were in the organization.

______5. Soon she became dependent on what her peers told her about work behavior and norms.

______6. She soon came to feel that she *wanted* to be a part of the organization .

______7. Her supervisor commented on the strength of the linkage between her and the firm.

______8. After several years, however, she began to wonder if she was really staying because it would be too hard to leave.

______9. She noticed that most employees really did follow and accept the norms established by the group.

_____10. But her boss and a few senior executives did have a tendency to deviate whenever they felt like it.

Short Answer Questions

Fill-in the missing word(s).

1. As a result of social influence, people often feel or act ____________ than they would as independent operators.

2. The use of idiosyncrasy credits allows a ____________ member of a group to be a nonconformist.

3. In some piecerate pay situations, workers will sometimes _____________ about their output to prevent pressure from their co-workers.

4. _____________ provide alternative sources of information to the group consensus and change potential reward and punishment patterns.

5. Many doubting members will _____________ to group norms just to avoid trouble and to obtain rewards.

6. People seldom join organizations without _____________ about what membership will be like.

7. Stereotypes about organizations are often communicated by _____________ .

8. Debasement experiences most commonly occur in _____________ jobs.

9. Many strong cultures reflect the values of the organization's _____________ .

10. _____________ experiences may be designed to illustrate how group members must depend upon each other.

ANSWER SHEET FOR CHAPTER 9

PRE-TESTING YOUR UNDERSTANDING OF THE CHAPTER

Key Concepts Matching

1. H	2. E	3. B	4. F	5. I	6. G	7. P	8. N	9. D	10. M
11. L	12. O	13. K	14. A	15. C	16. J				

True/False Questions

1. T	2. F	3. F	4. T	5. T	6. F	7. F	8. T	9. F	10. T
11. F	12. T	13. F	14. T	15. F	16. F	17. F	18. T	19. T	20. F

Multiple-Choice Questions

1. A	2. C	3. D	4. B	5. B	6. D	7. C	8. A	9. B	10. D

POST-TESTING FOR EXAMS

True/False Questions

1. T	2. T	3. F	4. T	5. F	6. T	7. F	8. T	9. F	10. F

Multiple-Choice Questions

1. D	2. A	3. D	4. B	5. D	6. B	7. C	8. C	9. A	10. D
11. B	12. B	13. A	14. A	15. D	16. A	17. D	18. C	19. A	20. B

Application Situations Exercise

1. M	2. D	3. L	4. O	5. H	6. A	7. K	8. C	9. N	10. G

Short Answer Questions

1. differently	2. high status	3. lie	4. dissenters
5. conform	6. expectations	7. the media	8. entry-level
9. founder	10. debasement		

CASE STUDY

BOIVIN REALTIES LTD.

Isabelle Rondeau and Michel Quennec were comparing notes over their beers at the Peel Pub in downtown Montreal, a practice dating back to when they had first met in college. Isabelle and Michel had each graduated with a BA, and exactly one year ago, each had accepted an offer of employment from Boivin Realties Ltd. It had been a pretty good year for both Isabelle and Michel, though it was hard for them to believe they really worked for the same company.

Company Overview

Boivin Realties Ltd. is a real estate brokerage firm founded in 1982 by Henri Boivin. The firm operates eight branch offices in southern Quebec dealing in residential real estate, although two offices have recently become involved in commercial real estate. The largest branch office, located in Sherbrooke and run by Henri Boivin, also serves as the head office. The head office formulates company policy and procedures, sets marketing strategy and budgets in conjunction with the branches, trains new sales agents, and reviews branch office reports on listings, sales and so forth. Henri Boivin, however, is a strong believer in decentralization: he allows his branch managers a great deal of latitude in running their offices.

In a typical branch office, the manager has one branch administrator and from 15 to 24 real estate agents reporting directly to him or her. The branch administrator serves as an office manager, and has one receptionist/secretary and from one to three part-time secretaries (depending on the season) reporting to him or her. The branch administrator also has "dotted line" responsibility over the sales agents, in that he or she must coordinate certain branch activities such as the scheduling of agents, preparation of documents, and the maintenance of listing files. The sales agents are responsible for all "field work," which includes hosting "open houses" at residences up for sale, escorting prospective buyers to available residences, facilitating negotiations between buyers and sellers and arranging inspections of properties.

The Interview

Two Montreal offices of Boivin, Westmount and St. Henri, were looking for new sales agents. Isabelle was interviewed by the manager of the Westmount office, and Michel, by the manager of the St. Henri office. The tone of the interviews was much the same. The managers spoke primarily of the unlimited potential of a sales agent to make money, as pay was based entirely on commissions. A commission of 6 percent was charged on each sale: the seller's agent and the agency with which the agent was affiliated split 3 percent, as did the buyer's agent and agency. If the buyer did not have an agent, then the seller's agent and agency received the entire commission.

The branch managers also noted the very flexible hours and almost complete autonomy that sales agents enjoyed. Isabelle and Michel were told that a good sales agent had to be a "self-starter" and be "good with people." One of the managers also stressed the "professionalism" and "high status" that real estate agents enjoyed in the local community.

Source: Case prepared by Blake E. Ashforth, Concordia University. Used with permission.

Both Isabelle and Michel generally liked what they heard, although Isabelle was somewhat concerned about what appeared to be limited opportunities for advancement in the company. She did not express her concern, however, for fear of appearing uninterested in he sales agent position. Michel was concerned about not generating sufficient sales to make ends meet while he was learning the ropes, but decided the short-term risk was worth the potential long-term gain. Isabelle and Michel accepted offers of employment shortly after their interviews.

The Westmount Office

Although both were hired as sales agents, their experiences at Boivin differed markedly. Isabelle and two other recent college graduates, John and Mark, were hired by the Westmount office, located in a very affluent area of Montreal. Given the high price of houses in the area, competition among real estate agencies was extremely high. Most agents had some higher education, and several had MAs or PHDs.

Following standard procedure for new recruits, Isabelle, John and Mark were sent to Sherbrooke for training. This training focused on the technical aspects of the trade necessary to pass the provincial licensing examination, such as real estate law, methods of financing purchases, and how to prepare an offer to buy. More "social" aspects of real estate, such as how to solicit new clients or "show" a house, were only briefly reviewed.

Upon their return to Westmount, Isabelle and her co-workers spent two more weeks training under the branch administrator. Several days were spent mastering technical tools, such as the office equipment and technical volumes on tax codes and property descriptions. The remainder of the two weeks was spent learning the social aspects of real estate. Role plays were frequently used, where the recruits were paired off and would assume the role of agent and seller or buyer and their performances were then evaluated by the branch administrator.

Isabelle and her co-workers found these exercises to be generally helpful when they began to actually deal with sellers and buyers, although they still encountered problems. Clients were not always as friendly and patient as their co-workers had been in the role plays, and often asked questions or requested favors that the new agents did not know how to handle. The sales agents also found it difficult investing often enormous amounts of time and energy in a client, only to have the client take their house off the market, or decide not to buy after all, or "get cold feet" and cancel an apparent deal at the last minute. They were also surprised at the sheer number of evenings and weekends that had to be devoted to field work.

Isabelle found the uncertainty associated with her performance to be especially disconcerting. Since most contact with clients occurred outside the office, the only reliable feedback was her sales figures. Yet she was never certain how "good" her figures actually were, or what actions on her part had actually persuaded a client to buy or sell. When she asked the branch administrator what was a reasonable sales target for someone of her experience, she was told to "just do your best." The branch manager did not comment on the performance of a new agent beyond vague messages like, "How's it going?" or "It's been a rough month, hasn't it?"

Over the course of time, it became readily evident that Isabelle, John and Mark had developed a very strong friendship. They could frequently be seen laughing together over some remark, sitting next to one another during the biweekly staff meetings, and eating lunch together. If one of the three had a problem or question, he or she invariably first approached one of the other two. Remarked one veteran agent: "I think they're joined at the hip."

This behavior, however, was not uncommon at Westmount, as the office contained several such cliques. One day, shortly after Isabelle arrived, the branch manager was disturbed by a loud and heated discussion between two sales agents. One was accusing the other of "sabotaging" his sale. Apparently, it was a common practice in one agent's group - but not the other's - to offer a client a discount on the sales commission if the client was also buying from this agent. The client had learned of this disparity and threatened to change agencies unless the agent offered a discount. The manager stepped in and settled the dispute, although a palpable chill remained between the agents and between their groups. When Isabelle asked the branch administrator if this sort of incident was common, she was told:

"Not really. We have some personality clashes here, but people here try not to get in each other's way." She went on to say that because an agent generally worked alone, these "clashes" did not hurt the company.

The St. Henri Office
Michel and one other person, Francine, were hired by the St. Henri office. Although not far from Westmount, the two districts are separated by a major expressway, and St. Henri enjoys far less affluence. As residences sell for a fraction of the price of Westmount residences, there is far less competition between the real estate agencies located in St. Henri. Many of the veteran agents are retirees from other occupations who entered real estate "for something to do" or to supplement their retirement income.

Like Isabelle and her co-workers, Michel and Francine received their initial training from the Sherbrooke office. That, however, is where the similarities ended. Upon their return from Sherbrooke, Michel and Francine were introduced by the branch manager to the other staff members in the office at the time. He then led them to a pair of desks, each bare except for a telephone, and said, "Get Suzanne [the receptionist/secretary] to fix you up with pens and stuff. I know you're new, so just do the best you can for now. Watch how the other guys do it. If you need me, you know where to find me."

Michel and Francine each tried to utilized what they had learned at Sherbrooke. They quickly found, however, that the general lessons did not translate well into the specific skills needed to interact with sellers and buyers and address their many and varied concerns. There were also a number of rude surprises. For example, Francine received a call from a homeowner who expressed an interest in selling. When Francine arrived at the home, she found an agent from a rival agency. Apparently, the homeowner had contacted two agencies in the hope of getting a better deal from one. Francine was so shocked that she berated the homeowner and lost the listing.

Francine became increasingly frustrated at her apparent inability to sell a listing or to interest prospective buyers in a home. As she put it: "Every day I beat my head against the wall." She was also discouraged with what she called the "feast or famine" nature of the business, referring to the wide fluctuations in pay-checks. After two and a half months at St. Henri, Francine quit.

Michel was also becoming frustrated with the trial and error method of learning. He had, however, developed a very warm relationship with Suzanne, the receptionist/secretary, and she provided some useful tips, such as when best to approach the manger with questions and how to circumvent some of the paperwork. One day, however, Michel came to realize what a truly invaluable source of information she was. Michel had periodically summoned the nerve to ask several of the more successful veteran agents questions about field work. Often, however, the replies were curt and uninformative. After one particularly painful rebuff, Suzanne suggested the Michel not be quite as "brash" and also, that he instead focus his attention upon Jean, a somewhat less successful, but more receptive sales agent.

Michel followed her advice, and was soon accompanying the agent on showings, listing presentations, and other aspects of field work. Jean revealed a number of "tricks of the trade," such as showing homes that were progressively more consistent with a client's expressed preferences in order to hone in on a sale, and progressively more expensive in order to whet a client's appetite for a larger purchase, or securing a listing by assuring a prospective client that his or her home could be sold for an unrealistically high price, and then later persuading him or her to decrease the price due to the "slow market." On several occasions, Michel told Jean that he was uncomfortable with certain practices which he considered to be "pretty slimy." Jean had little patience for such remarks, and usually responded along the lines of, "Given me a break, everyone does it," or "Do you want to sell or not?"

As Michel began to learn Jean's tricks of the trade, he attempted them himself, with Jean providing feedback. Though Michel's "hit rate" began improving, Michel still wondered from time to time whether he would ever enjoy the success of Jean and some of the other veteran agents. Whenever Jean seemed to sense Michel's pessimism, he would say something like "Don't worry. The only difference between me and you is 12 years experience."

As the friendship between Michel and Jean deepened, Jean started inviting Michel to outings with the other agents. Michel was surprised to discover that the veterans at St. Henri did a fair amount of socializing together. They frequently met for drinks after work, backyard barbecues, and some met for a weekly poker game. Michel found them to be far more relaxed and personable than he had originally thought them to be. Two incidents in particular stood out in his mind.:

The first occurred shortly after Michel began accompanying Jean in the field. Jean had suggested that Michel show one particular client several houses that were up for sale. Along the way, the client began to ask Michel increasingly difficult questions about zoning restrictions, construction materials, and the like, and increasingly bizarre questions about the location of fallout shelters, the sex habits of the neighbors and on and on. Michel was barely able to contain his exasperation, especially when the client insisted on accompanying Michel back to the office. As Michel entered the office, he was greeted with the loud laughter of his colleagues. The "client," it turned out, was himself a Boivin sales agent from another office.

The second incident occurred when Michel fell ill. He had several homes to show and was very worried that he might lose the listings. Jean told him not to worry. Michel's colleagues showed the homes in his place, and when one home actually sold, the colleague refused any compensation from Michel.

A Toast

It had been a fairly productive year for both Isabelle and Michel, but a long year, too. As they touched their beer glasses in a mock toast, Isabelle said: "Well, Michel, we survived. Let's hope the ride is a little smoother from here on."

1. In what respects were the initial job interviews accurate and inaccurate? What effects might this have had on Isabelle and Michel?

2. What are the likely advantages and disadvantages of having Isabelle and her colleagues receive their training at Westmount as a group? Under what conditions is such training desirable?

3. What are the likely advantages and disadvantages of having Michel receive most of his training from a veteran sales agent? Under what conditions is such training desirable?

4. The mentoring process at the St. Henri office was informal. Should it be formalized, that is, should specific agents be required to train recruits? Why or why not?

5. Why do you think Michel's colleagues pulled the bizarre stunt with the fake client? What risks do such stunts entail?

6. Outline and justify a socialization program to help newcomers fit in, feel at home and become productive sales agents at Boivin.

CHAPTER 10

LEADERSHIP

LEARNING OBJECTIVES

- DEFINE AND DISCUSS THE ROLE OF BOTH FORMAL AND EMERGENT LEADERSHIP.
- EXPLAIN AND CRITICALLY EVALUATE THE TRAIT APPROACH TO LEADERSHIP.
- EXPLAIN THE CONCEPTS OF CONSIDERATION AND INITIATING STRUCTURE AND THEIR CONSEQUENCES.
- EVALUATE THE USE OF LEADER REWARD VERSUS LEADER PUNISHMENT BEHAVIORS.
- DESCRIBE AND EVALUATE FIEDLER'S CONTINGENCY THEORY.
- DESCRIBE AND EVALUATE HOUSE'S PATH-GOAL THEORY.
- EXPLAIN HOW AND WHEN TO USE PARTICIPATIVE LEADERSHIP.
- DISCUSS THE MERITS OF TRANSFORMATIONAL LEADERSHIP AND CHARISMA.
- EXPLAIN THE CONCEPTS OF LEADERSHIP NEUTRALIZERS AND SUBSTITUTES.

KEY CONCEPTS

Leadership

Traits

Task Leader

Social-emotional leader

Consideration

Initiating structure

Leader reward behavior

Leader punishment behavior

Fiedler's Contingency Theory

Least Preferred Co-Worker (LPC)

House's Path-Goal Theory

Participative leadership

Transformational leadership

Charisma

Neutralizers of leadership

Substitutes for leadership

CHAPTER SUMMARY

Key concepts are identified by **bold** *faced type.*

I. What is Leadership?

Leadership is the influence that particular individuals exert upon the goal achievement of others in an organizational context.

Although any organizational member can influence other members, individuals with titles such as manager, executive supervisor, and department head are in assigned leadership roles and are expected to exert formal leadership.

II. The (Somewhat Elusive) Search for Leadership Traits

A. Research on Leadership Traits

During World War I, the US military began to search for those traits which would help in identifying future officers. **Traits** are personal characteristics of the individual, including physical characteristics, social background, intellectual ability, personality, task orientation, and social skills. After many studies by many organizations, no conclusive results have been found.

B. Problems With the Trait Approach

In many cases it is difficult to determine if traits make the leader or if opportunity for leadership produces the traits. So, the biggest weakness of the trait approach to leadership is its failure to take into account the situation in which leadership occurs.

III. Lessons from Emergent Leadership

After discouragement with trait approach studies, psychologists began to investigate what leaders do in group settings. These studies concentrated on emergent leadership or the behaviors in which certain group members engage that cause them to become leaders.

Two leadership roles were apparent. The **task leader** is a leader who is concerned with accomplishing a task by organizing others, planning strategy, and dividing labor. The **social-emotional leader** is a leader who is concerned with reducing tension, patching up disagreements, settling arguments, and maintaining morale.

Both of these functions are important leadership roles, and the needs of the group will determine which of these roles a leader will play at a given time.

IV. The Behavior of Assigned Leaders

A. Consideration and Initiating Structure

The most involved, systematic study of leadership so far, begun at Ohio State University in the 1970s, revealed two basic types of leadership behavior. **Consideration** involves the extent to which the leader is approachable and shows personal concern for subordinates. **Initiating structure** involves the degree to which the leader concentrates on group goal attainment.

B. The Consequences of Consideration and Structure

In general, the effects of consideration and initiating structure depend upon characteristics of the task, the subordinate, and the setting in which the work is performed. These contingencies will determine which behavior is most appropriate and when it is to be employed.

C. Leader Reward and Punishment Behaviors

Two additional leader behaviors are being studied widely. **Leader reward behavior** involves providing subordinates with compliments, tangible benefits, and deserved special treatment. **Leader punishment behavior** involves the use of reprimands or unfavorable task assignments and the active withholding of raises, promotions, and other rewards.

V. Situational Theories of Leadership

A. Fiedler's Contingency Theory

Fred Fiedler has developed a situational theory of leadership called **Fiedler's Contingency Theory** which argues that the association between *leadership orientation* and *group effectiveness* is contingent upon the extent to which the *situation* is *favorable* for the exertion of influence.

Leadership Orientation: Fiedler has measured leadership orientation by having leaders describe their **Least Preferred Co-worker (LPC)**, a current or past co-worker with whom the leader has had a difficult time accomplishing a task. Fiedler has argued that the LPC score reveals a personality trait that reflects the leader's motivational structure.

Situational Favorableness: This is the "contingency" part of Contingency Theory. Factors affecting situational favorableness include: leader-member relations, task structure, and position power. In general the situation is most favorable for leadership when leader-member relations are good, the task is structured, and the leader has strong position power.

Although there is reasonable support for the Fiedler's Contingency Theory, several studies have concluded that the evidence is contradictory and that the theory needs some adjustment.

B. House's Path-Goal Theory

House's Path-Goal Theory is concerned with the situations under which various leader behaviors (directive, supportive, participative, achievement-oriented) are most effective. According to House, the effective leader forms a *connection between subordinate goals and organizational goals.*

Leader Behavior: Path-Goal Theory is concerned with four specific kinds of leader behavior:

- Directive behavior - essentially identical to initiating structure
- Supportive behavior - essentially identical to consideration
- Participative behavior - leaders consult with subordinates
- Achievement-oriented behavior - leaders encourage subordinates to strive for a high level of goal accomplishment.

Situational Factors: This theory also deals with subordinate characteristics and environmental factors of work. Thus, subordinates who are high need achievers, prefer to be told what to do, or who feel that they have low task abilities each respond best to certain types of leadership. Also, according to the theory, the effectiveness of leadership depends upon the particular work environment. Thus, routine tasks, challenging but ambiguous tasks, and frustrating, dissatisfying jobs each require specific leader behaviors for effective leadership to take place.

In general, there is some research support for the situational propositions of this theory as well as evidence that this theory is more effective in predicting subordinate job satisfaction and acceptance of the leader than in predicting subordinate performance.

VI. Participative Leadership

A. What is Participation?

Participative leadership involves subordinates in making work related decisions. Participative leadership should not, however, be confused with abdication of leadership, which is almost always ineffective.

B. Potential Advantages of Participative Leadership

Participation can increase the *motivation* of subordinates. It can often increase the *quality* of the work, and it can increase the *acceptance* of decisions involving fairness issues, because the workers themselves will have been involved.

C. Potential Problems of Participative Leadership

Some of the difficulties of participative leadership include the *time and energy* involved, the perceived *loss of power* by leaders, and a *lack of receptivity or knowledge* on the part of subordinates.

D. A Situational Model of Participation

Victor Vroom and Arthur Jago have developed a model (the decision tree) which is frequently used in management development seminars.

This model takes into account various degrees of participation that can be exhibited by the leader as well as the various degrees of behavior exhibited by the work group. By taking a problem through the decision tree, the leader can determine the correct degree of participation for the problem solving situation.

E. Does Participation Work?

In general, employees who participate in job-related decisions are more satisfied than those who do not. However, the effects of participation on productivity are still open to question.

VII. Transformational Leadership and Charisma

Certain leaders throughout history are know for **transformational leadership** which is providing followers with a new vision that instills true commitment. Three qualities set transformational leaders apart: intellectual stimulation, individualized consideration, and charisma.

Charisma is a term stemming from a Greek word meaning favored or gifted. Leaders like Winston Churchill, Martin Luther King, Nelson Mandela and Abraham Lincoln are examples of charismatic leaders who possess traits of self-confidence, dominance, and a strong conviction in their own beliefs. Dave Thomas of Wendy's restaurants is a charismatic leader who commands strong loyalty and devotion from his employees.

VIII. Gender, Culture, and Leadership Style

Research suggests that there are few differences in leadership style between men and women in organizational settings, with one exception - women have a tendency to be more participative. This may be because of negative reactions to women adopting stereotypically male styles such as directive or authoritarian.

Power distance and the degree of individualism in a society may both impact the effectiveness of leader behaviors in cross cultural contexts.

IX. Does Leadership Matter?

A. Pros and Cons of Leader Influence

Leadership is still important today because of changing environments, differing needs of organization members, and the fact that organizations do not have a rule or policy for every contingency.

Leadership can be constrained, however, because of external factors beyond the leader's control as well as rigid selection or promotion policies that leave the leaders with no free hands.

B. Leadership Neutralizes and Substitutes

Neutralizers of leadership are factors present in the work setting which reduce the opportunities for leaders to exert influence.

Substitutes for leadership are those factors which can take the place of active leadership, making it unnecessary or redundant.

PRE-TESTING YOUR UNDERSTANDING OF THE CHAPTER

Key Concepts Matching

Match the letter of the key concepts with the appropriate definitions.

A. Charisma
B. Consideration
C. Fiedler's Contingency Theory
D. House's Path-Goal Theory
E. Initiating structure
F. Leader punishment behavior
G. Leader reward behavior
H. Leadership
I. Least Preferred Co-worker (LPC)
J. Neutralizers of leadership
K. Participative leadership
L. Social-emotional leader
M. Substitute for leadership
N. Task leader
O. Traits
P. Transformational leadership

______1. That which occurs when particular individuals exert influence upon others in an organizational context.

______2. Personal characteristics of the individual, including physical characteristics, social background, intellectual ability, personality, task orientation, and social skills.

______3. The concept that the association between leadership orientation and group effectiveness is contingent upon the extent to which the situation is favorable for the exertion of influence.

______4. A leader most concerned with accomplishing the task at hand.

______5. A leader nominated because he or she is the most liked person in the group.

______6. The extent to which the leader is approachable and shows personal concerns for subordinates.

______7. The degree to which the leader concentrates on group goal attainment.

______8. Providing subordinates with compliments, tangible benefits, and deserved special treatment.

______9. Involves the use of reprimands, unfavorable task assignments, and the active withholding of raises, promotions, and other rewards.

______10. A theory which measures leadership orientation by having leaders describe the co-workers they liked the least.

______11. A theory concerned with the situations under which various leader behaviors are most effective.

______12. Leadership which involves subordinates in making work-related decisions.

______13. Leadership which decisively changes the beliefs and attitudes of followers to correspond to a new vision.

______14. A term stemming from a Greek word meaning favored or gifted.

______15. Tasks or organizational characteristics which can operate to reduce the opportunities for leaders to exert influence.

______16. Tasks or organizational characteristics which can operate to make leadership unnecessary or redundant.

True/False Questions

Circle the letter of the correct answer.

T F 1. In general, traits themselves are no indication of leadership ability.
T F 2. A social-emotional leader is one most feared by group members.
T F 3. Leader reward behavior involves giving the leader large bonuses for especially effective leadership.
T F 4. Leader punishment behavior involves punishing leaders for their failures.
T F 5. Fred Fiedler was a pioneer in the study of contingency theory of leadership.
T F 6. Good leaders are effective regardless of the situations involved.
T F 7. LPC refers to the lowest percentage correlation in statistics.
T F 8. The Path-Goal theory is concerned with the easiest and most rapid ways to reach a goal.
T F 9. In participative behavior, leaders consult with subordinates about their work related matters and opinions.
T F 10. Supportive behavior and consideration are essentially identical.
T F 11. Generally, participation can increase the motivation of subordinates.
T F 12. A hospital emergency room is a good place for participative leadership.
T F 13. A decision tree is a chart on which group members hang suggestions.
T F 14. Jack Welsh has been chairman of General Motors since 1981.
T F 15. Leadership can be limited by external factors beyond the leader's control.
T F 16. Calvin Coolidge is often listed as an example of a charismatic leader.
T F 17. Individuals with titles in organizations are expected to influence and direct subordinates.
T F 18. Generally, good leaders should be good speakers and communicators.
T F 19. When rewards to subordinates are contingent upon performance, they perform at a high level and experience job satisfaction.
T F 20. Really good leaders should NOT be influenced by subordinate behavior.

Multiple-Choice Questions

Select the correct answer.

______1. All of the following have been considered to be successful leaders *except*
A. Henry Ford..
B. Martin Luther King.
C. Joan of Arc.
D. Herbert Hoover.

______2. In a given group, the _________ could most likely become the emergent leader.
A. person who talks the most
B. most silent person
C. richest person
D. tallest person

______3. The person most liked by group members who is nominated for leadership is known as
A. the charismatic leader.
B. the social-emotional leader.
C. the transformational leader.
D. the emergent leader.

______4. All of the following are components of the behavior of assigned leaders *except*
A. consideration.
B. initiating structure.
C. reward and punishment behaviors.
E. capricious, unpredictable behavior.

______5. All of the following are involved with situational favorableness *except*
A. leader-member relations.
B. task structure.
C. environmental concerns.
D. position power.

______6. The LPC measure stands for
A. least preferred co-worker.
B. lowest percentage curve.
C. least proven clause.
D. latest pop craze.

______7. Robert House was a pioneer in the development of
A. LPC theory.
B. the decision tree.
C. path-goal theory.
D. none of the above.

______8. All of the following are involved in path-goal theory *except*
A. directive behavior.
B. initial behavior.
C. supportive behavior.
D. participative behavior.

______9. In general, encouraging participation will ________ the motivation of workers.
A. increase
B. decrease
C. have no effect on
D. alter

______10. All of the following could be problems of participative leadership *except*
B. jealousy.
A. loss of power.
C. lack of receptivity or knowledge.
D. cohesiveness.

POST-TESTING FOR EXAMS

True/False Questions

Circle the letter of the correct answer.

T F 1. A leader who describes an LPC favorably is considered to be relationship oriented.
T F 2. Contingency theory deals with the situations and their effects on leadership.
T F 3. The more favorable the position power, the least favorable will be the leadership situation.
T F 4. Robert House was a pioneer in the development of the Path-Goal theory.
T F 5. Good leaders should not be concerned about workers' perception of fairness.
T F 6. Charisma is a Latin term meaning stubborn and inflexible.
T F 7. There are situations in organizations when neutralizers of leadership can serve as substitutes for leadership.
T F 8. Vroom and Jago are pioneers in the study of participative leadership models.
T F 9. Leader reward behavior is generally less effective than leader punishment behavior.
T F 10. Certain definite traits are now known to guarantee effective leadership across various situations.

Multiple-Choice Questions

Select the correct answer.

______1. All of the following are shown in the Vroom & Jago decision tree *except*
A. quality requirement.
B. quantity requirement.
C. leader information.
D. subordinate information.

______2. Steven Jobs was the founder and CEO of
A. Apple Computer.
B. American Motors.
C. Digital Computer.
D. Drake Business Schools.

______3. All of the following are qualities of transformational leaders *except*
A. intellectual stimulation.
B. inherent knowledge.
C. charisma.
D. individualized consideration.

______4. Prominent traits shared by charismatic leaders include all of the following *except*
A. self-confidence.
B. dominance.
C. doubts.
D. strong convictions.

______5. All of the following US Presidents were considered charismatic *except*
A. Jefferson.
B. Lincoln.
C. Kennedy.
D. Ford.

______6. All of the following are pioneers in the study of leadership *except*
A. Freud..
B. Vroom.
C. Jago.
D. Fiedler.

______7. Trait theories of leadership did not receive serious scientific attention until
A. 1972.
B. 1850.
C. the 1900s.
D. the 1800s.

______8. All of the following are considered to be individual traits *except*
A. physical characteristics.
B. intellectual ability.
C. personality.
D. family background.

______9. All of the following relate to leadership models *except*
A. Fiedler's contingency theory.
B. House's path-goal theory.
C. Maslow's hierarchy of needs.
D. Vroom and Jago's decision tree.

______10. According to House, the most important activities of leaders are those that clarify the paths of various goals of interest to
A. subordinates.
B. managers.
C. leaders.
D. stockholders.

______11. Subordinates who are high need achievers should work well under
A. direct leadership style.
B. achievement-oriented leadership.
C. participative leadership style.
D. supportive leadership style.

______12. All of the following are advantages of participative leadership *except*
A. increased motivation.
B. more quality.
C. use of more time and energy.
D. more acceptance.

______13. All of the following are various degrees of participation that can be exhibited by the leader (according to Vroom and Jago) *except*
A. accepting.
B. autocratic.
C. consultative.
D. group.

______14. Cross cultural transferability of leadership theories may be hampered by differences in
A. language.
B. power distance.
C. political climate.
D. workforce participation of women

______15. According to Fiedler, favorableness depends upon all of the following *except*
A. the structure of the task.
B. the position power of the leader.
C. the relative easiness of the task.
D. the degree of satisfaction in the relationship between the leader and the group.

______16. Participation works under all of the following conditions *except*
A. when workers are given special bonuses.
B. when the task is reasonably complex.
C. when workers desire participation.
D. when workers are intelligent and knowledgeable.

______17. Neutralizers are factors that make leadership attempts
A. more effective.
B. useless.
C. less effective.
D. more participatory.

______18. House was a pioneer in the development of
A. contingency theory of leadership.
B. hierarchy of needs theory.
C. the decision tree.
D. the path-goal theory of leadership.

______19. In general the trait approach to leadership is
A. the best predictor of leaders.
B. at best an uncertain way of selecting leaders.
C. the latest trend in leadership studies.
D. easily managed by computers.

______20. As a result of reading this chapter, you should realize that
A. the trait approach is the best leadership approach.
B. contingency methods seem to produce the best results.
C. scientists know how to develop good leaders.
D. leadership is no longer of importance today.

Application Situations Exercise

Match the key concepts with the statements that best describe them.

A. Charisma
B. Consideration
C. Fiedler's Contingency Theory
D. House's Path-Goal Theory
E. Initiating structure
F. Leader punishment behavior
G. Leader reward behavior
H. Leadership
I. Least Preferred Co-worker (LPC)
J. Neutralizers of leadership
K. Participative leadership
L. Social-emotional leader
M. Substitute for leadership
N. Task leader
O. Traits
P. Transformational leadership

______1. Our boss always wanted to get the job at hand finished as quickly as possible.

______2. The boss did give us bonuses and praise when we did the job well.

______3. But when the boss was disappointed in our performance, we received reprimands and unfavorable task assignments.

______4. The boss once tried involving all of us in making work-related decisions.

______5. We were once even asked to elect our own group leader, so we picked the most popular person.

______6. This person was a very friendly and concerned person.

______7. This boss preferred a leader who was less people oriented and more task oriented.

______8. We always wondered what characteristics would or wouldn't make for good leadership.

______9. Perhaps the situation helps create the leader.

_____10. Anyway, we think that in the future, computers will take over what leaders do today.

Short Answer Questions

Fill-in the missing word(s).

1. The trait approach fails to take into account the ______________ in which leadership occurs.

2. When subordinates lack knowledge as to how to perform a job, ______________ becomes important for leadership.

3. Leadership always contains ______________ between leaders and followers with both parties able to influence each other.

4. The effective leader (according to House) favors a connection between _______________ goals and organizational goals.

5. Participative leadership should not be confused with the _______________ of leadership.

6. As leaders, women tend to adopt more _______________ behaviors than men.

7. _______________ involves treating subordinates as distinct individuals and showing concern for their personal development.

8. When neutralizers and substitutes are present, the impact of _______________ is reduced.

9. Two important facets of emotional leadership are the task function and the _______________.

10. Many historical leaders and figures are said to be _______________.

ANSWER SHEET FOR CHAPTER 10

PRE-TESTING YOUR UNDERSTANDING OF THE CHAPTER

Key Concepts Matching

1. H	2. O	3. C	4. N	5. L	6. B	7. E	8. G	9. F	10. I
11. D	12. K	13. P	14. A	15. J	16. M				

True/False Questions

1. T	2. F	3. F	4. F	5. T	6. F	7. F	8. F	9. T	10. T
11. T	12. F	13. F	14. F	15. T	16. F	17. T	18. T	19. T	20. F

Multiple-Choice Questions

1. D	2. A	3. B	4. D	5. C	6. A	7. C	8. B	9. A	10. D

POST-TESTING FOR EXAMS

True/False Questions

1. T	2. T	3. F	4. T	5. F	6. F	7. T	8. T	9. F	10. F

Multiple-Choice Questions

1. B	2. A	3. B	4. C	5. D	6. A	7. C	8. D	9. C	10. A
11. B	12. C	13. A	14. B	15. C	16. A	17. C	18. D	19. B	20. B

Application Situations Exercise

1. N	2. G	3. F	4. K	5. L	6. B	7. E	8. O	9. C	10. M

Short Answer Questions

1. situation
2. initiating structure
3. interaction
4. subordinate
5. abdication
6. participative or democratic
7. individualized consideration
8. formal leadership
9. socio-emotional functions
10. charismatic

Case Study

Jean Hall's Dilemma

Jean Hall had worked for the Contronica Corporation for about five years. She was 29 years old, was single, and had acquired a B.B.A. and M.B.A. from the University of Florida, where she majored in finance and management. Her performance at Contronica, first as an analyst in the Corporate Planning group, and then as a consultant in the Management Audit Department, was typically described by her supervisors and co-workers as "excellent" or "outstanding." She was recognized as having exceptional analytical ability, and the studies she completed for Contronica were regarded by at least one of the company's division managers as "models in their own right." Jean was affable and openly communicative in her relationships with people; she seemed to be generally well liked in return and had been considered "one of the team" in both departments in which she had worked.

Despite this, Jean had begun to experience some self-doubt and anxiety in the last few days. A month earlier she received a promotion as director of the Management Audit Department, a middle management position which reported to the Vice-President of Administration. Her predecessor, Roger Davis, had been transferred to cover an important line position left vacant by the sudden death of the incumbent.

The function of the Management Audit Department was to conduct reviews and studies of the systems and general operations of the various divisions throughout the company with the objective of recommending, and assisting in implementing, changes to improve the effectiveness or efficiency of these divisions. These studies were conducted on a pre-arranged rotational basis, or by invitation of the divisions. In effect, the department worked as in-house resource group and consulting arm of the company.

Jean's anxiety stemmed from the task which had been thrust upon her and her department, and from her uncertainty concerning the leadership approach she should use in getting the job accomplished. Only three weeks after assuming her new position, she received a hurried phone call from her superior, Bill Handelman, the Vice-President of Administration. Handelman had received feedback from the Marketing Division to the effect that the company was losing literally "hundreds of thousands" of dollar sales volume as a result of an apparent failure to meet delivery dates on orders for the company's new portable fax machine. Both the Marketing and Manufacturing personnel seemed to agree that the problem was in the production and inventory control system which had been installed by an external management consulting firm some three years earlier. The company's President had also learned of the problem and was "hopping mad." Jean was directed by Handelman to "get you and your department working on that problem...and fast. We need action and solutions...no delays...no blue-sky fooling around." While Handelman's own manner could largely be explained by the pressure he himself felt in the circumstances, nonetheless, it was not totally unrepresentative of the approach of the corporation's top executives to management problems. As one middle manager stated "they (top management) are very, very 'hard nosed.'"

Source: This case is an adaptation from "Montronics Corporation: The New Manager's Dilemma," by Professor Peter E. Pitsalis, Concordia University, Montreal, 1991. All names and other selected data have been disguised. Used by permission.

From her own experience and from the preliminary investigations she conducted, Jean knew that the real underlying cause for the company's problem might not necessarily lie in the production and inventory control system. As far as she was concerned, the causes still had to be determined; there would likely be numerous obstacles for which there were probably no pre-packaged solutions. Jean personally did not know very much about the production and control system used in the company. Most of her own experience had been acquired working on problems related to procurement, distributions, sales forecasting, and the like. However, she had a good opinion of the people now working for her. She had an opportunity to get to know most of them as colleagues in the previous three years. In her view, they had both the competence and breadth of technical knowledge to respond to the situation.

There were 17 people working for Jean, about half men and half women: four consultants, nine analysts, and four audit assistants with the duties of the latter including secretarial work. All of the consultants and analysts had university degrees, mostly in business, but some in engineering and science. Two of the four consultants were themselves M.B.A.'s. Jean knew that at least three of the analysts and one of the consultants had done some work in the Manufacturing Division on production control problems, so she could count on their knowledge and input.

On reflection, Jean was convinced that interpersonal relations among members of her department were generally quite good. There was some competition among some of them, and conflict was evident at times, but none of it was out of the ordinary. Jean perceived most of the members of the department to be responsible and reasonably cognizant of, and committed to, the goals of the department. There were a few natural or informal sub-group formations or cliques in the department, but the sharing of information and technical know-how was not blocked because of this. Jean felt that this openness could in part be explained by the procedures used in the department for assigning personnel to the study projects.

Traditionally, the Management Audit Department assigned two or three main teams to a study. One of the consultants usually served as the project leader. Teams would thus be formed around a study. One of the consultants usually served as the project leader. Teams would thus be formed around a study, and when the work was completed the members would be separately re-assigned to other projects. In this way, over a period of six months or a year, each member of the department would have had task interactions with most of the other members. Because of the rotating nature of the assignments, each consultant could expect to occasionally work under the team leadership of one of the other consultants. The leadership behavior of these consultants varied considerably: Two appeared to be task and job oriented; one of them appeared to stress participation and interpersonal relations; the fourth seemed to exhibit varying degrees of both orientations.

While Jean had not perceived any clear relationship between leadership behaviors and team performance, it was not, she was certain because such relationships did not exist. In running the department as a whole, Jean's predecessor, Roger Davis, had clearly been of the "hard nose," directive tradition. This was illustrated in the manner with which he frequently established objectives and schedules for the study teams, occasionally omitting to even get input from the team members for the purpose. Yet he had not been particularly disliked by the department. It seemed to Jean that reaction to her predecessor's approach varied from resentment and frustration on the one hand to mild disinterest and acceptance on the other. As a measure of its performance, the department appeared to have won the acceptance of top management and in the previous two years had generated proposals that resulted in significant improvements and dollar savings for the company. These savings were more than 12 times greater than the costs associated with running the department. To some of the top management group, Davis had been the corporate "golden boy."

As a co-worker, Jean had had good working relationships with other members of the department as previously indicated. As their "new" boss however, she was not certain about the extent to which she had their loyalty, confidence and support. There were indications of at least some mild resentment on the part of three consultants over their having lost out in the competition for the directorship of the Management Audit Department. Jean's performance in the company however, had put her in a good position; at the time of her appointment to her new job she was given "full authority to hire, fire, and run the department as she saw fit, so long as she produced results."

Jean pondered this situation and was trying to determine what leadership approach would be most effective. She knew that she was very much "on trial" by top management and by her own subordinates. To the extent that she could produce results by solving the order delivery problem she and her department would look good in the eyes of the top executives. On the other hand, the initial perceptions of her managerial approach by the subordinates in the department would be very much influenced by her style with the project team members - and these initial perceptions, Jean knew, might very well affect the tenor of her relationships in the department in the future.

1. Describe the role conflict (ch. 8) currently being faced by Jean Hall.

2. Use House's Path-Goal Theory to analyze the leadership situation confronting Jean. Which leadership style does the theory suggest?

3. Use Fiedler's Contingency Theory to analyze the leadership situation confronting Jean. Which leadership style does the theory suggest?

4. Run the portable fax problem through the Vroom and Jago decision tree. What level of participation is indicated?

5. Discuss the merits of transformational or charismatic leadership in this setting.

6. Are there any factors at Contronica that might neutralize Jean Hall's attempts at leadership? Are there any substitutes for leadership in this setting? Does "leadership matter" in the Management Audit Department?

7. What should Jean Hall do now?

CHAPTER 1l

COMMUNICATION

LEARNING OBJECTIVES

- DEFINE COMMUNICATION AND EXPLAIN WHY COMMUNICATION BY THE STRICT CHAIN OF COMMAND IS OFTEN INEFFECTIVE.
- DISCUSS BARRIERS TO EFFECTIVE SUPERIOR-SUBORDINATE COMMUNICATION.
- EXPLAIN THE ORGANIZATIONAL GRAPEVINE AND DISCUSS ITS MAIN FEATURES.
- REVIEW THE ROLE OF BOTH VERBAL AND NONVERBAL COMMUNICATION AT WORK.
- DISCUSS HOW COMMUNICATION DIFFERS ACROSS CULTURES AND HOW IT IS INFLUENCED BY CULTURAL CONTEXT.
- GENERATE SOME PERSONAL APPROACHES TO IMPROVING COMMUNICATION.
- DISCUSS SOME ORGANIZATIONAL APPROACHES TO IMPROVING COMMUNICATION.

KEY CONCEPTS

Communication

Effective communication

Chain of command

Downward communication

Upward communication

Horizontal communication

Filtering

Open door policy

Mum effect

Grapevine

Rumor

Jargon

Nonverbal communication

Body language

Cultural context

Congruence

Active listening

Information richness

360 degree feedback

Employee surveys

Suggestion systems

CHAPTER SUMMARY

Key concepts are identified by **bold** *faced type.*

I. What is Communication?

Communication is the process by which information is exchanged between a sender and a receiver.
The sender must encode his or her thoughts into some form that can be transmitted to the receiver. And the receiver must perceive the message and accurately decode it to achieve understanding.

Effective communication occurs when the right people receive the right information in a timely manner.

II. The Importance of Communication

Organizational goals will not be accomplished without communication among group members. Communication is also necessary for organizational effectiveness. As individuals move up the organization's hierarchy they spend more time communicating.

III. The Basics of Organizational Communication

A. Communication by Strict Chain of Command

When communication in companies flows in accordance with an organization chart, we say that communication follows the **chain of command** or lines of authority and formal reporting relationships.

In **downward communication**, information flows from the top of the organization toward the bottom. In **upward communication**, information flows from the bottom of the organization toward the top. **Horizontal communication** refers to information that flows between departments or functional units, usually as a means of coordinating effort.

B. Deficiencies in the Chain of Command

1. Informal Communication

Much organizational communication occurs during informal meetings on golf courses or lunch rooms. This type of communication might not benefit the organization since inaccurate rumors might be spread.

2. Filtering

At times, effective communication using the chain of command is inhibited by **filtering**, which is the tendency for a message to be watered down or stopped altogether at some point during transmission. Subordinates use upward filtering to keep negative performance information out of their supervisor's hands. Supervisors use downward filtering to play the "information is power" card.

To prevent this filtering, some organizations have an **open-door policy** in which any organizational member can communicate directly with a manager without going through the chain of command. Managers may also wish to go outside normal channels if information has broad applications.

3. Slowness

Even when the chain of command relays information accurately, it is painfully slow. Responsiveness to customers and decisions involving cross functional inputs are areas of particular difficulty.

IV. Superior-Subordinate Communication

Communication consisting of one-to-one exchanges between a boss and a subordinate is known as superior-subordinate exchange. Most employees preferred their immediate supervisors as the source of most organizational information.

A. How Good Is Superior-Subordinate Communication?

Research indicates that superiors and subordinates often disagree in their perceptions of such fundamental workplace issues as subordinate use of time, how long it takes to learn a job, pay, authority, subordinate skills and abilities, performance, and the superior's leadership style.

These differences indicate a lack of openness in communication which could contribute to role conflict and ambiguity and result in less worker satisfaction.

B. Barriers to Effective Superior-Subordinate Communication

Among the factors which contribute to communication problems are the following: conflicting role demands between social-emotional needs of workers and task business needs of managers; the **mum effect** or tendency to avoid communicating unfavorable news to others; status effects in which superiors tend to devalue communication with subordinates; and time constraints which prevent superiors from spending much time with a given subordinate.

V. The Grapevine

A. Characteristics of the Grapevine

The grapevine is an organization's informal communication network. Although the grapevine is generally thought of as involving word of mouth, written notes, e-mail and fax messages have may also be involved. Organizations may have several loosely coordinated grapevine systems, and the grapevine may transmit information relevant to the performance of the organization as well as personal gossip.

B. Who Participates in the Grapevine?

Extroverts are more likely to pass on information than introverts. The physical location and task elements of members are also related to their opportunities to participate in the grapevine. Locations that receive a lot of traffic or employees that must travel through the organization in the course of their jobs both facilitate the operation of the grapevine.

C. Pros and Cons of the Grapevine

At times, the grapevine can be a regular substitute for formal communication either by managerial default or as a deliberate attempt to "test the waters" on some proposed initiative by "leaking" information. The grapevine can also add a little interest and diversion to the work setting.

A problem can occur in the grapevine when it helps spread too many rumors. A **rumor** is an unverified belief that is in general circulation. When false rumors get out of hand, companies must institute rumor control through early and accurate communication.

VI. The Verbal Language of Work

Jargon is the special language used by job holders or members of particular organizations to communicate. Although it is efficient for communicating with peers and insiders, jargon can serve as a barrier to communicating with outsiders and the general public, as well as adding to the burden of spouses attempting to relate to their partner's career issues.

VII. The Nonverbal Language of Work

Nonverbal communication refers to the transmission of messages by some medium other than speech or writing. It can be a highly relevant part of the communication process since the information provided is sometimes "the real stuff" while words serve as a smoke screen.

A. Body Language

Body language is nonverbal communication that occurs by means of the sender's bodily motions and facial expressions or the sender's physical location in relation to the receiver. When a contradiction exists between verbal behavior and body language, we tend to rely on the messages sent through body language. Research demonstrates that body language is an important communicator in an employment interview situation.

B. Props, Artifacts, and Costumes

Nonverbal communication can also occur through the use of various objects such as props, artifacts or costumes. Holding an object can communicate nonverbally. The placement of office desks or flowers can also communicate messages in a nonverbal fashion.

Research has also shown that the clothes we wear are indeed forms of nonverbal communication. Thus, proper clothing can enhance one's esteem and self-confidence, while improper clothing will hurt the image of a worker in the eyes of executives and supervisors.

VIII. Cross-Cultural Communication

A. Language Differences

When people share the same language, communication is generally better. Today with English becoming the language of international business, global communication is spreading. Despite this, executives should seek to learn second languages in order to understand the viewpoints of the people of different trading partners.

B. Nonverbal Communication Across Cultures

People in different nations generally are good at decoding basic, simple emotions in facial expressions. Gestures and gaze do not translate well across cultures.

In some countries, people stand close to and touch each other. In other nations these activities are considered signs of rudeness.

C. Etiquette and Politeness Across Cultures

Cultures differ considerably in how etiquette and politeness are expressed. Learning these differences is important for managers who seek to deal with their counterparts in other nations.

D. Social Conventions Across Cultures

These are cross cultural differences in the directness of business dealings, in the "proper" degree of loudness of speech, in punctuality, and in the practice of nepotism. All of these should be taken into account when dealing with people of other nations.

E. Cultural Context

Cultural context is the cultural information that surrounds a communication episode. Some cultures, including many Oriental, Latin American, African and Arab cultures are high-context cultures meaning that communication is highly influenced by the context in which it takes place. This is in contrast to low-context cultures like North America, Australia, Northern Europe (except France), and Scandinavia, where more meaning resides in the message than the context. These differences are important in many business situations, especially cross-cultural negotiations.

IX. Personal Approaches to Improving Communication

A. Basic Principles of Effective Communication

Several basic principles of effective communication apply to upward, downward, horizontal, and outside communication:

- Take the Time: Developing an awareness of context factors and selecting the appropriate medium to ensure good communication take time.
- Be Accepting of the Other Person: Empathy will go much farther than arrogance.

- Don't Confuse the Person With the Problem: Focus on behaviors rather than attributing motives. Try to be descriptive instead of evaluative.
- Say What You Feel: **Congruence** is the condition in which a person's words, thoughts, feelings, and actions all contain the same message.
- Listen Actively: **Active listening** is a technique for improving the accuracy of information reception by paying close attention to the sender.
- Give Timely and Specific Feedback: Speed maximizes the reinforcement potential of the message and explicitness maximizes its usefulness to the recipient.

B. When in Rome...

In addition to the basic principles above, several others are particularly useful in a cross-cultural communication situation:

- Assume Differences Until You Know Otherwise: Projection and a foreign speaker's good command of English can tempt to assume that culture is not an issue.
- Recognize Differences *Within* Cultures: Avoid culture based stereotypes and be alert for occupational and social class differences that may be more difficult to recognize.
- Watch Your Language (and Theirs): Speak slowly, clearly and avoid clichés, jargon and slang. Don't assume that those who are very fluent in English are necessarily smarter, more skilled or more honest than those who are not.

X. Organizational Approaches to Improving Communication

A. Choosing the Correct Medium

Information richness is the potential information-carrying capacity of a communication medium. It is therefore necessary to choose the correct medium to convey your intended message. A good rule to follow is that less routine messages require richer communications media.

B. 360 Degree Feedback

Often a part of a total quality management system (TQM), **360 degree feedback** is performance appraisal that uses the input of superiors, subordinates, peers, and clients or customers of the appraised individual.

C. Employee Surveys and Survey Feedback

Employee surveys are anonymous questionnaires that enable employees to state their candid opinions and attitudes about an organization and its practices. Downward communication can be enhanced when survey results are fed back to employees along with management responses and any plans for changes.

D. Suggestion Systems and Query Systems

Suggestion systems are programs designed to enhance upward communication by soliciting ideas for improved work operations from employees. Query systems provide a formal means of answering questions that employees may have about the organization. An example might be a column of questions and answers in an employee newsletter.

E. Telephone Hotlines and TV Networks

Telephone hotlines may be query systems in which employees can call in for answers to their questions. More common are news format hotlines that provide up-dated employee information. Some large organizations such as Ford Motor Company have expanded this concept to company-owned TV networks.

F. Management Training

The evidence suggests that proper training can improve the communication skills of managers. Training should emphasize the use of models to demonstrate specific skills in effective use followed by role-playing and reinforcement. Being able to communicate effectively downward can have the effect of increasing upward communication in return.

PRE-TESTING YOUR UNDERSTANDING OF THE CHAPTER

Key Concepts Matching

Match the letter of the key concepts with the appropriate definitions.

A. Active listening
B. Body language
C. Chain of command
D. Communication
E. Congruence
F. Cultural context
G. Downward communication
H. Effective communication
I. Employee surveys
J. Filtering
K. Grapevine
L. Horizontal communication
M. Information richness
N. Jargon
O. Mum effect
P. Nonverbal communication
Q. Open door policy
R. Rumor
S. Suggestion systems
T. 360 degree feedback
U. Upward communication

______1. The process by which information is exchanged between a sender and a receiver.

______2. Performance appraisal that uses the input of superiors, subordinates, peers, and clients or customers of the appraised individual.

______3. A system in which organizational members communicate according to lines of authority and reporting relationships.

______4. Communication that flows from the top of the organization toward the bottom.

______5. Communication that flows from the bottom of the organization toward the top.

______6. Communication that occurs between departments as functional units, usually as a means of coordinating effort.

______7. Communication which occurs when the right people receive the right information in a timely manner.

______8. The tendency for a message to be watered down or stopped altogether at some point during transmission.

______9. A policy established by managers in which any organizational member below them can communicate directly without going through the chain.

_____10. The tendency to avoid communicating unfavorable news to others.

_____11. The informal communication network that exists in any organization.

_____12. An unverified belief that is in general circulation.

_____13. Specialized language that associates use to communicate with each other.

_____14. The transmission of messages by some medium other than speech or writing.

_____15. The nonverbal communication that occurs by means of the sender's body motions and facial expressions or the sender's physical location in relation to the receiver.

_____16. The potential information carrying capacity of a communication medium.

_____17. A technique for improving the accuracy of information reception by paying close attention to the sender.

_____18. Questions that reliably tap employee concerns and provide information useful for practical purposes.

_____19. Systems designed to enhance upward communication by soliciting ideas for improved operations from nonmanagerial employees.

_____20. A condition in which a person's words, thoughts, feelings, and actions all contain the same message.

_____21. The cultural information that surrounds a communication episode.

True/False Questions

Circle the letter of the correct answer.

T F 1. The wall thermostat in your house and your furnace are constantly engaged in communication.
T F 2. Communication is no longer important in organizations.
T F 3. In horizontal communication, organizations communicate with each other.
T F 4. Effective communication occurs when the boss gives clear orders.
T F 5. Filtering occurs when a message is watered down or stopped altogether at some point during transmission.
T F 6. In most organizations, the immediate supervisor is the preferred source of communication.
T F 7. The open door policy refers to plant layouts in which offices have no doors.
T F 8. The mum effect takes place when superiors prevent subordinates from speaking.
T F 9. Time constraints can often affect communication.
T F 10. Superiors tend to place high values on communications with subordinates.
T F 11. The grapevine refers to company garden projects.
T F 12. Rumors are usually accurate depictions of real events.
T F 13. Jargon is language used by company insiders to communicate with outsiders.
T F 14. Relaxation is an example of body language.
T F 15. When contradictions exist between verbal behavior and body language, we tend to rely more on the body language message.
T F 16. Props and costumes can also be used in body language.
T F 17. Clothing is also an effective method of communication.
T F 18. Cross cultural communication is easily achieved with computers.
T F 19. Speaking the same language is usually a guarantee of effective communication.
T F 20. Germany is an example of a high context culture.

Multiple-Choice Questions

Select the correct answer.

______1. All of the following are types of communication *except*
A. horizontal communication.
B. command communication.
C. upward communication.
D. downward communication.

______2. Communication between departments or functional units of companies is known as
A. upward communication.
B. downward communication.
C. horizontal communication.
D. command communication.

______3. All of the following are inhibiting factors in communication except
A. conflicting role demands.
B. status effects.
C. suggestion systems.
D. time.

______4. Raised eyebrows and shrugs are examples of
A. body language.
B. poor communication.
C. good communication.
D. all-channel communication.

______5. All of the following may be used in nonverbal communication *except*
A. props.
B. artifacts.
C. costumes.
D. cue cards.

______6. An American businessman dealing with a French business would be engaging in
A. horizontal communication.
B. cross-cultural communication.
C. all-channel communication.
D. international diplomacy.

______7. All of the following might be involved in nonverbal communication *except*
A. gestures.
B. gaze.
C. touch.
D. phone messages.

______8. All of the following might be used to improve organizational communication *except*

A. TV networks.
B. 90 degree feedback.
C. surveys and feedback.
D. suggestion systems.

______9. All of the following are necessary for communication *except*

A. messages.
B. senders.
C. filters.
D. receivers.

______10. Lack of openness in communication

A. reduces subordinate satisfaction.
B. increases subordinate satisfaction.
C. has no effect on subordinate satisfaction.
D. shows good management control.

POST-TESTING FOR EXAMS

True/False Questions

Circle the letter of the correct answer.

T F 1. Paying attention to facial expressions will often help in cross- cultural communication.
T F 2. Cultures differ considerably in how etiquette and politeness are expressed.
T F 3. Social conventions are aids in improving cross cultural communications.
T F 4. The medium of communication is of no consequence in organizational communication.
T F 5. Information richness refers to the volume and amount of data in a given message.
T F 6. Exit interviews are conducted to aid in firing future workers.
T F 7. Surveys of current employees are useful means of upward communication.
T F 8. Query systems question employees about the behavior of their peers.
T F 9. Proper training can improve the communication skills of supervisors.
T F 10. More communication is not always better communication.

Multiple-Choice Questions

Select the correct answer.

______1. A message from the CEO to factory workers is an example of
A. upward communication.
B. downward communication.
C. horizontal communication.
D. good supervision.

______2. All of the following are necessary for effective communication to occur <u>except</u>
A. the right people.
B. the right information.
C. the right environment.
D. a message in a timely manner.

______3. Communication following strict lines of authority and reporting relationships is known as
A. chain of command.
B. open door policy.
C. effective communication.
D. filtering.

______4. The most preferred source of information about organizational issues is
A. top executives.
B. the grapevine.
C. immediate supervisors.
D. mass meetings.

______5. Physicians' not letting patients know about terminal illnesses are practicing
A. the mum effect.
B. effective communication.
C. nonverbal communication.
D. filtering.

______6. At least ______ of the grapevine on organizational matters is considered to be correct.
A. 75%
B. 25%
C. 50%
D. 20%

______7. Rumors are likely to spread fastest in all of the following instances *except* when
A. the information is important to those involved.
B. the information is ambiguous.
C. the recipient is emotionally involved.
D. the recipient is not concerned about the information.

______8. Relaxation is demonstrated by all of the following actions *except*
A. a lack of fidgeting and nervous activity.
B. a tensing of muscles.
C. a reclining, non-erect seating position.
D. casual, asymmetric placement of arms and legs.

______9. Senders communicate liking and interest in the receiver *except* when they
A. maintain eye contact with the receiver.
B. lean forward during the interaction.
C. lean away during the interaction.
D. touch the receiver during the interaction.

______10. John Malloy is a pioneer in the study of
A. verbal communication.
B. body language.
C. wardrobe engineering.
D. employee surveys.

______11. The Japanese people have ______ different ways of saying no.
A. ten
B. sixteen
C. five
D. twenty

______12. People in all of the following countries tend to touch each other as an adjunct to conversation *except* those in
A. Arab countries.
B. South European countries.
C. Latin American countries.
D. North American countries.

______13. The potential information carrying capacity of a communication medium is known as
A. all-channel communication.
B. overload.
C. information richness.
D. surplus communication.

______14. Surveys of attitudes of current employees can provide a useful means of
A. downward communication.
B. upward communication.
C. rumor filtering
D. management control.

______15. All of the following are methods of enhancing upward communication *except*
A. suggestion systems.
B. hotlines.
C. query systems.
D. exit interviews.

______16. Exit interviews are usually conducted by all of the following *except*
A. the person's superiors.
B. a management representative.
C. a personnel representative.
D. a person's subordinates.

______17. Jargon is most effective when communicating
A. to outside groups.
B. among experienced associates.
C. cross culturally.
D. to new organizational members.

______18. Studies of production workers indicate that they participate in between 16 and _______communication episodes per hour.
A. 25
B. 30
C. 46
D. 35

______19. People communicating on a golf course might indulge in
A. informal communication.
B. downward communication.
C. horizontal communication.
D. rumor.

______20. Conflicting role demands might include being
A. mentor and friend of a co-worker.
B. boss and friend of a co-worker.
C. friend and teacher of a co-worker.
D. assistant to an executive.

Application Situations Exercise

Match the key concepts with the statements that best describe them.

A. Active listening
B. Body language
C. Chain of command
D. Communication
E. Congruence
F. Cultural context
G. Downward communication
H. Effective communication
I. Employee surveys
J. Filtering
K. Grapevine
L. Horizontal communication
M. Information richness
N. Jargon
O. Mum effect
P. Nonverbal communication
Q. Open door policy
R. Rumor
S. Suggestion systems
T. 360 degree feedback
U. Upward communication

______1. The boss wanted to improve our exchanges of information within the company.

______2. So the boss sent messages to employees.

______3. But the boss didn't receive any messages from the employees.

______4. At times, messages from the boss were being watered down and even stopped by middle managers.

______5. We would have liked a policy in which we could visit the boss directly without going through intermediaries.

______6. But the boss did ask us for ideas on how to improve our communication and company morale.

______7. We suggested more use of our informal organizational network.

______8. We also suggested the elimination of unverified beliefs that were generally circulating throughout the company.

______9. When we sent a delegation, the boss wouldn't look at us or even smile when he saw us.

_____10. The delegation was so upset that it wouldn't tell the workers about the boss's hostile reaction.

Short Answer Questions

Fill-in the missing word(s).

1. Organizations are ___________ for accomplishing goals through group effort.

2. The content of many managerial jobs is composed almost exclusively of ___________ tasks.

3. Superior-subordinate communication consists of a ___________ exchange of information between a boss and a subordinate.

4. The ___________ is the actual source and the preferred source of most organizational information.

5. Hiring one's own children for a job is an example of ___________ .

6. Jargon can often serve as a ___________ to communicating with others.

7. According to Malloy, a black raincoat signals ___________ .

8. In Latin American nations, people tend to more ___________ than in North American countries.

9. ___________ that vary across cultures can often lead to communication problems.

10. A good employee survey should always provide for ___________ responses.

ANSWER SHEET FOR CHAPTER 11

PRE-TESTING YOUR UNDERSTANDING OF THE CHAPTER

Key Concepts Matching

1. D 2. T 3. C 4. G 5. U 6. L 7. H 8. J 9. Q 10. O
11. K 12. R 13. N 14. P 15. B 16. M 17. A 18. I 19. S 20. E 21. F

True/False Questions

1. T 2. F 3. F 4. F 5. T 6. T 7. F 8. F 9. T 10. F
11. F 12. F 13. F 14. T 15. T 16. T 17. T 18. F 19. F 20. T

Multiple-Choice Questions

1. B 2. C 3. C 4. A 5. D 6. B 7. D 8. B 9. C 10. A

POST-TESTING FOR EXAMS

True/False Questions

1. T 2. T 3. F 4. F 5. F 6. F 7. T 8. F 9. T 10. T

Multiple-Choice Questions

1. B 2. C 3. A 4. C 5. A 6. A 7. D 8. B 9. C 10. C 11. B 12. D
13. C 14. B 15. D 16. D 17. B 18. C 19. A 20. B

Application Situations Exercise

1. D 2. G 3. U 4. J 5. Q 6. S 7. K 8. R 9. B 10. O

Short Answer Questions

1. social inventions 2. communication 3. one-to-one 4. immediate supervisor
5. nepotism 6. barrier 7. "lower middle class"
8. touch each other 9. social conventions 10. anonymous

CASE STUDY

ADCO PHARMACY

The events occurred in the Sherbrooke Street branch of a large Montréal-based pharmacy chain called ADCO. "Pharmacy" was perhaps a misnomer, since the stores, in addition to drugs, sold everything from expensive perfumes to magazines to snack foods to motor oil to household cleaning products. The Sherbrooke Street store was staffed by a manager, an assistant manager, a pharmacist, and a large crew of young workers, most of whom were college students who worked part-time.

Mr. Rollins, the manager of the store, was fifty-two years old and had been with ADCO for sixteen years, managing stores in a number of locations as the chain grew with the demand for larger self-service drug emporiums. Mr. Rollins always prided himself with concern for customer opinion, and he tried to be a visible and helpful manager despite the fact that the store was large and essentially self-service in nature. Besides this important public relations function, his major tasks were ordering drugs and other goods and working with the pharmacist to ensure the security of the prescription drug stock.

Cindy Nellis has been the assistant manager at the Sherbrooke Street branch for two years. Twenty-four years old and a part-time student, her job primarily involved maintaining the work schedule for the rest of the staff and deploying them on various tasks throughout the store. This was a critical function. The profits stemming from the dispensing of prescription drugs were fairly constant, since they were under the sole control of the pharmacist. However, the overall profitability of the store was highly dependent upon the efficient deployment and motivation of the rest of the staff, since the operation was fairly labor intensive.

The mostly student staff at ADCO unpacked received goods, priced them, and stocked the shelves. In addition, they engaged in "housekeeping" and the operation of the cash registers. Although the work was far from exciting, the store received a large amount of student traffic, and it was often possible to say "hello" to one's friends and chat for a few minutes while one worked. In addition, most of the staff enjoyed listening to FM 95 ("The Big Five") as they worked. The hard rock station was played over the store's public address system and was audible in all parts of the store, as all ADCO stores employed some kind of background music. Cindy Nellis had long ago taken informal control of the "sounds," tuning in FM 95 every morning to "keep the staff awake." Quite by coincidence, the ADCO chain featured frequent advertisements and promotions on the station. During the day, it was not uncommon for the student help to be seen mouthing the words to popular rock tunes or snapping their fingers as they worked in time to the music.

One day, Mrs. Zima, a senior citizen and long-time patron of the store, in to refill a medical prescription, accosted Mr. Rollins and complained that "the music is so loud I can't think." Mr. Rollins expressed concern and told her that everything would be taken care of. At the end of the day he saw Cindy Nellis and told her that there had been customer complaints about the rock music and that she should from now on tune the radio to another station, an "easy listening" station that he occasionally listened to at home.

The next morning, Cindy found the station after some searching (she had never heard of it before). Within fifteen minutes, the student staff began to complain about the music to Cindy, who informed them that they would just have to accept the change. During the week, the complaints continued, and Cindy found that she had to begin supervising much more closely

---

Source: Case prepared by Gary Johns

than usual. Twice, she had to "hustle employees up" when she found them lounging around rather than pricing goods or stacking shelves. Both took the opportunity to complain yet again about the music, citing boredom for their lax performance. Once, Cindy had to stop a loud bickering match between two employees who had always gotten along well together. During a break, several employees speculated that Mr. Rollins didn't like rock music because his nephew had been in trouble with the police over drugs. Whether the music was as bad as the employees said or not, Cindy became convinced that it was damaging productivity. Besides, she thought, ADCO didn't even advertise on the easy listening station.

About two weeks after the radio station had been switched, Mr. Rollins asked Cindy to see him in his office.

"Cindy," he said, "I think you've lost control of the staff. Housekeeping has gone from bad to worse, the shelves just aren't being stocked effectively, and we have conflict that we've never had before. And sales are down, too. What's going on? You know I'm always open to suggestions."

Cindy wondered whether Mr. Rolling would believe that the problems were due to radio music.

1. How effective is communication at the Sherbrooke Street branch of ADCO? Cite specific examples where ineffective communication occurred.

2. Is there evidence of the mum effect in the case?

3. Most of the communication occurred via the store's formal chain of command. Was this appropriate?

4. Is Cindy correct? Is radio music the problem?

5. How should Mr. Rollins and Cindy Nellis resolve the current state of affairs?

CHAPTER 12

DECISION MAKING

LEARNING OBJECTIVES

- DEFINE DECISION MAKING AND DIFFERENTIATE WELL-STRUCTURED AND ILL-STRUCTURED PROBLEMS.
- DISCUSS THE IMPACT OF FRAMING AND COGNITIVE BIASES ON THE DECISION PROCESS.
- EXPLAIN THE PROCESS OF ESCALATION OF COMMITMENT TO AN APPARENTLY FAILING COURSE OF ACTION.
- COMPARE AND CONTRAST PERFECTLY RATIONAL DECISION MAKING WITH DECISION MAKING UNDER BOUNDED RATIONALITY.
- SUMMARIZE THE PROS AND CONS OF USING GROUPS TO MAKE DECISIONS.
- EXPLAIN THE GROUPTHINK PHENOMENON.
- REVIEW HOW GROUPS HANDLE RISK WHEN MAKING DECISIONS.
- DISCUSS TECHNIQUES FOR IMPROVING ORGANIZATIONAL DECISION MAKING.
- EXPLAIN THE PROMISE AND PROBLEMS OF ELECTRONIC DECISION-MAKING GROUPS.

KEY CONCEPTS:

Decision making

Problem

Well-structured problem

Program

Ill-structured problem

Perfect rationality

Bounded rationality

Sunk costs

Escalation of commitment

Framing

Cognitive biases

Confirmation bias

Information overload

Maximization

Anchoring effect

Satisficing

Devil's advocate

Brainstorming

Hindsight

Diffusion of responsibility

Groupthink

Risky shift

Conservative shift

Nominal group technique

Delphi technique

Electronic groups

Electronic brainstorming

CHAPTER SUMMARY

Key concepts are identified by **bold** *faced type.*

I. What is Decision Making?

Decision making is the process of developing a commitment to some course of action. This process involves making a choice, and it also involves the commitment of resources such as time, money or personnel.

A **problem** exists when a gap is perceived between some existing state and some desired state. Decision making is also a process of problem solving.

A. Well-Structured Problems

In a **well-structured problem**, the existing state is clean, the desired state is clear, and how to get from one state to the other is fairly obvious. Organizations prefer a **program** or standardized way of solving a problem, when dealing with well-structured problems.

B. Ill-Structured Problems

In an **ill-structured problem**, the existing and desired states are unclear, and the method of getting to the desired state is unknown. These problems are usually unique, complex, and have not been encountered before. In dealing with these problems, organizations use nonprogrammed decision making which means they are likely to implement a full rational decision model.

II. The Complete Decision Maker - A Rational Decision-Making Model

A. Perfect Versus Bounded Rationality

The use of **perfect rationality** involves a decision strategy that is completely informed, perfectly logical, and oriented toward economic gain.

These characteristics do not exist in real life. Instead executives use **bounded rationality**, a decision strategy that relies on limited information and that reflects time constraints and political considerations.

Framing and cognitive biases both illustrate the operation of bounded rationality. **Framing** refers to aspects of the presentation of information about a problem that are assumed by decision makers. **Cognitive biases** are tendencies to acquire and process information in an error-prone way.

B. Problem Identification and Framing

Bounded rationality can lead to several difficulties involved in problem identification:

- perceptual defense: we may have difficulty "seeing" problems that might have unpleasant repercussions for us.
- problem defined in terms of functional specialty: if we are in Marketing, we may tend to view too many problems as being "marketing problems".
- problem defined in terms of solution: jumping to conclusions that short-circuiting the full decision process.
- problem diagnosed in terms of symptoms: failure to get below surface indicators that leads us to not address the "real" problem.

C. Information Search

Once a problem has been identified, a search for information is started. Bounded rationality again suggests that problems can exist that are not encompassed by the rational model:

- Too little information: Decision makers may collect insufficient information to make a good decision because people are mentally lazy and tend to use whatever information is available in memory. Unfortunately, our memory is more selective then representative - we remember vivid, recent events. Overconfidence is also a problem and it is reinforced by **confirmation biases**: the tendency to seek out information that conforms to one's own definition of or solution to a problem.
- Too much information: **Information overload** is the reception of more information than is necessary to make effective decisions. Curiously, even as overload causes decision quality to deteriorate, decision makers become more confident of their decisions. The ease of adding someone's name to an e-mail message can result in overload there too.

D. Alternative Development, Evaluation and Choice

At times a decision maker may exhibit **maximization** which is the choice of a decision alternative with the greatest expected value. Unfortunately, the decision maker operating under bounded rationality may not know all alternative solutions and may be ignorant of the ultimate values and probabilities of success for known alternatives.

People in general are weak intuitive statisticians. They have trouble with base rates, sample size, probability estimates of multiple event scenarios, and the revision of estimates. An example of this last problem is **the anchoring effect**: the inadequate adjustment of subsequent estimates from an initial estimate that serves as an anchor. This occurs even when subsequent estimates are far more sophisticated than the original, naive estimate.

As a consequence of the overwhelming complexity of rational decision making, the decision maker operating under bounded rationality relies on **satisficing**: they establish an adequate level of acceptability for a solution to a problem and then screen solutions until one that exceeds this level is found.

E. Risky Business

The role of risk in decision making is also fertile ground for the issue of framing. Research by Kahneman and Tversky shows that when people view a problem as a choice between losses, they tend to make risky decisions, rolling the dice in the face of a sure loss. When people frame the alternatives as a choice between gains, they tend to make conservative decisions, protecting the sure win.

A study of senior executives also reached some interesting conclusions:

- perceived themselves as riskier than their behavior demonstrated
- more risk-averse with their own money that the firm's
- no one was uniformly risky in all domains, i.e. no evidence of a "risky personality"
- bankers, older managers and longer tenured managers were more risk-averse
- higher-level executives and those from smaller firms took more risks
- the most successful executives took the most risks

F. Solution Implementation

Once a decision is reached, the solution must be carried out. Decision makers often depend upon others to implement decisions, and it might be difficult to anticipate their motivation or ability to do so.

G. Solution Evaluation

Once decisions are made, people tend to be overconfident about their validity. Thus organizations often try to justify a faulty decision.

At times, **sunk costs**, or permanent losses of resources increased as the result of a decision, organizations will keep "throwing good money after bad." The term **escalation of commitment** describes the tendency to invest additional resources in an apparently failing course of action. Since changing one's mind is often perceived as a weakness, many wrong decisions continue to be endorsed in the name of consistency.

Attempts to prevent the escalation of commitment might include the following:

- Reframe the problem from one of spending to one of saving.
- Set specific goals that must be met before additional resources are released.
- Evaluate managers on decision process instead of outcomes.

The careful evaluation of decisions is also inhibited by **hindsight** or the tendency to review a decision-making process to find out what was done right or wrong. People practicing hindsight are exhibiting the knew-it-all-along effect which assumes after the fact that we knew all along what the outcome of a decision would be.

The attribution process is also at fault here. Poor decision outcomes are attributed to external interference. Favorable decision outcomes are attributed to internal competency!

H. Rational Decision Making - A Summary

Research shows that for complex, unfamiliar decisions the rational model provides a pretty good picture of how people actually make decisions. However, the rational decision-making process is often short-circuited through the biases discussed above or by subject area experts who use the process as a rough guide only.

III. Group Decision Making

A. Why Use Groups?

Groups are used in decision making because they can often improve decision quality and enhance decision acceptance and commitment. The argument that groups make higher-quality decisions is based on several assumptions:

- groups are *more vigilant* than individuals
- groups can *generate more ideas* than individuals
- groups can *evaluate ideas better* than individuals

The enhanced decision acceptance and commitment of groups is also based on several assumptions:

- people *wish to be involved* in decisions that affect them
- people *better understand* a decision in which they have participated
- commitment increases with the *investment of personal time and energy* in the decision process

A weakness in the use of groups can occur because of **diffusion of responsibility**, a term which describes the ability for group members to share the burden of the negative consequences of a poor decision.

B. Do Groups Actually Make Higher-Quality Decisions Than Individuals?

In general, groups usually produce more and better solutions to problems than individuals working alone. More specifically, groups should perform better than individuals when:

- group members *differ in relevant skills and abilities*, but not enough to cause conflict
- some *division of labor* can occur
- the greater *memory capacity* of groups is important to the task
- individual *member expertise can be weighted and combined*

C. Disadvantages of Group Decision Making

Among the disadvantages to the use of groups are the additional time necessary relative to individual decision making; the potential for conflict and political infighting to occur; and the possibility that a dominant individual or small coalition will work against group processes.

The most serious potential disadvantage, however, is **groupthink** a term which describes the capacity for group pressure to damage the mental efficiency, reality testing, and moral judgment of decision-making groups. Group cohesiveness that is too high, excessive concern for approval from the group and isolation of the group from other sources of information can lead to groupthink.

D. How Do Groups Handle Risk?

Research into group decision making processes has explored two apparently contradictory tendencies. **Risky shift** is the tendency for groups to make riskier decisions than the average risk initially advocated by their members. **Conservative shift** is the tendency for groups to make less risky decisions than the average risk initially advocated by their individual members. Both phenomena are seen to occur because group discussion seems to polarize or exaggerate the initial position of the group by supplying new arguments and setting the stage for one-upmanship behaviors.

IV. Improving Decision Making in Organizations

A. Training Decision Leaders

When decision leaders are trained, they can be more effective in guiding groups to effective decisions. Role-playing is an effective technique for such training.

B. Stimulating and Managing Controversy

Although full-blown controversy is to be avoided, some managed controversy can avoid the dangers of groupthink and escalation of commitment. A **devil's advocate** is a person appointed to identify and challenge the weaknesses of a proposed plan or strategy.

C. Brainstorming

Brainstorming is an attempt to increase the number of creative solution alternatives to problems by focusing on idea generation rather than evaluation. Despite its acceptance into common usage, brainstorming is not an effective group technique for idea generation. In general, an equivalent number of single individuals will come up with more ideas working on their own.

D. Nominal Group Technique

Unlike brainstorming, **nominal group technique** (NGT) is a structured group decision-making technique in which ideas are generated without group interaction and then systematically evaluated by the group.

E. The Delphi Technique

The **Delphi technique** is a method of pooling a large number of expert judgments by using a series of increasingly refined questionnaires. A major drawback of this method is the time involved.

V. Electronic Decision-Making Groups - Promise and Problems

Electronic groups are decision-making groups whose members are linked electronically rather than face-to-face. Such groups confer anonymity, mask non-verbal communication, and allow more than one person to speak at the same time.

A. Electronic Brainstorming

Electronic brainstorming involves the use of computer-mediated technology to improve traditional brainstorming practices. As a consequence of the advantages above, such groups have been found to perform better than face-to-face groups in terms of quantity and quality of ideas.

B. Beyond Brainstorming

Preliminary research on the behavior of electronic groups indicates several trends: such groups tend to be more egalitarian, but are also subject to flaming. Existing groups may see improved speed, but new groups may take longer to form. Finally, electronic groups appear to make more extreme decisions than face-to-face groups, especially when it comes to risk.

PRE-TESTING YOUR UNDERSTANDING OF THE CHAPTER

Key Concepts Matching

Match the letter of the key concept with the appropriate definitions.

A. Anchoring effect
B. Bounded rationality
C. Brainstorming
D. Cognitive biases
E. Confirmation bias
F. Conservative shift
G. Decision making
H. Delphi technique
I. Devil's advocate
J. Diffusion of responsibility
K. Electronic brainstorming
L. Electronic groups
M. Escalation of commitment
N. Framing
O. Groupthink
P. Hindsight
Q. Ill-structured problem
R. Information overload
S. Maximization
T. Nominal group technique
U. Perfect rationality
V. Problem
W. Program
X. Risky shift
Y. Satisficing
Z. Sunk costs
& Well-structured problem

______ 1. The process of developing a commitment to some course of action.

______ 2. The perception of a gap between some existing state and a desired state.

______ 3. An example of an economic person who is a perfectly cool, calculating decision maker.

______ 4. Limitations on rational action imposed by capacity to acquire and process information as well as time and political restraints.

______ 5. The reception of more information than is necessary to make effective decisions.

______ 6. The choice of an alternative with the greatest expected value.

______ 7. The establishing of an adequate level for a solution.

______ 8. Permanent losses of resources increased as a result of a decision.

______ 9. Devotion of more and more resources to actions implied by a decision.

_____ 10. The tendency to assume after the fact that we knew all along what the outcome of a decision would be.

_____ 11. Problems in which the existing state is clear, the desired state is clear, and how to get from one state to the other is fairly obvious.

_____ 12. A standardized way of solving a problem.

_____ 13. Problems in which the existing and desired states are unclear, and the method of getting to the desired state is unknown.

_____ 14. Tendencies to acquire and process information in an error-prone way.

_____ 15. The tendency in groups for each member to share the burden of negative consequences with no individual singled out for punishment.

_____ 16. That which happens when group pressures lead to reduced mental efficiency, poor testing of reality, and lax moral judgments.

_____ 17. The tendency of groups to advocate riskier courses of action than the average risk initially advocated by their members.

_____ 18. The tendency of groups to reach decisions that were less risky than those of the individual members before interaction.

_____ 19. The tendency to seek out information that conforms to one's own definition of or solution to a problem.

_____ 20. A person whose role is to challenge the weaknesses of the plan or strategy and state why it should not be adopted.

_____ 21. A decision making technique that focuses on the generation of ideas rather than the evaluation of ideas.

_____ 22. A technique that is concerned with the generation of ideas as well as their evaluation.

_____ 23. A decision making technique that uses questionnaires mailed to experts who provide information for organizational decision makers.

_____ 24. The use of computer mediated-technology to improve upon traditional brainstorming techniques.

_____ 25. Decision-making groups whose members are linked electronically rather than face-to-face.

_____ 26. Aspects of the presentation of information about a problem that are assumed by decision makers.

_____ 27. The inadequate adjustment of subsequent estimates from an initial estimate that serves as an anchor.

True/False Questions

Circle the letter of the correct answer.

T	F	1. Decision making involves making choices among several action alternatives.
T	F	2. Perfect rationality is usually perfectly logical and is concerned primarily with economic gain.
T	F	3. Perceptual defense refers to goggles and eye-glasses during dangerous work.
T	F	4. Too much information can often damage the quality of decisions.
T	F	5. Generally, people tend to be overconfident about the adequacy of their decisions.

T F 6. Changing one's mind and reversing previous decisions are usually perceived to be signs of strength.

T F 7. Many of us take personal responsibility for successful outcomes and deny responsibility for failures.

T F 8. Well-structured problems are those with simple answers.

T F 9. Ill-structured problems are usual ones that occur frequently.

T F 10. Many organizational decisions are made by groups instead of individuals.

T F 11. Generally, groups do produce better decisions than individuals working alone.

T F 12. Groups usually work more rapidly than individuals can.

T F 13. The anchoring effect describes how people "dig in their heels" on some decisions.

T F 14. How a problem is framed can change our answer to it completely.

T F 15. Cognitive biases are often decision-making short-cuts that cause errors in our thinking.

T F 16. Electronic brainstorming generates more ideas of better quality than equivalent sized face-to-face groups.

T F 17. Controversy is never necessary in corporate decision making.

T F 18. Brainstorming involves Nobel Prize winners in round table discussions.

T F 19. Individuals working alone tend to produce more ideas than when in groups.

T F 20. Nominal Group Technique carefully separates the generation of ideas from their evaluation.

Multiple-Choice Questions

Select the correct answer.

______ 1. All of the following are factors in decision making *except*

A. choice.
B. process.
C. resources.
D. resolve.

______ 2. All of the following are characteristics of Economic Person *except*

A. being completely informal.
B. being perfectly logical.
C. being concerned about ethics.
D. seeking only economic gain.

______ 3. All of the following are difficulties in problem identification *except*

A. perceptual offense.
B. perceptual defense.
C. problems diagnosed in terms of symptoms.
D. problems defined in terms of solutions.

______ 4. The perfectly rational decision maker can do all of the following *except*

A. know the ultimate value of each alternative.
B. conceive of all alternatives.
C. predict unknown factors.
D. know the probability that each alternative will work.

______ 5. The saying, "throwing good money after bad" is a description of
A. escalation of commitment.
B. groupthink.
C. maximization.
D. satisficing.

______ 6. Armchair quarterbacks are individuals who exhibit
A. foresight.
B. hindsight.
C. beer breath.
D. Delphi technique.

______ 7. All of the following are attributes of well-structured problems *except* that
A. the existing state is clear.
B. the desired state is clear.
C. going from one state to the other is clear.
D. pleasing all executives is clear.

______ 8. All of the following are assumptions about group decision making *except* that
A. groups are less vigilant less than individuals.
B. groups can generate more ideas than individuals.
C. groups are more vigilant than individuals.
D. groups can evaluate ideas better than individuals.

______ 9. All of the following are disadvantages of group decision making *except*
A. inefficient use of time.
B. more cohesiveness.
C. groupthink.
D. conflict.

______ 10. All of the following are symptoms of groupthink *except*
A. mindguards.
B. self-censorship.
C. satisficing.
D. rationalization.

POST-TESTING FOR EXAMS

True/False Questions

Circle the letter of the correct answer.

T F 1. The Delphi technique is a very rapid method of decision making.
T F 2. Satisficing means seeking the maximum outcomes of any decision.
T F 3. The devil's advocate is a religious cult leader.
T F 4. NASA was involved in faulty decision making concerning the space shuttle Challenger.
T F 5. Bounded rationality refers to limits placed by corporate executives.
T F 6. Organizational members often obtain more information than is necessary for adequate decisions.
T F 7. Sunk costs are temporary losses of resources as a result of a weak decisions.
T F 8. Generally, the most successful executives are those who take the most risk.
T F 9. Hindsight refers to the knowledge we have before we make a decision.
T F 10. Groupthink is a positive outcome and factor in group decision making.

Multiple-Choice Questions

Select the correct answer.

______ 1. All of the following constitute difficulties in problem definition *except*
A. perceptual defense.
B. problem defined in terms of functional specialty.
C. problem diagnosed in terms of symptoms.
D. solutions defined by problems.

______ 2. NASA has recently been involved with Perkin-Elmer because of
A. Russian cosmonauts.
B. a landing on Mars.
C. the Hubble telescope.
D. the X-files.

______ 3. All of the following are potential benefits of electronic groups *except*
A. more than one person can speak at once.
B. flaming.
C. established groups operate faster.
D. they are more egalitarian.

______ 4. All of the following are methods of improving decision making in organizations *except*
A. training decision leaders.
B. stimulating controversy.
C. eliminating controversy.
D. brainstorming.

______ 5. The Delphi technique was developed by
A. General Motors.
B. The Rand Corporation.
C. Coca-Cola.
D. Apple Computers.

______ 6. A problem exists when a gap is perceived between
A. some existing state and a desired state.
B. some previous state and a present state.
C. an ideal state and a real state.
D. none of the above.

______ 7. A marketing manager's failure to identify a sales problem is an example of
A. conservative shift.
B. bounded rationality.
C. perceptual defense.
D. perfect rationality.

______ 8. A program is a __________ way of solving a problem.
A. risky
B. conservative
C. standardized
D. random

______ 9. Other terms for programs include all of the following *except*
A. rules.
B. regulations.
C. responsibilities.
D. procedures.

______ 10. Research on information gathering and use supports all of the following *except*
A. overloaded decision makers are less satisfied about the quality of their decisions.
B. decision makers tend to gather a lot of information that has no relevance.
C. decision makers ignore available information and request additional information.
D. information is often gathered *after* a decision is made to provide justification for it.

______ 11. People are especially weak intuitive statisticians in all of these areas *except*
A. base rates.
B. sample sizes.
C. calculation using formulas.
D. probability estimation.

______ 12. When the speed of arriving at a solution to a problem is a prime factor, organizations should
A. avoid using groups.
B. ignore sunk costs.
C. adopt the Delphi technique.
D. appoint a devil's advocate.

______ 13. Discussion leaders should be trained to develop all of the following skills *except* to
A. wait out pauses.
B. play the devil's advocate.
C. draw out all group members.
D. ask stimulating questions.

______ 14. Weaknesses of brainstorming include all of the following *except*
A. inhibition.
B. domination by a weak member.
C. physical limitations.
D. creative solutions.

______ 15. The Delphi technique involves extensive use of
A. questionnaires.
B. face-to-face meetings.
C. brainstorming.
D. escalation of commitment.

______ 16. Groups are often employed for all of the following reasons *except*
A. decision acceptance.
B. decision ambiguity.
C. decision quality.
D. diffusion of responsibility.

______ 17. All of the following are problem areas for electronic groups *except*
A. the expression of extreme views.
B. the difficulties experienced by new groups in reaching consensus.
C. electronic groups make more risky decisions.
D. men are five times more likely to make the first proposal in electronic discussions.

______ 18. During brainstorming all of the following events occur *except* that members are not allowed to
A. operate in a free-wheeling manner.
B. feed off each other's suggestions.
C. criticize each other's ideas.
D. voice any ideas that come to mind.

______ 19. When satisficing occurs, the decision maker has
A. reached the maximum solution.
B. accepted a minimal solution.
C. rejected all solutions.
D. established an adequate level of solution acceptability.

______ 20. After reading this chapter you should realize that decision making is
A. easily done with computers.
B. a difficult and uncertain process.
C. no longer of importance.
D. best left to government officials.

Application Situations Exercise

Match the key concepts with the statements that best describe them.

A.	Anchoring effect	O.	Groupthink
B.	Bounded rationality	P.	Hindsight
C.	Brainstorming	Q.	Ill-structured problem
D.	Cognitive biases	R.	Information overload
E.	Confirmation bias	S.	Maximization
F.	Conservative shift	T.	Nominal group technique
G.	Decision making	U.	Perfect rationality
H.	Delphi technique	V.	Problem
I.	Devil's advocate	W.	Program
J.	Diffusion of responsibility	X.	Risky shift
K.	Electronic brainstorming	Y.	Satisficing
L.	Electronic groups	Z.	Sunk costs
M.	Escalation of commitment	&	Well-structured problem
N.	Framing		

______ 1. Our computers kept grinding out more information than we could ever use.

______ 2. So the boss tried to decide what to do.

______ 3. At first, she formed a group and told us to throw out ideas freely and without criticism.

______ 4. We argued for hours, but were not willing to be blamed as individuals for giving the boss a bad suggestion.

______ 5. Some in the group said they know the computers would hurt the company long before the organization went in for data processing.

______ 6. Others suggested buying bigger and better computers and getting even more information.

______ 7. A few suggested taking risks by doing away with computers altogether.

______ 8. Some suggested sending questionnaires to outside experts.

______ 9. Most of us recognized a gap between what existed and what we hoped would exist.

______ 10. All of us finally reached a decision that seemed to please all a little, but that didn't really make any of us happy.

Short Answer Questions

Fill-in the missing word(s).

1. Decision makers tend to think that ______________ information is always better.

2. People often tend to be ______________ about the adequacy of their decisions.

3. When things go poorly, we tend to blame an ______________ for the failures.

4. Decision makers continue to use ______________ even when they have become ineffective.

5. Both risky and ______________ shifts are often possible in group decision making.

6. When a real estate agent allows a client's asking price to unduly influence their professional evaluation of a house, ______________ is probably operating.

7. Programmed decision making is effective so long as ______________ do not change.

8. Claiming that one knew the results before the actions were taken is an example of ____________.

9. It is very important to be aware of what reference point you are using when you ____________ decision alternatives.

10. Setting clear goals for a project in advance that must be met before additional resources will be committed should help to guard against ______________.

ANSWER SHEET FOR CHAPTER 12

PRE-TESTING YOUR UNDERSTANDING OF THE CHAPTER

Key Concepts Matching

1. G	2. V	3. U	4. B	5. R	6. S	7. Y	8. Z	9. M	10. P
11. &	12. W	13. Q	14. D	15. J	16. O	17. X	18. F	19. E	20. I
21. C	22. T	23. H	24. K	25. L	26. N	27. A			

True/False Questions

1. T	2. T	3. F	4. T	5. T	6. F	7. T	8. F	9. F	10. T
11. T	12. F	13. F	14. T	15. T	16. T	17. F	18. F	19. T	20. T

Multiple-Choice Questions

1. D	2. C	3. A	4. C	5. A	6. B	7. D	8. A	9. B	10. C

POST-TESTING FOR EXAMS

True/False Questions

1. F	2. F	3. F	4. T	5. F	6. T	7. F	8. T	9. F	10. F

Multiple-Choice Questions

1. D	2. C	3. B	4. C	5. B	6. A	7. C	8. C	9. C	10. A
11. C	12. A	13. B	14. D	15. A	16. B	17. D	18. C	19. D	20. B

Application Situations Exercise

1. R	2. G	3. C	4. J	5. P	6. M	7. X	8. H	9. V	10. Y

Short Answer Questions

1. more	2. overconfident	3. external factor	4. programs
5. conservative	6. the anchor effect	7. conditions	8. hindsight
9. frame	10. escalation of commitment		

EXERCISE FOR CHAPTER 12

DECISION MAKING

Advanced Preparation: To be completed before class

It is generally agreed that the trend is toward increasing levels of participative management. The big problem issue facing managers today is determining when to make the decision alone, when to use participation, and when to let the group make the decision. This exercise will give you practice as a manager at determining when to use participation and when not to.

For the ten situations below decide which of the three styles you would use for that unique situation.
Place the letter A, P, or L on the line before each situation's number.

A- autocratic, make the decision alone without subordinate input.
P- participative, make the decision based on subordinate input.
L- laissez-faire, allow the group to make the decision, you may be a group member.

_______ 1. You have developed a new work procedure that will increase productivity. Your boss likes the idea and wants you to try it within a few weeks. You view your employees as fairly capable, and believe that they will be receptive to the change.

_______ 2. The industry of your product has new competition. Your organization's revenues have been dropping. You have been told to lay off three of your ten employees in two weeks. You have been the supervisor for over one year. Normally, your employees are very capable.

_______ 3. Your department has been facing a problem for several months. Many solutions have been tried and failed. You finally thought of a solution, but you are not sure of the possible consequences of the change required or the acceptance of the highly capable employees.

_______ 4. Flex time has become popular in your organization. Some departments let each employee start and end work when they choose. However, because of the cooperative effort of your employees they must all work the same eight hours. You are not sure of the level of interest in changing the hours. Your employees are a very capable group and like to make decisions.

_______ 5. The technology in your industry is changing faster than the members of your organization can keep up with. Top management hired a consultant who has given the recommended decision. You have two weeks to make your decision. Your employees are capable, they enjoy participating in the decision making process.

_______ 6. Your boss called you on the telephone to tell you that someone has requested an order for your department's product with a very short delivery date. She asked you to call her back with the decision about taking the order in fifteen minutes. Looking over the work schedule, you realize that it will be very difficult to deliver the order on time. Your employees will have to push hard to make it. They are cooperative, capable, and enjoy being involved in decision making.

_______ 7. A change has been handed down from top management. How you implement it is your decision. The change takes effect in one month. It will personally affect everyone in your department. Their acceptance is critical to the success of the change. Your employees are usually not too interested in being involved in making decisions.

_______ 8. You believe that productivity in your department could be increased. You have thought of some ways that may work, but your not sure of them. Your employees are very experienced; almost all of them have been in the department longer than you have.

_______ 9. Top management has decided to make a change that will affect all of your employees. You know that they will be upset because it will cause them hardship. One or two may even quit. The change goes into effect in thirty days. Your employees are very capable.

______ 10. A customer has offered you a contract for your product with a quick delivery date. The offer is open for two days. Meeting the contract deadline would require employees to work nights and weekends for six weeks. You can not require them to work overtime. Filling this profitable contract could help get you the raise you want and feel you deserve. However, if you take the contract and don't deliver on time it will hurt your chances of getting a big raise. Your employees are very capable.

In-Class Part of Exercise 12

Objective:

To gain a better understanding when and when not to use groups in decision making.

Option A: (3-8 minutes)

The instructor simply gives the students the recommended answers to the advanced preparation.

Option B: (7-15 minutes)

The instructor calls on students for their decision making style answers (advanced preparation). The instructor may or may not ask for volunteers.

Option C: (12-20 minutes)

1. Break into groups of four to six and share your answers to the preparation. Come to an agreement on the recommended group answer.
2. The instructor goes over the recommended answers.

Conclusion:

The instructor may lead a class discussion and/or make concluding remarks.

Application: (2-4 minutes)

What have I learned through this exercise? How will I use this knowledge in the future?

Sharing:

Volunteers give their answers to the application section.

Copyright 1987, Robert N. Lussier, used with permission

CHAPTER 13

POWER, POLITICS, AND ETHICS

LEARNING OBJECTIVES

- DEFINE POWER AND REVIEW THE BASES OF INDIVIDUAL POWER.
- EXPLAIN HOW PEOPLE OBTAIN POWER IN ORGANIZATIONS.
- DISCUSS THE CONCEPT OF EMPOWERMENT.
- REVIEW VARIOUS INFLUENCE TACTICS.
- PROVIDE A PROFILE OF POWER SEEKERS.
- EXPLAIN STRATEGIC CONTINGENCIES AND DISCUSS HOW SUB-UNITS OBTAIN POWER.
- DEFINE ORGANIZATIONAL POLITICS AND DISCUSS ITS VARIOUS FORMS.
- DEFINE ETHICS AND REVIEW THE ETHICAL DILEMMAS THAT MANAGERS FACE.

KEY CONCEPTS

Power

Legitimate power

Reward power

Coercive power

Referent power

Expert power

Empowerment

Influence tactics

Subunit power

Strategic contingencies

Organizational politics

Machiavellianism

Networking

Ethics

Stakeholders

CHAPTER SUMMARY

Key concepts are identified by **bold** *faced type.*

I. What Is Power?

Power is the capacity to influence others who are in a state of dependence. This does not necessarily imply that a poor relationship exists between the exerciser of power and the target, as most friendships involve reciprocal influence processes.

Power can flow in any direction in an organization, although members at higher levels typically have more power. Power is a broad concept that applies to individuals as well as to groups.

II. The Bases of Individual Power

A. Legitimate Power

Legitimate power derives from a person's position or job in the organization. This power works because people have been socialized to accept its influence. Even across various cultures, employees cite legitimate power as a major reason for following their boss's directions.

B. Reward Power

Reward power exists when the power holders can exert influence by providing positive outcomes and preventing negative outcomes. It is often used to back up legitimate power.

C. Coercive Power

Coercive power is available when the power holder can exert influence by the use of punishment and threats. Although it too is employed as a support for legitimate power, its use by managers is generally ineffective.

D. Referent Power

Referent power exists when the power holder is well liked by others. It is potent because it stems from identification with the power holder, and anyone in the company may possess this power.

E. Expert Power

Expert power is derived from having special information or expertise that is valued by the organization. This power can be accrued by lower-level organizational members, and is especially likely to exist for those members in scientific and technical areas.

III. How Do People Obtain Power?

A. Doing the Right Things

Power may be obtained through extraordinary activities or through excellent performances in unusual or nonroutine activities which might include risk taking or managing great changes.

These activities will fail to produce power if no one knows about them. Therefore, people who seek power must try to publicize their efforts and ensure that they are visible.

Work done must be relevant to the needs of the organization for power to accrue. Therefore being in the right place at the right time and doing the right things are important in the effort to gain power.

B. Cultivating the Right People

To obtain power, one must develop informal relationships with various groups of people. These include: outsiders, subordinates, peers, and superiors.

All of these groups can play a part in helping one obtain and hold power.

IV. Empowerment-Putting Power Where It's Needed

Power need not be seen as something of fixed quantity which must necessarily be in short supply at the bottom of the organization if it is largely held at the top. **Empowerment** gives people the authority, opportunity, and motivation to take initiative and solve organizational problems.

Authority comes from pushing legitimate power down to lower levels so that decisions can be made by those with the information to make them. Opportunity means freedom from bureaucratic barriers. The motivation part of empowerment works when people are intrinsically motivated by power and opportunity and see their rewards linked to their performance.

V. Influence Tactics-Putting Power to Work

Power is the *potential* to influence others. **Influence tactics** are tactics that are used to convert power into actual influence over others. These tactics include assertiveness, ingratiation, rationality, exchange, upward appeal, and coalition foundation. Which tactics are used may be influenced by the power bases of the individual exercising power , by the hierarchical level of the target and by gender.

VI. Who Wants Power?

The old concepts of power seekers were that they were neurotics covering up feelings of inferiority, striving to compensate for childhood deprivations or substituting power for lack of affection.

Yet, according to psychologist David McClelland, some individuals have power needs which can make them effective managers when used in a responsible and controlled manner. McClelland calls these *institutional managers* because they use their power for the good of the institution. He stresses the greater effectiveness of these individuals with *personal power managers*, who use their power for personal gain, and *affiliative managers*, who are more concerned with being liked.

People who want power and can't get it often feel helpless and alienated from their work.

VII. Controlling Strategic Contingencies - How Subunits Obtain Power

Subunit power is the degree of power held by various organizational subunits, such as departments. They obtain this power through the control of **strategic contingencies**: critical factors affecting organizational effectiveness that are controlled by a key subunit. The conditions under which such control confers power involve scarcity, uncertainty, centrality and substitutability.

A. Scarcity

When resources such as budget dollars become scarce, subunits able to secure additional resources from outside the organization can obtain power. For example, university departments like engineering and medicine that have the ability to bring in external funding gain power in this way.

B. Uncertainty

Since organizations dislike uncertainty, those subunits with the ability to cope with the unexpected are most likely to obtain power. The intervention of governments into human resource policies in recent years has allowed personnel departments in organizations to gain power by coping with the attendant uncertainties.

C. Centrality

Subunits whose activities are most central to the work flow of the organization are more apt to obtain power than those whose activities are more peripheral. This explains the relatively greater power of line departments such as production and sales over staff areas like personnel.

D. Substitutability

If the expertise of a subunit's staff is nonsubstitutable, it can acquire power. One factor here is the general labor market for particular occupations. For example, engineers will have more power when there are few of them, than when their numbers increase. Having refined technical skills also impacts substitutability as does the ability of an organization to subcontract for skills outside.

E. The Irrational Face of Power

According to the strategic contingencies view, power gravitates to where it is needed to solve pressing organizational problems. However, once a subunit gets power, it may seek to hold it, even in the clear face of the knowledge that it is no longer in the best interests of the organization as a whole for it to do so.

VIII. Organizational Politics - Using and Abusing Power

A. The Basics of Organizational Politics

Organizational politics is the pursuit of self-interest in an organization, whether or not this self-interest corresponds to organizational goals. Generally, this activity is self-conscious and intentional, and it is possible for benefits to accrue to the organization even though outcomes are achieved by questionable tactics. A means/ends matrix may be used to explore these relationships.

B. Machiavellianism - The Harder Side of Politics

Machiavellianism is a set of cynical beliefs about human nature, morality, and the permissibility of using various tactics to achieve one's ends. For example, compared with "low machs", "high Machs" are more likely to advocate the use of lying and deceit to achieve desired goals. High Machs are especially adept at getting their way when situations are unstructured and face-to-face dealing under emotional circumstances is the mode of interaction.

C. Networking - The Softer Side of Politics

Networking is defined as establishing good relations with key organizational members and/or outsiders in order to accomplish one's goals. In essence, networking involves developing informal social contacts to enlist the cooperation of others when their support is necessary. The value of informal contacts has been cited as one of the downsides of telecommuting: Those who work at home feel "out of the loop".

D. Defensiveness-Reactive Politics

Political behavior can also be directed to the defense or protection of self-interest. At times, the best ways to reduce threats to one's own power are to avoid taking action that wouldn't be in one's best interest or to avoid blame for potentially damaging events.

Ashforth and Lee suggest that avoiding action may be accomplished by stalling, overconforming, buck passing, playing dumb, or depersonalizing. Avoiding blame can involve the behaviors of buffing, scapegoating, and justifying.

IX. Ethics in Organizations

Ethics can be defined as systematic thinking about the moral consequences of decisions. Moral consequences can be framed in terms of the potential for harm to any stakeholders in the decision. **Stakeholders** are people inside or outside of an organization who have the potential to be affected by organizational decisions.

A. The Nature of Ethical Dilemmas

A recent survey indicated that conflicts of interest, questionable gift giving and sexual harassment are the most frequent dilemmas encountered. A standardized set of moral standards for decision making that managers can strive to achieve can help them to deal with such dilemmas: honest communication, fair treatment, legitimate special consideration, fair competition, responsibility to the organization, corporate social responsibility, and respect for law.

B. Causes of Unethical Behavior

Although difficult to research, evidence does suggest the following causes:

- Gain: The anticipation of healthy reinforcement ($$$$) can't be underestimated!
- Role Conflict: An individual's "bureaucratic" role may be in conflict with their role as a member of a profession. The conflict provides a point of leverage for an unscrupulous boss.
- Competition: Extreme competition for scarce resources and the absence of competition (monopoly power) may both lead to unethical practices.
- Personality: An individual with a strong economic value orientation, who had a high need for personal power (especially a "high Mach"), but a relatively unsophisticated understanding of moral issues would be a strong bet for unethical behavior.

Organizational and Industry Culture: The ethical values of a given organization are often shaped by how the behavior of highly visible role models is rewarded. Also, some industries seem to have more ethical crises than others, although competition may be a factor.

C. Is Playing Politics Ethical?

Different stakeholders such as political opponents, subordinates, and the organization itself have legitimate interests when politics are played. Although politics are natural in all organizations, by definition, they promote an individual's *self-interest*. Thus, whether or not the playing of politics is ethical may depend upon the ends that one pursues (in the case of the organization) as well as the influence means that are used (in the case of who "gets hurt" along the way).

D. Employing Ethical Guidelines

There is evidence that formal education in ethics does have a positive impact on ethical attitudes. Here are a few simple guidelines that should help in the ethical screening of decisions:

- Identify the stakeholders.
- Identify the cost & benefit impacts of the decision on them.
- Consider the relevant moral expectations.
- Be familiar with common ethical dilemmas in your role or profession.
- Discuss ethical matters with stakeholders and others.
- Convert your ethical judgments into appropriate action.

PRE-TESTING YOUR UNDERSTANDING OF THE CHAPTER

Key Concepts Matching

Match the letter of the key concepts with the appropriate definitions.

A.	Coercive power	I.	Organizational politics
B.	Empowerment	J.	Power
C.	Ethics	K.	Referent power
D.	Expert power	L.	Reward power
E.	Influence tactics	M.	Stakeholders
F.	Legitimate power	N.	Strategic contingencies
G.	Machiavellianism	O.	Subunit power
H.	Networking		

______ 1. The capacity to influence others who are in a state of dependency.

______ 2. Power which derives from a person's position or job in the organization.

______ 3. Power which exists when the power holder can exert influence by providing positive outcomes and preventing negative outcomes.

______ 4. Power through which the power holder can exert influence by the use of punishment and threat.

______ 5. Power which exists when the power holder is well liked by others.

______ 6. Power which exists through special expertise that is valued by the organizations.

______ 7. Power exerted through organizational departments.

______ 8. The concept that the work performed by other subunits is contingent on the activities and performance of a key subunit.

______ 9. The pursuit of self-interest within an organization, whether or not this self-interest corresponds to organizational goals.

______ 10. A set of cynical beliefs about human nature, morality, and the permissibility of using various tactics to achieve one's ends.

______ 11. Establishing good relations with key organizational members and/or outsiders in order to accomplish one's goals.

______ 12. Giving people the authority, opportunity, and motivation to take initiative and solve organizational problems.

______ 13. Systematic thinking about the moral consequences of decisions.

______ 14. Tactics that are used to convert power into actual influence over others.

______ 15. People inside or outside an organization who have the potential to be affected by organizational decisions.

True/False Questions

Circle the letter of the correct answer.

T F 1. In the past, textbooks devoted extensive coverage to the topics of power, politics and conflict.
T F 2. Power can flow only from the top down in an organization.
T F 3. Legitimate power derives from a person's position in an organization.
T F 4. Generally, managers have more reward power than subordinates.
T F 5. Coercive power is an effective method of influencing worker behavior.
T F 6. Extraordinary activities will fail to generate power if no one knows about them.
T F 7. "Its not what you know, it's who you know" is generally true today in organizations.
T F 8. Cultivating relationships with subordinates is a poor method of enhancing power.
T F 9. Liaisons with key superiors represent an excellent way of obtaining power.
T F 10. People who seek power without success tend to become model employees.
T F 11. Differences in subunit power tend to decrease when resources become scarce.
T F 12. Organizations generally look forward to the unknown.
T F 13. Most political maneuvering occurs at middle or upper management levels rather than at lower levels.
T F 14. Machiavellianism generally uses ethical methods to achieve legitimate corporate goals.
T F 15. Empowerment inevitably results in a decrease in the power of upper level managers.
T F 16. It is impossible to teach people how to be more ethical in their business dealings.
T F 17. In general, we are readily influenced by people we like.
T F 18. Expert power is really of little value to top managers.
T F 19. In general, everyone wants power.
T F 20. Stakeholders to a decision could include everyone from the decision maker themselves to an "innocent bystander".

Multiple-Choice Questions

Select the correct answer.

______ 1. All of the following are bases of power *except*
A. legitimate power.
B. nominal power.
C. reward power.
D. expert power.

______ 2. All of the following are methods of obtaining power *except*
A. doing the right things.
B. visible activities.
C. relevant activities.
D. asking for it.

______ 3. One can obtain power by cultivating all of the following groups *except*
A. peers.
B. superiors.
C. whistle-blowers.
D. outsiders.

______ 4. According to old images, power seekers had all of the following traits *except* that
A. they seek power as a substitute for affection.
B. they seek power to help the company.
C. they are neurotics.
E. they are striving to compensate for childhood deprivation.

______ 5. All of the following are means by which subunits obtain power *except*
A. uncertainty.
B. centrality.
C. cohesiveness.
D. scarcity.

______ 6. All of the following are concepts of organizational politics *except* those of
A. nonsanctioned means/nonsanctioned ends.
B. sanctioned means/sanctioned ends.
C. sanctioned means/nonsanctioned ends.
D. nonsanctioned means/sanctioned ends.

______ 7. All of the following traits are associated with Machiavellianism *except* those of
A. altruism.
B. self-esteem and confidence.
C. self-interest behavior.
D. cool and calculating behavior.

______ 8. Empowerment means giving people all of the following *except*
A. authority.
B. close supervision.
C. opportunity.
D. motivation to take initiative.

______ 9. All of the following are influence tactics *except*
A. ingratiation.
B. exchange.
C. individual competence.
D. coalition formation.

______ 10. All of the following are among causes of unethical behavior *except*
A. ambiguous legislation.
B. competition.
C. role conflict.
D. personality.

POST-TESTING FOR EXAMS

True/False Questions

Circle the letter of the correct answer.

T F 1. Despite the tactics used, organizational politics can sometimes help an organization.
T F 2. Machiavellian activities are usually carried out in an emotional manner.
T F 3. "High Machs" are airplanes that fly at supersonic speeds.
T F 4. Networking is an effort to coerce others for one's own ends.
T F 5. A survey of companies found executive salaries a major source of ethical concern.
T F 6. When essentially no competition exists, there is a strong tendency to make unethical decisions.
T F 7. Buffing is a way of avoiding blame in organizations.
T F 8. There is no evidence that formal education in ethics has an impact on ethical attitudes.
T F 9. Flattery can be a successful influence tactic in organizations.
T F 10. It is impossible to gain power by cultivating relationships with one's subordinates.

Multiple-Choice Questions

Select the correct answer.

_____ 1. A CEO might be expected to possess
A. legitimate power.
B. coercive power
C. reward power.
D. all of the above.

_____ 2. A popular fellow employee has
A. reward power.
B. legitimate power.
C. referent power.
D. expert power.

_____ 3. A surgeon whose work is reported in a newspaper is engaging in
A. extraordinary activities.
B. visible activities.
C. relevant activities.
D. showmanship.

_____ 4. Mark Jorgensen was an employee of
A. General Motors.
B. Burroughs.
C. Prudential.
D. Chrysler.

_____ 5. According the McClelland the most effective managers have all of the following traits *except*
A. disregard for people.
B. a high power need.
C. a participative leadership style.
D. seeking to achieve organizational goals.

_____ 6. All of the following are more likely to stimulate political activity *except*
A. budget allocation.
B. reorganization.
C. purchasing equipment.
D. personnel changes.

_____ 7. All of the following are aspects of defensiveness-reactive politics *except*
A. stalling.
B. ingratiation.
C. overconforming.
D. scapegoating.

_____ 8. A person called in for consultation has
A. expert power.
B. referent power.
C. legitimate power.
D. reward power.

_____ 9. Some subunits are more prone to politicking than others because
A. clear goals might provoke less political activity than vague goals.
B. complex tasks might provoke more political activity than simple tasks.
C. most political maneuvering happens among middle managers.
D. scarce resources provoke political activity.

_____ 10. In general, political activity is
A. done through ignorance.
B. anticipating resistance.
C. self-conscious and intentional.
D. happily received in organizations.

_____ 11. All of the following are conditions under which subunits can control strategic contingencies *except*
A. scarcity.
B. centrality.
C. uncertainty
D. clarity.

_____ 12. The term Machiavellianism comes from the writings of
A. a corporate psychologist.
B. a contemporary Italian official.
C. a 16th century Italian official.
D. a business executive.

_____ 13. All of the following groups are <u>stakeholders</u> when politics are being employed *except*
A. opponents
B. other companies.
C. the organization itself.
D. subordinates or co-workers.

_____ 14. When a manager agrees to recommend a raise for a subordinate if she increases her net sales 30% in the next six months, we have a case of
A. sanctioned means/unsanctioned ends.
B. unsanctioned means/unsanctioned ends.
C. unsanctioned means/sanctioned ends.
D. sanctioned means/sanctioned ends.

_____ 15. McClelland identified all of the following *except*
A. administrative managers.
B. institutional managers.
C. personal power managers.
D. affiliative managers.

_____ 16. A subunit can achieve centrality in all of the following ways *except*
A. when it influences the work of other subunits.
B. when its services lose their importance.
C. when it impacts a company's key services.
D. when it has immediate impact.

_____ 17. In the 1990s there is again a shortage of
A. lawyers.
B. teachers.
C. engineers and scientists.
D. factory workers.

_____ 18. Most political activity occurs among
A. upper management levels.
B. middle and upper management levels.
C. lower management levels.
D. employee-worker levels.

_____ 19. Establishing good relations with key organizational members is an example of
A. Machiavellianism.
B. compromise.
C. networking.
D. problem solving.

_____ 20. The increase in personnel department power due to increased government intervention relates to the strategic contingency of
A. uncertainty.
B. centrality.
C. substitutability.
D. scarcity.

Application Situations Exercise

Match the key concept with the statements that best describes them.

A.	Coercive power	I.	Organizational politics
B.	Empowerment	J.	Power
C.	Ethics	K.	Referent power
D.	Expert power	L.	Reward power
E.	Influence tactics	M.	Stakeholders
F.	Legitimate power	N.	Strategic contingencies
G.	Machiavellianism	O.	Subunit power
H.	Networking		

_____ 1. Our manager wanted to call in outside experts to solve a production problem.

_____ 2. I would have disagreed, but didn't want to be assigned to "Siberia".

_____ 3. But the boss was in charge, so she called the shots.

_____ 4. Some people felt that she was just pursuing her own ends at the expense of the company.

_____ 5. But it soon became clear that her objective was to give the production people some authority of their own so they would take the initiative to solve their own problems.

_____ 6. She gathered together everyone that might be affected by the decisions being made.

_____ 7. It was apparent that she had established good relations with the key players.

_____ 8. I asked if she had done any systematic thinking about the moral consequences of the decisions at hand, since production already had so much power in the organization.

_____ 9. She said that she felt that Production's control over critical factors affecting organizational effectiveness meant that they would always have a great deal of power.

____ 10. She is a true charismatic leader.

Short Answer Questions

Fill-in the missing word(s).

1. Expert power is especially common among lower-level members in ______________ areas.

2. Under empowerment, freedom from bureaucratic barriers is referred to as ______________ .

3. The basic sources of uncertainty exist mainly in an organization's ______________ .

4. The most easily identified stakeholders in organizational politics ______________ .

5. The pursuit of nonsanctioned ends is always ______________ .

6. Liaisons with ______________ represent the best way of obtaining power through cultivating others.

7. Mentors are especially important today for ______________ junior executives.

8. In the 1970s increased government intervention into ______________ policies began.

9. Of all the bases of power, ______________ is most consistently associated with subordinate effectiveness.

10. The case of Mark Jorgeson and Prudential involved his dismissal for being a ____________.

ANSWER SHEET FOR CHAPTER 13

PRE-TESTING YOUR UNDERSTANDING OF THE CHAPTER

Key Concepts Matching

1. J 2. F 3. L 4. A 5. K 6. D 7. O 8. N 9. I 10. G
11. H 12. B 13. C 14. E 15. M

True/False Questions

1. T 2. F 3. T 4. T 5. F 6. T 7. T 8. F 9. T 10. F
11. F 12. F 13. T 14. F 15. F 16. F 17. T 18. F 19. F 20. T

Multiple-Choice Questions

1. B 2. D 3. C 4. B 5. C 6. B 7. A 8. B 9. C 10. A

POST-TESTING FOR EXAMS

True/False Questions

1. T 2. F 3. F 4. F 5. F 6. T 7. T 8. F 9. T 10. F

Multiple-Choice Questions

1. D 2. C 3. B 4. C 5. A 6. C 7. B 8. A 9. A 10. C
11. D 12. C 13. B 14. D 15. A 16. B 17. C 18. B 19. C 20. A

Application Situations Exercise

1. D 2. A 3. F 4. I 5. B 6. M 7. H 8. C 9. N 10. K

Short Answer Questions

1. scientific / technical 2. opportunity 3. environment 4. political opponents
5. dysfunctional 6. key superiors 7. female 8. personnel
9. expertise 10. whistle-blower

CASE STUDY

MANAGING THE MARKETING DEPARTMENT

Richard Walsh's first career had been that of a researcher for a small Halifax market research firm. He had begun this job with a fresh M.B.A. degree, dividing his time between working long hours, getting married, and beginning a family. At the research firm Walsh was recognized as bright and competent, but he was also seen as somewhat arrogant and egotistical. Walsh liked to flaunt his intellect, and he frequently strung multisyllabic words together as if he were an Oxford University don. He prided himself on keeping up with the latest marketing research techniques emanating from the top universities, and he frequently gave rambling lectures about the virtues or vices of some new technique to the perplexed staff of the firm.

At the age of thirty-seven Richard Walsh made a radical career change. Selling the family home, he and his family moved to Ontario and he enrolled in a Ph.D. program at a university with a reasonable reputation. The move had been carefully planned, and the family lived in a small rented apartment and conserved resources to support Richard's endeavour. As a graduate student he was perceived as fairly intelligent, but argumentative. After three and one half years, Walsh received his Ph.D. degree and took a job as assistant professor at Collins College. He felt he could have gone to a much more prestigious school, but he told his friends that his wife and children really wanted to return to the Maritimes. "Besides, I'll build that place into a powerhouse or else move on to UBC," he laughed.

When Richard arrived at Collins College, the dean of the business school immediately appointed him coordinator of the marketing area. At the time, faculty at Collins were organized by teaching areas and not separated into formal departments. There were only two other marketing professors, both older individuals who did not hold Ph.D.s, and the dean was eager to put Ph.D.s in the coordination positions to take advantage of their more recent university experience for curriculum development. Both of Walsh's senior colleagues were happy to be relieved of the coordination job, since it cut into their consulting time, and were very supportive of their new colleague.

Richard took to the coordinator's job with relish. He updated many course descriptions and introduced two new courses in his specialty, marketing research. In addition, he revised the scheduling of the marketing courses, taking pains to incorporate the time preferences of his two senior colleagues. Richard quickly acquired a reputation as an effective if long-winded speaker at faculty meetings, where he showed an impressive command of the language. During his first three years at Collins, his prestige among faculty was aided considerably by the publication of several works from his Ph.D. dissertation. Two of these were technical notes in prestigious marketing journals and the other was a monograph put out by an obscure Toronto publisher. Since the publication efforts of Collins faculty were almost nil, this activity was noticed. Privately, Richard's two marketing colleagues described the monograph as brilliant, although both admitted they really didn't understand it very well.

Richard's fourth year at Collins was an important one for him. He was promoted to associate professor, received tenure, and was appointed chairperson of the newly formed marketing department. The business school at Collins was going to be expanded, and the dean felt that formal departments would be necessary as the school grew in size. Richard's appointment was enthusiastically supported by his two older colleagues, who had consistently deferred to his judgment during his years as coordinator.

Source: Case prepared by Gary Johns

The key task of the new department chairpersons was to hire additional faculty and to make decisions about the renewal of their contracts. Previously, these tasks had been performed directly by the dean. The dean was particularly interested in increasing the research and publication output of the business school, and Richard readily agreed. "After all," he said, "I'm the only person around here publishing in the top journals. We need more of that."

During the next few years, Collins's chairpersons were generally successful in recruiting new faculty. Most departments hired new Ph.D.s or individuals in the very last stages of their doctoral dissertations. Although they were not from exceptional schools, most turned out to be good teachers and active researchers and publishers. Gradually, the reputation of the Collins business school was increasing throughout Canada.

In the marketing department, Richard Walsh employed a somewhat different recruiting strategy. He tended to hire Ph.D. students who were in the very early phases of their dissertations. They were usually from the better schools, and Richard said that they had great potential for building an "intellectual core" in the department. His senior marketing colleagues agreed. When someone asked Richard how he managed to attract people from the better schools to the relatively modest Collins campus he replied that he looked for those who were "poverty stricken." "You'd be surprised what a job offer will do to a poor graduate student with a whole dissertation to complete," he grinned.

Some of the new marketing faculty complained that their teaching loads were heavier than they had expected, and that Richard had been vague about this when they were being recruited. In the other departments new recruits were given a reprieve from committees so they could devote their time to getting their teaching and research off to a good start. Richard, on the other hand, assigned new recruits to several committees so they could "get the feel of the college."

Over the years, successive new recruits in marketing experienced considerable difficulty in completing their dissertations. Although some surreptitiously looked for jobs elsewhere, they soon learned that it was difficult to obtain another position without having finished their Ph.D.s. Richard was very sympathetic to their difficulties, and he frequently recounted the privations he and his family had endured during his graduate study. In addition he was always willing to provide frank and lengthy critiques of the dissertation work they had accomplished.

New recruits were hired under two-year contracts, and a decision was made early in the second year as to whether they would be renewed for another two years. Although the chairpersons had the final say in this matter, it was standard practice in all departments to convene a department meeting to evaluate those up for renewal and to vote on renewal decisions. At the first renewal meeting for each candidate, Richard spoke forcefully in favor of contract renewal, citing his or her "great potential." Consistently, the two senior members agreed with Richard, as did the junior members (who were often in the same boat as the person on whom they were voting). Thus, over the years, first renewals occurred in spite of incomplete dissertations.

Second renewal decisions were made early in a faculty member's fourth year at Collins. By this time, most had completed their dissertations or were very close to doing so. Richard's approach to second renewal decisions varied considerably from that used in first renewal decisions. Typically, he began second-renewal meetings with an eloquent speech about maintaining the quality of the department and increasing its research and publication efforts.

"After all," he said, "We don't want to end up granting tenure to someone who will never publish anything." Invariably, those up for renewal had achieved no publications, and Richard spoke against their renewal. His senior colleagues always agreed, as did all of the junior members who were awaiting their own first renewal decisions. This group consistently carried the vote, and no junior member lasted more than four years in the Collins marketing department.

Jack Ross, dean of the school of business at Collins, sat in his office and wondered what to do about the marketing department. During his reign as dean, Ross felt that he had generally been successful in increasing the quality of the school. However, he had gradually come to see the marketing department as a weak link in the chain. Although marketing had hired some promising people, turnover was high because of nonrenewals, and publication productivity was low. Even Richard Walsh hadn't published anything since his success years ago.

Recently, a delegation of the other chairpersons had complained to Ross that their departments were not receiving enough travel money to cover the presentation of research papers at learned conferences. They had implied (though not said directly) that the marketing department received too much travel money. Ross knew that almost all of marketing's travel allocation was spent by Richard Walsh, who frequently attended conferences for recruiting purposes. However, the dean had begun to wonder about Walsh's recruiting strategy. For years, he had been unable to hire anyone in his own specialty, marketing research, even though another person in this area was desperately needed. Furthermore, Walsh never seemed to follow up on leads provided by the dean for experienced, well-published marketing professors who might be attracted to Collins.

Jack Ross worried about what he should say to Richard Walsh.

1. Is power an issue in *Managing the Marketing Department?* If so, who has power over whom?

2. What bases of individual power does Richard Walsh command?

3. How did Richard Walsh acquire the power he holds?

4. Why did Richard Walsh engage in his unique hiring and contract renewal strategy? What are his motives? Is he a Machiavellian?

5. Is there evidence of organizational politics in the case? Defend your answer.

6. Is conflict an issue in this case? Explain your answer.

7. What should Dean Ross do about the marketing department?

CHAPTER 14

CONFLICT AND STRESS

LEARNING OBJECTIVES

- DEFINE INTERPERSONAL CONFLICT AND REVIEW ITS CAUSES IN ORGANIZATIONS.
- EXPLAIN THE PROCESS BY WHICH CONFLICT OCCURS.
- DISCUSS THE VARIOUS MODES OF MANAGING CONFLICT.
- REVIEW A RANGE OF NEGOTIATION TECHNIQUES.
- DISCUSS THE MERITS OF STIMULATING CONFLICT.
- DISTINGUISH AMONG STRESSORS, STRESS, AND STRESS REACTIONS.
- DISCUSS THE ROLE THAT PERSONALITY PLAYS IN STRESS.
- REVIEW THE SOURCE OF STRESS ENCOUNTERED BY VARIOUS ORGANIZATIONAL ROLE OCCUPANTS.
- DESCRIBE BEHAVIORAL, PSYCHOLOGICAL, AND PHYSIOLOGICAL REACTIONS TO STRESS.
- DISCUSS TECHNIQUES FOR REDUCING OR COPING WITH STRESS.

KEY CONCEPTS

Interpersonal conflict

Avoiding

Accommodating

Competing

Compromise

Collaborating

Stress reactions

Type A behavior pattern

Role overload

Boundary roles

Job demands-job control model

Burnout

Negotiation

Distributive negotiation

Integrative negotiation

Superordinate goals

Conflict stimulation

Stressors

Stress

Defense mechanisms

Rationalization

Projection

Displacement

Reaction formation

Compensation

Repression

CHAPTER SUMMARY

Key concepts are identified by **bold** *faced type.*

I. What Is Conflict?

Interpersonal conflict is a process that occurs when one person, group, or organizational subunit frustrates the goal attainment of another. In its classic form, conflict often involves antagonistic attitudes and behaviors such as name calling, sabotage, or even physical aggression.

II. Causes of Organizational Conflict

It is possible to isolate a number of factors that contribute to organizational conflict:

A. Group Identification and Intergroup Bias

This is the tendency of people to develop a more positive view of their own "in-group" and a less positive view of "out-groups" of which they are not a member. This tendency appears to develop even when group membership is essentially arbitrary.

B. Interdependence

When individuals or subunits are dependent upon each other to accomplish their goals, the potential for conflict exists. The potential for the abuse of power in such relationships and the on-going need for coordination are both potential problem areas.

C. Differences in Power, Status, and Culture

If dependence is not mutual, an imbalance in power can arise and the potential for conflict increases. Status differences have the greatest potential for conflict when a reversal of expected roles occurs; that is, when a high status person like an executive, finds themselves being educated on computer usage by their administrative assistant. The clash between differing organizational cultures provides fertile ground for conflict as fundamental beliefs and values collide. Mass hirings, acquisitions or mergers often create such conditions.

D. Ambiguity

Ambiguous goals, jurisdictions, or performance criteria can lead to conflict. Under such circumstances, the formal and informal rules that govern interaction break down and it may be difficult to determine responsibility.

E. Scarce Resources

Differences in power are magnified when common resources are in short supply. Resources may also act as buffers in sufficient quantities which, when removed, allow conflict to surface.

III. Types of Conflict

Most organizational conflicts boil down to disputes over goals, facts, and procedures. Recognizing that a conflict is over goal definition, rather than a simple question of fact will go a long way toward approaching its resolution in an appropriate manner. It is also important to understand that framing issues may mean that different people categorize the same problem as different types of conflict. Trying to see the conflict from your opponent's frame of reference is also a useful step toward resolution.

IV. The Conflict Process

As a conflict develops, "winning" becomes very important, the parties conceal information from each other, each group becomes more cohesive, contact with the opposite party is discouraged, negative stereotypes develop and aggressive leaders may emerge. Based on these internal dynamics, the process begins to run "on its own steam"!

V. Modes of Managing Conflict

Conflict expert Kenneth Thomas has developed a set of 5 conflict management styles or strategies based on a combination of the degree of assertiveness shown and the degree of cooperation with the other party which is demonstrated.

A. Avoiding

Avoiding is a conflict management style characterized by low assertiveness of one's own interests and low cooperation with the other party. This is the "hiding the head in the sand" response to conflict.

B. Accommodating

Accommodating is a conflict management style in which one party cooperates with the other party while not asserting one's own interests. This may be seen as a sign of weakness.

C. Competing

Competing is a conflict management style that maximizes assertiveness and minimizes cooperation. The conflict tends to be framed in strict win-lose terms.

D. Compromise

Compromise is a conflict management style that combines intermediate levels of assertiveness and cooperation. This tends to be a satisficing approach - neither true competition nor true accommodation.

E. Collaborating

Collaborating is a conflict management style that maximizes both assertiveness and cooperation. Collaboration works as a problem-solving approach where the object is to determine a win-win solution to the conflict.

VI. Managing Conflict With Negotiation

Negotiation is a decision-making process among independent parties who do not share identical preferences. Labor and management negotiate over wages and conditions, but job applicants also negotiate for starting salaries, employees negotiate for better job assignments, and people with sick kids negotiate to leave work early.

Distributive negotiation is a win-lose negotiation in which a fixed amount of assets is divided between parties. **Integrative negotiation** is a win-win negotiation that assumes that mutual problem solving can enlarge the assets to be divided between the parties.

A. Distributive Negotiation Tactics

Reaching an acceptable resolution in distributive negotiation involves both parties arriving at a point in the "settlement range", an area of overlap between each party's target and their resistance point. Several techniques can influence how that point is determined:

- Threats and Promises: Threats consist of implying that punishment will be forthcoming if the opponent does not concede to your position. Promises are pledges that concessions will lead to rewards in the future.
- Firmness versus Concessions: Intransigence - not moving - is often met by the same and the negotiations are deadlocked. A series of small concessions early in the process will often be matched.
- Persuasion: Verbal persuasion often (1) asserts the technical merit of the party's position in terms of the quality of the goods or services involved and (2) asserts the fairness of the party's position on price.

B. Integrative Negotiation Tactics

The effort and creativity required to move past "fixed-pie" bargaining can be well worth the effort. A number of factors can help to make it happen:

- Copious Information Exchange: Parties need to give away noncritical information early to start the ball rolling, ask lots of questions and listen to the answers. Trust must be built slowly so that "positions" will give way to the communication of true interests.
- Framing Differences as Opportunities: Differences need not represent mutually exclusive options. Explore them for the opportunity to satisfy both parties without compromise.
- Cutting Costs: If you can somehow cut the costs that the other party associates with an agreement, the chance of an integrative settlement increases.
- Increasing Resources: The ultimate solution to "fixed-pie" bargaining is to have the parties use their combined power to obtain greater resources which they can then divide.
- Introducing Superordinate Goals: Superordinate goals are attractive outcomes that can be achieved only by collaboration. Neither party can achieve the goal on its own.

C. Third Party Involvement

Third parties may be involved between negotiating parties when an impasse is reached (labor/management disputes) or may be involved from the start as a normal part of the process of bargaining (real estate agents). Two approaches to third party involvement are mediation and arbitration:

- Mediation: This occurs when a neutral third party helps to facilitate a negotiated agreement by aiding the process / atmosphere of bargaining or by intervening in the content of the negotiation.
- Arbitration: This occurs when a third party is given the authority to dictate the terms of settlement of a dispute. In *conventional arbitration*, the arbitrator can choose any outcome, such as splitting the difference between the parties. In *final offer arbitration*, each party makes a final offer and the arbitrator chooses one of them.

D. Some Final Words on Negotiation

- Interests Versus Positions: Try to stay focused on underlying interests, yours and theirs, not just stated positions.
- Credibility: Credibility of negotiators is key, but will vary depending on the type of negotiation (distributive versus integrative) and the cultural context (In the east, age and seniority carries more weight than technical expertise).
- Maintaining Face: Good negotiators avoid personalizing the problem, try to have some empathy for their counterpart, and avoid passing gratuitous insults.
- Constituency Effects: The use of high status negotiators is a good hedge against the inevitable pressure from constituencies to escalate conflict.

VII. Is All Conflict Bad?

Some experts feel that conflict creates change which is necessary for adaptation and survival. Therefore, while some conflict is functional and some dysfunctional, it must be properly managed.

Conflict stimulation is a strategy of increasing conflict in order to motivate change. This can occur when peaceful relationships take precedence over organizational goals or when differences are suppressed or down played. Both *scarcity* and *ambiguity* can be manipulated by managers to stimulate the organization.

VIII. A Model of Stress in Organizations

A. Stressors

Stressors are environmental events or conditions that have the potential to induce stress. These can include a person's job, a person's co-workers, conditions like extreme heat and cold, as well as the hostility of others. A person's personality often determines whether or not a stressor will actually induce stress.

B. Stress

Stress is a psychological reaction to the demands inherent in a stressor that has the potential to make a person feel tense or anxious. All stress is not intrinsically bad since moderate levels of stress can serve as stimulation.

C. Stress Reactions

Stress reactions are the behavioral, psychological, and physiological consequences of stress. Some of these reactions are passive such as high blood pressure. Others are active attempts to <u>cope</u> with some aspect of the stress episode.

Reactions that are useful for the individual in dealing with stress may be very costly for the organization. Hence, organizations should be interested in the stress their employees experience.

D. Personality and Stress

Personality can affect both the extent to which potential stressors are perceived as stressful and the types of stress reactions that occur. Two key personality traits are locus of control and Type A behavior pattern:

- Locus of Control: Compared with internals, externals are more likely to feel anxious in the face of potential stressors since they feel less in control. Internals are also more likely to confront stressors directly, while externals are more prone to simple anxiety-reduction strategies that only work in the short term.
- Type A Behavior Pattern: **Type A behavior pattern** is a personality pattern that includes aggressiveness, ambitiousness, competitiveness, hostility, impatience, and a sense of time urgency. The major component in Type A behavior that contributes to negative physiological reactions is hostility and repressed anger. Paradoxically, these individuals often do achieve higher level jobs in organizations as a result of their achievement orientation and long work hours despite their heightened tendencies to suffer heart attacks and high levels of blood pressure.

IX. Stressors in Organizational Life

A. Executive and Managerial Stressors

- Role Overload: **Role overload** occurs when too many tasks must be performed in too short a time period. This is an especially common stressor for managers. Management is an ongoing process, and few managers get time to rest or even to think about a new work strategy. Some executives even ignore threats to their health in combating role overload.

- Heavy Responsibility: Since managers also have heavy responsibilities, they to must always be aware of the consequences of their actions. Hence, firing employees, million dollar decisions, closing a money-losing plant, or ending a strike can all serve as stressors to executives.

B. Operative-Level Stressors

- Poor Physical Working Conditions: Operative-level employees are more likely than managers and professionals to be exposed to physically unpleasant or dangerous working conditions.
- Poor Job Design: The educational level of the North American work force has been rising steadily, yet many workers still find themselves in boring, frustrating, and repetitive jobs. The **job demands-job control model** is a model that asserts that jobs promote high stress when they make high demands while offering little control over work decisions.

C. Boundary Role Stressors and Burnout

- **Boundary roles** are positions in which organizational members are required to interact with members of other organizations or with the public.
- **Burnout** is emotional exhaustion, depersonalization, and reduced personal accomplishment among those who work with people. Teachers, nurses, social workers, and paramedics, and police are especially likely candidates for burnout.

D. Some General Stressors

- Interpersonal conflict: The entire range of conflict, from personality clashes to intergroup strife, is especially likely to cause stress when it leads to real or perceived attacks on our self-esteem or integrity.
- Work-Family Conflict: Increases in dual career families, single parent families, and lifespans are all contributing to conflicting demands of work and family. Many managers remain unaware of the impact of these changes on child-care and elder-care concerns and there is evidence to suggest that these demands still fall disproportionately on women's shoulders with career limiting results.
- Job Insecurity: No level of the organization is immune to this stressor. Technological changes threaten the operative level. Professionals may find themselves "overqualified" in a narrow specialty no longer required. Executives are often let go as organizations thin their ranks.
- Role Ambiguity: Stress often results from the lack of direction which exists when the goals of one's job or the methods of performing it are unclear.

X. Reactions to Organizational Stress

A. Behavioral Reactions to Stress

- Problem Solving: In general, problem solving is directed toward terminating the stressor or reducing its potency. Some examples include: delegation, time management, talking it out, asking for help, and searching for alternatives.
- Withdrawal: In organizations, withdrawal takes the form of absence or turnover.
- Use of Addictive Substances: Smoking, drinking and drug use represent the least satisfactory behavioral response to stress.

B. Psychological Reactions to Stress

Defense mechanisms are psychological attempts to reduce the anxiety associated with stress. These might include:
- **Rationalization**: attributing socially acceptable reasons or motives to one's actions.
- **Projection**: attributing one's own undesirable ideas and motives to others.
- **Displacement** : directing feelings of anger at a "safe" target rather than expressing them where they may be punished.
- **Reaction formation**: expressing oneself in a manner that is directly opposite to the way one truly feels.
- **Compensation**: applying one's skills in a particular area to make up for failure in another area.
- **Repression**: The prevention of threatening ideas from becoming conscious.

C. Physiological Reactions to Stress

There is evidence that work stress is associated with electrocardiogram irregularities and elevated levels of blood pressure, cholesterol, and pulse. Stress has also been associated with the onset of diseases such as respiratory and bacterial infections.

XI. Reducing and Coping with Stress

A. Prepare for Stress

Realistic job previews are effective ways of helping individuals prepare for the stress of their new jobs. Seminars training films, lectures, use of sponsor families, and trail runs are some of the methods used to prepare individuals for the stressors ahead.

B. Job Redesign and Staffing

When jobs are enriched or executives are given needed assistance, stressors can be reduced. Job postings and promotions from within are methods of dealing with stress by allowing current employees to move horizontally or laterally to escape boring or routine work.

C. Social Support

One's spouse, family, and friends as well as co-workers can provide needed support to stress-prone individuals.

D. "Family Friendly" Personnel Policies

In order to reduce stress associated with dual careers, child care, and elder care, many organizations are beginning to institute "family friendly" personnel policies. These policies usually include some combination of formalized social support (newsletters, support groups), material support (corporate daycare), and increased flexibility (flextime, job sharing) to adapt to employee needs.

E. Stress-Management Programs

Some organizations use programs involving meditation, biofeedback, skills training in time management, muscle relaxation exercises and positive thinking techniques to help employees manage work related stress.

F. Fitness Programs

Many organizations feel that physical exercise can reduce stress and counter its negative effects. Hence, many companies now provide gyms, pools, tracks and trainers to aid workers. So far, research indicates that these programs do serve to reduce stress and lower absenteeism. Worker health and job performance have also been improved through these programs.

PRE-TESTING YOUR UNDERSTANDING OF THE CHAPTER

Key Concepts Matching

Match the letter of the key concepts with the appropriate definitions.

A. Accommodating
B. Avoiding
C. Boundary roles
D. Burnout
E. Collaborating
F. Compensation
G. Competing
H. Compromise
I. Conflict stimulation
J. Defense mechanisms
K. Displacement
L. Distributive negotiation
M. Integrative negotiation
N. Interpersonal conflict
O. Job demands-job control model
P. Negotiation
Q. Projection
R. Rationalization
S. Reaction formation
T. Repression
U. Role overload
V. Stress
W. Stress reactions
X. Stressors
Y. Superordinate goals
Z. Type A behavior pattern

______ 1. Environmental events or conditions that have the potential to induce stress.

______ 2. A psychological reaction to the demands inherent in a stressor that has the potential to make a person feel tense or anxious because the person does not feel capable of coping with these demands.

______ 3. The behavioral, psychological, and physiological consequences of stress.

______ 4. Individuals who tend to be aggressive and ambitious with easily aroused hostility, and a sense of time urgency.

______ 5. That which occurs when too many tasks must be performed in too short a time period.

______ 6. Positions in which organizational members are required to interact with members of other organizations with the public.

______ 7. A combination of "emotional exhaustion, depersonalization, and reduced personal accomplishment that can occur among individuals who work with people in some capacity".

______ 8. A conflict management style in which one cooperates with the other party while not asserting one's own interests.

______ 9. Psychological attempts to reduce anxiety associated with stress.

______ 10. The attribution of socially acceptable reasons or motives to one's actions so that they will appear reasonable and sensible, at least to oneself.

______ 11. Attributing one's own undesirable ideas and motives to others so that they seem less negative.

______ 12. Directing feelings of anger at a "safe" target rather than expressing them where they may be punished.

______ 13. Expressing oneself in a manner that is directly opposite to the way one truly feels, rather than risking negative reactions to one's true position.

______ 14. Applying one's skills in a particular area to make up for failure in another area.

______ 15. Preventing threatening ideas from becoming conscious so that the stressor need not be confronted.

______ 16. A conflict management style characterized by low assertiveness of one's own interests and low cooperation with the other party.

______ 17. A conflict management style that maximizes both assertiveness and cooperation.

______ 18. A conflict management style that maximizes assertiveness and minimizes cooperation.

______ 19. A conflict management style that combines intermediate levels of assertiveness and cooperation.

______ 20. A strategy of increasing conflict in order to motivate change.

______ 21. Win-lose negotiation in which a fixed amount of assets is divided between parties.

______ 22. Win-win negotiation that assumes that mutual problem solving can enlarge the assets to be divided between the parties.

______ 23. A process that occurs when one person, group, or organizational subunit frustrates the goal attainment of another.

______ 24. A model that asserts that jobs promote high stress when they make high demands while offering little control over work decisions.

______ 25. A decision-making process among independent parties who do not share identical preferences.

______ 26. Attractive outcomes that can be achieved only by collaboration.

True/False Questions

Circle the letter of the correct answer.

T F 1. Stress itself is not always a bad thing.
T F 2. Superordinate goals are outcomes that can be achieved only by competition.
T F 3. Type A people are usually calm and friendly individuals.
T F 4. The major components of type A behaviors are hostility and repressed anger.
T F 5. When different cultures develop in an organization, overt conflict can result.

T F 6. Poor physical conditions are no longer causes of stress.
T F 7. At times, conflict stimulation will result in changes that benefit the organizations.
T F 8. Secure employment is an important goal for almost everyone.
T F 9. Using addictive substances is a socially acceptable reaction to stress.
T F 10. Projection and rationalization are behavioral reactions to stress.
T F 11. Work stress can cause heart problems and high blood pressure.
T F 12. Realistic job previews are of no value in preparing for stress.
T F 13. The support of others can often help us deal with stress.
T F 14. Fitness programs are a waste of company time.
T F 15. Problem solving is an ineffective way of coping with stress.
T F 16. A common psychological reaction to stress is the use of defense mechanisms.
T F 17. Reaction formation involves the build up of negative emotions.
T F 18. Repression involves preventing hostile individuals from speaking.
T F 19. Increasing salaries is the most effective way of reducing stress.
T F 20. The goal of problem solving is to leave each party in better condition that it was when the conflict began.

Multiple-Choice Questions

Select the correct answer.

_____ 1. Conflict can erupt when parties differ significantly in all of the following *except*
A. power.
B. status.
C. culture.
D. superordinate goals.

_____ 2. An advocate of the use of conflict has suggested that
A. conflict > change > adaptation > survival
B. conflict - change = survival.
C. conflict + change = adaptation.
D. conflict > change.

_____ 3. All of the following are involved in stress management programs *except*
A. meditation.
B. projection.
C. biofeedback training.
D. skills training in time management.

_____ 4. All of the following might be stressors in organizational life except
A. role overload.
B. lack of authority.
C. defense mechanisms.
D. heavy responsibility.

_____ 5. Burnout is most often experienced through
A. boundary-role stressors.
B. operative-level stressors.
C. professional stressors.
D. organizational stressors.

_____ 6. Which of the following career occupants are more apt to encounter boundary role stressors than others?
A. salespeople
B. laboratory technicians
C. installers
D. receptionists

_____ 7. All of the following are examples of general stressors *except*
A. job security.
B. role ambiguity.
C. interpersonal incompatibility.
D. job insecurity.

_____ 8. All of the following might be among behavioral reactions to stress *except*
A. problem solving.
B. use addictive substances.
C. withdrawal.
D. mediations.

_____ 9. All of the following might be employed in problem solving *except*
A. delegation.
B. denial.
C. talking it out.
D. time management.

____ 10. All of the following are common defense mechanisms *except*
A. projection.
B. rationalization.
C. restitution.
D. repression.

POST-TESTING FOR EXAMS

True/False Questions

Circle the letter of the correct answer.

T F 1. Reactions that might help an individual cope with stress can often be harmful to the organization.
T F 2. Type B individuals tend to impatient, aggressive and ambitious.
T F 3. Role overload is a common stressor for workers in American factories.
T F 4. Japanese workers spend more time at work than their European or American counterparts.
T F 5. Professionals in organizations often lack authority despite their expertise.
T F 6. Operatives are individuals who serve in managerial positions in organizations.
T F 7. Burnout is a positive reaction to stress.
T F 8. Jobs lower in an organization seem clearer in method and are less apt to produce ambiguity.
T F 9. The educational level of the North American work force has risen consistently over the years.
T F 10. Withdrawal from the stressor is one of the most basic reactions to stress.

Multiple-Choice Questions

Select the correct answer.

_____ 1. Among the following, the most likely stressor would be
A. a sabbatical.
B. a more responsible job.
C. job tenure.
D. good supervision.

_____ 2. Directing one's feelings of anger at a "safe target" is known as
A. repression.
B. compensation.
C. reaction formation.
D. displacement.

_____ 3. Applying one's skills in a particular area to make up for failure in another area is known as
A. compensation.
B. displacement.
C. repression.
D. reaction formation.

_____ 4. Physical exercise and fitness classes are examples of
A. stress management.
B. job redesign.
C. compensation.
D. problem solving.

_____ 5. The "Family Friendly" organization *doesn't* provide help with
A. elder care.
B. family planning.
C. day care.
D. flexible work schedules

_____ 6. Giving a busy executive an assistant is an example of
A. compensation.
B. job redesign.
C. stress management.
D. problem solving.

_____ 7. Preventing threatening ideas or emotions from becoming conscious is an example of
A. displacement.
B. compensation.
C. repression.
D. reaction formation.

_____ 8. All of the following involve the use of addictive substances *except*
A. smoking.
B. gum chewing.
C. drug use.
D. drinking.

_____ 9. Blaming others for one's own negative ideas is an example of
A. projection.
B. problem solving.
C. displacement.
D. reaction formation.

_____ 10. In conventional arbitration
A. the arbitrator must "split the difference" between the parties.
B. the arbitrator must choose one of the party's final offers.
C. settlements are based entirely on precedent.
D. the arbitrator can choose any outcome.

_____ 11. The groups most likely to experience poor physical working conditions are
A. operative level employees.
B. managers.
C. professionals.
D. top executives.

_____ 12. In negotiation, good advice about "maintaining face" refers to
A. knowing "when to hold 'em and when to fold 'em.".
B. restraining the leakage of nonverbal cues.
C. sustaining credibility.
D. having empathy for your opponent.

_____ 13. All of the following are the consequences of stress *except*
A. psychological consequences.
B. metaphysical consequences.
C. behavioral consequences.
D. physiological consequences.

_____ 14. All of the following are among managerial stressors *except*
A. role overload.
B. heavy responsibility.
C. government interference.
D. executive perquisites.

_____ 15. The area of party overlap in the model of distributive negotiation is called
A. Miller time.
B. the path of least resistance.
C. the settlement range.
D. there is no area of overlap in distributive negotiation.

_____ 16. All of the following might be examples of operative-level stressors *except*
A. easy jobs.
B. high demand-high control jobs.
C. boring jobs.
D. high demand-low control jobs.

_____ 17. The recommended behavioral method of coping with stress is
A. withdrawal.
B. problem solving.
C. use of addictive substances.
D. resignation.

_____ 18. _________ can be an effective conflict management technique when you are wrong.
A. Compromise.
B. Accommodating.
C. Collaborating.
D. Competing.

_____ 19. Inability to get along with one's co-workers is known as
A. type A behavior.
B. rationalization.
C. interpersonal incompatibility.
D. ambiguity.

_____ 20. All of the following occupations are normally thought of as stressful *except*
A. policemen.
B. firemen.
C. emergency room personnel.
D. florists.

Application Situations Exercise

Match the key concepts with the statements that best describe them.

A.	Accommodating	N.	Interpersonal conflict
B.	Avoiding	O.	Job demands-job control model
C.	Boundary roles	P.	Negotiation
D.	Burnout	Q.	Projection
E.	Collaborating	R.	Rationalization
F.	Compensation	S.	Reaction formation
G.	Competing	T.	Repression
H.	Compromise	U.	Role overload
I.	Conflict stimulation	V.	Stress
J.	Defense mechanisms	W.	Stress reactions
K.	Displacement	X.	Stressors
L.	Distributive negotiation	Y.	Superordinate goals
M.	Integrative negotiation	Z.	Type A behavior pattern

_____ 1. His work was making him sick and grouchy.

_____ 2. His job made high demands on him, but gave him little control over important decisions.

_____ 3. He sought to come to a decision with his boss about changes, but knew they had different preferences.

_____ 4. The boss was an aggressive, ambitious individual who was easily angered.

_____ 5. He was hoping that they would reach an agreement that would allow him to maximize both his own assertiveness and his cooperation with his boss.

_____ 6. At worst, he thought that he might have to settle for intermediate levels of both .

_____ 7. But his workplace remained full of conditions that increased his feelings of anxiety and tension.

_____ 8. When he couldn't cope, he felt depersonalized and emotionally exhausted.

_____ 9. He began to feel hostile toward the boss, and blamed the boss for being hostile towards him.

_____10. He finally began to praise the boss and the company in order to conceal his true anger and hostility.

Short Answer Questions

Fill-in the missing word(s).

1. The pressures placed on negotiators by the people they represent are called ____________ .

2. The process of ____________ occurs when a neutral third party helps to facilitate a negotiated agreement .

3. The labor / management agreement that helped to save Chrysler from bankruptcy in 1980 is a good example of introducing ____________.

4. Organizations that take positive steps to help employees with work-family conflict are called ____________.

5. In some cases, the organization and the profession compete for the ____________ of the professional.

6. One way to facilitate integrative negotiation is for the parties to use their ____________ clout to increase resources .

7. Burnout seems to be most common among people who entered their jobs with especially ____________ .

8. Many top corporations have greatly thinned their ____________ ranks in recent years.

9. Defense mechanisms concentrate on ____________ rather than confronting or dealing with the stressor.

10. Research shows that ____________ between organizational departments is particularly important for providing good customer service.

ANSWER SHEET FOR CHAPTER 14

PRE-TESTING YOUR UNDERSTANDING OF THE CHAPTER

Key Concepts Matching

1. X	2. V	3. W	4. Z	5. U	6. C	7. D	8. A	9. J	10. R
11. Q	12. K	13. S	14. F	15. T	16. B	17. E	18. G	19. H	20. I
21. L	22. M	23. N	24. O	25. P	26. Y				

True/False Questions

1. T	2. F	3. F	4. T	5. T	6. F	7. T	8. T	9. F	10. F
11. T	12. F	13. T	14. F	15. F	16. T	17. F	18. F	19. F	20. T

Multiple-Choice Questions

1. D	2. A	3. B	4. C	5. A	6. B	7. A	8. D	9. B	10. C

POST-TESTING FOR EXAMS

True/False Questions

1. T	2. F	3. F	4. T	5. T	6. F	7. F	8. T	9. T	10. T

Multiple-Choice Questions

1. B	2. D	3. A	4. A	5. B	6. B	7. C	8. B	9. A	10. D
11. A	12. D	13. B	14. D	15. C	16. B	17. B	18. B	19. C	20. D

Application Situations Exercise

1. W	2. O	3. P	4. Z	5. E	6. H	7. X	8. D	9. Q	10. S

Short Answer Questions

1. constituency effects	2. mediation	3. superordinate goals	4. family-friendly
5. loyalty	6. combined	7. high ideals	8. executives
9. anxiety reduction	10. collaboration		

CASE STUDY

WORK/FAMILY INTEGRATION STRESS

At the weekly manager's meeting, Alex, the Director of the systems group, commended Peter on behalf of the group for his recent performance on the reorganization project. Peter was pleased to receive this recognition from his colleagues. Alex then announced to the group that he was recommending Peter to the Executive Committee to lead the group on the new project . The team all agreed and supported the Director's recommendation.

Peter thanked the team for their confidence and support. He knew that this would be good for his career. But, he was also sick with the news and found it difficult to show enthusiasm. The reorganization project had required an enormous amount of time and energy from him. During the final 4 months, Peter worked 7 days a week and an average of 12 to 14 hours a day. He was drained physically and emotionally. In addition, there was every indication that the long hours were having a profoundly negative effect on his family. During the last month, the issue had come to a head when his 3 year old son had been briefly hospitalized after an accident at his daycare. He had slipped off a piece of equipment in the playground, caught his lower lip on a rough edge and as a result had ripped the lip partly off his face! The injury had required plastic surgery to repair the damage. His partner, Annie had been distraught. She had called him about the accident and promptly left work herself to take their son Ryan to the hospital.

Peter was also upset, but felt that he could not leave work right away. He had made commitments that couldn't be changed. When he was given this project by his previous Director, Will, he was told that it was critical for the department. There was a lot on the line and hitting the time lines wouldn't be easy. "If we screw up this one we're dead meat!" Will had yelled. Will had a reputation for giving this kind of message to his team leaders. He had the idea that by doing so, his managers would rise to the challenge and prove that they could beat impossible odds. In some way, it excited Peter to prove that the could beat the odds. He also knew what had happened to a fellow team leader, Adele when she had refused a project that was similarly "challenging". She had argued that as a single parent, she couldn't be away from her family for the extended hours and weekend work that the job would require. She enjoyed her work, but couldn't see why every project had to be run under such crisis conditions. Will told her, "Give what's required or put in for a transfer. Systems isn't a group for the faint or weak. Work and family are separate concerns and employees who are serious about their work and committed to the company don't need to have that explained to them!"

But Peter had still been really worried about little Ryan and knew that Annie was expecting him to meet her at the hospital. He had called his team to an emergency meeting and explained what had happened. His team was sympathetic and offered to cover the last part of the day.

Peter and Annie stayed with the child most of the night to soothe him as he was frightened and in pain. Once the child was sleeping the couple returned home to get some sleep. Early the next morning Annie returned to the hospital and Peter to the office. Peter then was faced

---

Source: Case written by Deborah Hurst, Faculty of Business Administration, Memorial University of Newfoundland, 1995. Used with permission.

with catching up with events from the previous day in addition to what he had planned for the current day. He dug in, but it was nearly midnight when he finally returned home. He learned as he opened the door that Ryan had had the surgery and was doing well. But he also learned that Annie was not thrilled to have shouldered the difficult day by herself and she laid this out to Peter in no uncertain terms. She also told him that Ryan wouldn't be going back to the daycare right away and that she didn't think she would be able to take another day off of work. "I think it's your turn," she said. "Don't think you're the only one with work piling up on their desk!"

He had refused saying that the reorganization project was in a very critical stage and the team had meetings scheduled all day the following day to deal with some of the most pressing concerns. A somewhat heated discussion had ensued and Annie had reluctantly agreed to take another day off work. The problem appeared to have been dealt with and Peter was happy to put it behind him.

But just one week prior to the end of the project, Annie had announced to Peter that if things didn't improve between them once the reorganization project was finished, she no longer wanted to continue in their relationship. "Over the last year, I could count the times we've sat down for a meal together on one hand. We don't see you on weekends. You don't take any responsibility for any of the household maintenance or childcare and it was pretty clear from your actions when Ryan got hurt just where your priorities lie." In Annie's opinion, if Peter cared so much more for his job then his family, then that would be what she would leave him with. She was at the end of her rope and he clearly had a choice to make.

1. Describe what stressors are active here.

2. Use the various modes of managing conflict to examine the confrontation between Peter and Annie. Can you suggest an improved approach?

3. Is the conflict between Peter and Annie amenable to negotiation? How would you suggest that they proceed?

4. Is this just Peter and Annie's problem? Does the organization have any responsibility here? How could the organization help?

5. As Peter, what will you do?

6. As Alex, how will you respond to Peter if he declines to accept the new project?

CHAPTER 15

ORGANIZATIONAL STRUCTURE

LEARNING OBJECTIVES

- DEFINE ORGANIZATIONAL STRUCTURE AND EXPLAIN HOW IT CORRESPONDS TO DIVISION OF LABOR.
- DISCUSS THE RELATIVE MERITS OF VARIOUS FORMS OF DEPARTMENTATION.
- REVIEW THE MORE BASIC AND MORE ELABORATE MEANS OF ACHIEVING ORGANIZATIONAL COORDINATION.
- DISCUSS THE NATURE AND CONSEQUENCES OF TRADITIONAL STRUCTURAL CHARACTERISTICS.
- EXPLAIN THE DISTINCTION BETWEEN ORGANIC AND MECHANISTIC STRUCTURES
- DISCUSS THE EMERGENCE OF NETWORK ORGANIZATIONS.
- REVIEW IMPORTANT CONSIDERATIONS CONCERNING DOWNSIZING.

KEY CONCEPTS

Organizational structure

Differentiation

Functional departmentation

Product departmentation

Matrix departmentation

Geographic departmentation

Customer departmentation

Hybrid departmentation

Coordination

Integration

Liaison role

Task force

Integrators

Span of Control

Flat organization

Tall organization

Formalization

Centralization

Complexity

Mechanistic structures

Organic structures

Network organization

Downsizing

CHAPTER SUMMARY

Key concepts are identified by **bold** *faced type.*

I. A Prologue: The Role of Organizational Structure

A firm could be well staffed with motivated members and properly led groups, but it could still fail if worker efforts are divided and uncoordinated.

Organizational structure intervenes between goals and accomplishments and thus influences organizational effectiveness.

II. What Is Organizational Structure?

Organizational structure is the manner in which an organization divides its labor into specific tasks and achieves coordination among these tasks.

III. The Division and Coordination of Labor

A. Vertical Division of Labor

The vertical division of labor is concerned primarily with apportioning authority for planning and decision making.

The issues of autonomy and control, and of communication are involved in the vertical division of labor. Thus, labor must be divided vertically enough to ensure proper control but not so much as to make vertical communication and coordination impossible.

B. Horizontal Division of Labor

The horizontal division of labor involves grouping the basic tasks that must be performed into jobs and then into departments so that the organizations can achieve its goals.

Job design is an important component in the horizontal division of labor. Also important is **differentiation** which is the tendency for managers in separate functions or departments to differ in terms of goals, time spans, and interpersonal styles.

C. Departmentation

One way of grouping jobs is to assign them to departments. This process called departmentation can be divided into several types:

- **Functional departmentation**: employees with closely related skills and responsibilities are assigned to the same department.
- **Product departmentation**: departments are formed on the basis of a particular product, product line, or service.
- **Matrix departmentation**: employees remain members of a functional department while also reporting to a product or project manager.
- **Geographic departmentation**: relatively self-contained units deliver the organization's products or services in specific geographic territories.
- **Customer departmentation**: relatively self-contained units deliver the organization's products or services to specific customer groups.
- **Hybrid departmentation**: the structure is based on some mixture of functional, product, geographic, or customer departmentation.

D. Basic Methods of Coordinating Divided Labor

Coordination is the process of facilitating timing, communication, and feedback.

The five basic methods include:
- Direct supervision in which designated supervisors coordinate the work of their subordinates.
- Standardization of work processes in which the jobs are so routine that the technology itself provides a means of coordination.
- Standardization of outputs can achieve coordination by ensuring that the work meets certain physical and economic standards.
- Standardization of skills can achieve coordination when technicians and professionals know what to expect of each other because of their standard training.
- Mutual adjustment relies upon informal communications to coordinate tasks.

E. Other Methods of Coordination

Integration is the process of obtaining coordination across different departments. The three basic methods are:

- **Liaison roles**: A person is assigned to help achieve coordination between his or her department and another department.
- **Task forces**: Temporary groups set up to solve coordination problems across several departments.
- **Integrators**: Organizational members permanently assigned to facilitate coordination between departments.

IV. Traditional Structural Characteristics

A. Span of Control

The **span of control** is the number of subordinates supervised by a manager. The larger the spans the less potential there is for direct supervision. Also, at upper corporate levels, spans are smaller than at lower levels.

B. Flat Versus Tall

Flat organization refers to an organization with relatively few levels in its hierarchy of authority.

Tall organization refers to an organization with relatively many levels in its hierarchy of authority.

C. Formalization

Formalization refers to the extent to which work roles are highly defined by the organization. Detailed job descriptions and thick procedure manuals are evidence of the trend.

D. Centralization

Centralization refers to the extent to which decision making power is localized in a particular part of the organization. In the most centralized organization, the power for all key decisions would rest in a single individual, such as the president.

E. Complexity

Complexity refers to the extent to which organizations divide labor vertically, horizontally, and geographically. The essential characteristic of complexity is variety, and as an organization grows in complexity it has more kinds of people performing more kinds of tasks in more places.

V. Employee Reactions to Structural Characteristics

There is no simple association between tallness or flatness and job satisfaction, although formalization often prompts job dissatisfaction for people occupying boundary roles.

Studies also indicate that spans that are too large can result in communication problems, while very small spans might reduce employee autonomy and provoke dissatisfaction.

VI. Summarizing Structure - Organic versus Mechanistic

Mechanistic structures are organizational structures characterized by tallness, specialization, centralization, and formalization. **Organic structures** are organizational structures characterized by flatness, low specialization, low formalization, and decentralization.

In general, more mechanistic structures are called for when an organization's environment is more stable and its technology is more routine. Organic structures tend to work better when the environment is less stable and the technology is less routine.

VII. Network Organizations

In **network organizations**, liaisons exist between specialist organizations that rely strongly on market mechanisms for coordination. Network organizations may take either stable or dynamic forms. The key advantage of the network organization is its flexibility and adaptability.

VIII. The Impact of Size

A. Size and Structure

In general, large organizations are more complex and less centralized than small organizations. Larger organizations have greater horizontal specialization and require more integrators and other coordination functions. Large organizations also rely more on formalization and often display greater vertical and geographic complexity.

B. Downsizing

During the 1980's and 1990's, millions of jobs have disappeared as organizations have attempted to increase efficiency and cut costs in an era of global competition, government deregulation, corporate raiding, changing consumer preferences, and advancing technologies. **Downsizing** is the intentional reduction of workforce size with the goal of improving organizational efficiency or effectiveness.

Downsizing usually results in a different organization, not just a smaller one. That is because there are different forces at work than those which drive growth. Also, white collar managerial and staff jobs have been hit hardest changing how organizations are structured. Downsizing is often accompanied by reducing horizontal and vertical complexity. Organizations become flatter and self-managed teams take over supervisory and quality control functions.

But there can be a downside to downsizing as well. Organizations have a tendency to become more formalized and centralized when threatened which works against needed flexibility in times of change. Firms may also be over-zealous in their cutting and end up sub-contracting work to consultants which may be both inferior in quality and more expensive. Removing levels from the organization may be a good idea, provided that it doesn't overload the remaining staff and that everyone is comfortable with the greater levels of delegation required. Finally, the process of downsizing must be considered. Surprising people with workforce cuts is likely to result in low morale, reduced productivity, and continuing distrust of management.

IX. A Footnote: Symptoms of Structural Problems

A list of symptoms of structural problems would include bad job design, the right hand doesn't know what the left is doing, persistent conflict between departments, slow response times, decisions made with incomplete information, and the proliferation of committees.

If an organization has too many of these symptoms, a review of organizational structure may be necessary.

PRE-TESTING YOUR UNDERSTANDING OF THE CHAPTER

Key Concepts Matching

Match the letter of the key concept with the appropriate definitions.

A. Centralization
B. Complexity
C. Coordination
D. Customer departmentation
E. Differentiation
F. Downsizing
G. Flat organization
H. Formalization
I. Functional departmentation
J. Geographic departmentation
K. Hybrid departmentation
L. Integration
M. Integrators
N. Liaison role
O. Matrix departmentation
P. Mechanistic structures
Q. Network organization
R. Organic structures
S. Organizational structure
T. Product departmentation
U. Span of Control
V. Tall organization
W. Task force

_____ 1. The manner in which an organization divides its labor into specific tasks and achieves coordination among these tasks.

_____ 2. The tendency for managers in separate functions or departments to differ in terms of goals, time spans, and interpersonal styles.

_____ 3. The location of workers with closely related skills and responsibilities in the same department.

_____ 4. The formation of departments on the basis of a particular product, product line, or service.

_____ 5. Relatively self-contained units delivering the organization's products or services in specific geographic territories.

_____ 6. Relatively self-contained units delivering the organization's products or services to specific customer groups.

_____ 7. Departmentation which involves a combination of other departmentation structures.

_____ 8. A process of facilitating timing, communication, and feedback.

_____ 9. The process of obtaining coordination across different departments.

_____10. A person in one department who is assigned to achieve coordination with another department.

_____ 11. Temporary groups set up to solve coordination problems across several departments.

_____ 12. Organizational members who are permanently installed between two departments that are in clear need of coordination.

_____ 13. The number of subordinates supervised by a superior.

_____ 14. An organization with relatively few levels in its hierarchy of authority.

_____ 15. An organization with relatively many levels in its hierarchy of authority.

_____ 16. The extent to which work roles are highly defined by the organization.

_____ 17. The extent to which decision-making power is localized in a particular part of the organization.

_____ 18. The extent to which organizations divide labor vertically, horizontally, and geographically.

_____ 19. The intentional reduction of workforce size with the goal of improving organizational efficiency.

_____ 20. Structures tending toward tallness, narrow spans, specialization, and high formalization.

_____ 21. Structures which rely upon less formalization, centralization and specialization.

_____ 22. Employees remain members of a functional department while also reporting to a product manager.

_____ 23. Liaisons between specialist organizations that rely strongly on market mechanisms for coordination.

True/False Questions

Circle the letter of the correct answer.

T F 1. The vertical division of labor apportions authority for planning and decision making.

T F 2. The horizontal division of labor involves grouping the basic tasks into jobs and departments so that the organization can achieve its goals.

T F 3. Differentiation is an unnatural and needless consequence of the vertical division of labor.

T F 4. Under functional departmentation workers with the same skills are located in different departments.

T F 5. Under customer departmentation different organizational units deliver its products or services to different customer groups.

T F 6. Direct supervision is a very basic form of coordination.

T F 7. Mutual adjustment relies upon informal communication to coordinate tasks.

T F 8. Integrators are individuals who investigate problems within departments.

T F 9. The larger the span of control, the more potential there is for direct supervision.

T F 10. A flat organization is a boring work place.

T F 11. Formalization refers to the extent to which work roles are defined by the organization.

T F 12. Centralization refers to the diffusion of decision-making power.

T F 13. A very complex organization will usually be tall.

T F 14. In general, large organizations are more complex than small ones.

T F 15. There is great correlation between tallness and flatness and job satisfaction.

T F 16. Some organizations have found that downsizing and contracting work out can be more expensive than using in-house staff..

T F 17. Mechanistic structures are the machines used in production.

T F 18. CBS, NBC and FOX are examples of network organizations.
T F 19. Organic structures are plants used to enrich executive offices.
T F 20. Downsizing attempts to shrink an organization's size without fundamentally changing it.

Multiple-Choice Questions

Select the correct answer.

_____ 1. All of the following are methods of coordinating divided labor except for standardization of
A. work processes.
B. work inputs.
C. work outputs.
D. skills.

_____ 2. All of the following are methods of achieving integration *except*
A. integrators.
B. task forces.
C. liaison roles.
D. negotiators.

_____ 3. All of the following methods of operation are more likely to be formed in formal organizations than in informal ones *except*
A. rules.
B. standard procedures.
C. flexible decision making.
D. regulations.

_____ 4. New United Motor Manufacturing (NUMMI) is operated by
A. Nissan.
B. Toyota.
C. General Motors.
D. Toyota and General Motors.

_____ 5. All of the following might be symptoms of structural problems *except*
A. bad job design.
B. job enrichment.
C. slow response times.
D. a proliferation of committees.

_____ 6. The two types of network organizations are
A. stable and dynamic.
B. mechanistic and organic.
C. tall and flat.
D. product and matrix.

_____ 7. All of the following are traditional structural characteristics *except*
A. flat versus tall.
B. formalization.
C. broad versus thin.
D. complexity.

_____ 8. All of the following are traditional methods of departmentation *except*
A. functional departmentation.
B. product departmentation.
C. customer departmentation.
D. ecological departmentation.

_____ 9. All of the following are the basic dimensions to the division of labor *except*
A. vertical division.
B. loose division.
C. horizontal division.
D. rigid division.

_____ 10. All of the following are advantages of functional departmentation *except*
A. poor coordination with the organization.
B. efficiency.
C. enhanced career ladders.
D. better communication within given departments.

POST-TESTING FOR EXAMS

True/False Questions

Circle the letter of the correct answer.

T F 1. Slow response times are symptoms of persistent conflict.

T F 2. A proliferation of committees is a sign of a good organizational structure.

T F 3. To achieve its goals, an organization has to divide labor among its members and then coordinate what has been divided.

T F 4. When faced with serious decline, organizations have a tendency to become more mechanistic.

T F 5. Titles are usually used to designate levels of command.

T F 6. As levels increase in a hierarchy, managers have more and more authority over more and more matters.

T F 7. As labor is divided vertically, communication becomes easier to achieve.

T F 8. As organizations grow horizontal, division of labor usually becomes more necessary.

T F 9. Functional departments are the least efficient types in companies.

T F 10. Hybrid departmentation involves ad hoc units set up to perform particular tasks.

Multiple-Choice Questions

Select the correct answer.

_____ 1. A hardware division of a computer firm is an example of
A. functional departmentation.
B. product departmentation.
C. hybrid departmentation.
D. differentiation.

_____ 2. All of the following organizations might exhibit geographic departmentation *except*
A. oil companies.
B. national retailers.
C. insurance companies.
D. neighborhood bakeries.

_____ 3. A good example of standardization of work processes is found in
A. automobile assembly lines.
B. operating rooms.
C. retail stores.
D. colleges.

_____ 4. Integrators are useful for dealing with conflicts within all of the following situations *except* when
A. departments are interdependent.
B. the environment is unambiguous.
C. the environment is ambiguous.
D. departments have diverse goals and orientations.

_____ 5. Evidence of formalization include all of the following *except*
A. written job descriptions.
B. thick procedures manuals.
C. detailed written instructions.
D. oral work rules.

_____ 6. Complexity refers to the extent to which organizations are divided in all of the following ways *except*
A. ecologically.
B. vertically.
C. horizontally.
D. geographically.

_____ 7. The individual firms that make up a network organization do all of the following *except*
A. share information.
B. customize their services to the network.
C. compete with each other.
D. pursue their own individual specializations.

_____ 8. One way to retain control as size increases the amount of decentralization in an organization is through
A. differentiation.
B. formalization.
C. matrix departmentation.
D. coordination.

_____ 9. The W. L. Gore company is successful because of its system of
A. non-management.
B. bureaucracy.
C. vertical integration.
D. horizontal integration.

_____ 10. Organic structure includes all of the following *except*
A. wide span of control.
B. low position-based authority.
C. wide range of compensation.
D. narrow range of skill levels.

_____ 11. All of the following workers are apt to be affected by formalization *except*
A. salespeople.
B. nurses.
C. courthouse desk clerks.
D. welfare officers.

_____ 12. Mutual adjustment relies upon _______________ to coordinate tasks.
A. upward communication
B. downward communication
C. informal communication
D. formal communication

_____ 13. All of the following are basic methods of job design *except*
A. forming an ABC department in which all workers do ABC work.
B. forming a separate A department, B department and C department.
C. forming an ABC department in which workers do any work they wish.
D. forming a separate A department, B department and C department.

_____ 14. In the vertical division of labor, the top position is usually held by the
A. supervisor.
B. president.
C. foreman.
D. manager.

_____ 15. All of the following are disadvantages of functional departmentation *except*
A. poor coordination and slow responses to organizational problems.
B. over-specialization.
C. open conflict between departments.
D. enhanced communication within departments.

_____ 16. All of the following are possible disadvantages to product departmentation *except*
A. economies of scale might be threatened.
B. flexibility.
C. professional development might suffer.
D. departments might work at cross purposes.

_____ 17. Surgeons, nurses, and anesthesiologists working together are exhibiting
A. standardization of skills.
B. standardization of outputs.
C. standardization of work processes.
D. direct supervision.

_____ 18. Downsizing has resulted in disproportionate reductions in
A. unionized jobs.
B. white collar managerial and staff jobs.
C. technical specialists.
D. senior executives.

_____ 19. As a rule, organic structures rely on all of the following techniques *except*
A. a tight bureaucracy.
B. informal command structures.
C. informal communication.
D. less specialization.

_____ 20. As a result of reading this chapter you should realize that
A. experts know how to organize all companies effectively.
B. there is no "one best way" to organize.
C. computers can solve organizational problems.
D. all successful firms have organized in the same fashion.

Application Situations Exercise

Match the key concepts with the statements that best describe them.

A. Centralization
B. Complexity
C. Coordination
D. Customer departmentation
E. Differentiation
F. Downsizing
G. Flat organization
H. Formalization
I. Functional departmentation
J. Geographic departmentation
K. Hybrid departmentation
L. Integration
M. Integrators
N. Liaison role
O. Matrix departmentation
P. Mechanistic structures
Q. Network organization
R. Organic structures
S. Organizational structure
T. Product departmentation
U. Span of Control
V. Tall organization
W. Task force

_____ 1. Our company set up a department arranged to work only on cellular telephones.

_____ 2. We arranged other departments to deliver their products mostly to physicians and hospitals.

_____ 3. We were worried that senior management was thinking of an intentional reduction of workforce size to improve efficiency and effectiveness.

_____ 4. So we argued that the real problem was the process of facilitating timing, communication, and feedback among work tasks.

_____ 5. After some disputes, the company appointed one person to achieve coordination and cooperation with other departments.

_____ 6. We obviously would have liked a structure with less formalization, less centralization, and more flexibility.

_____ 7. Our boss had twelve people reporting directly to her.

_____ 8. But the company had only five levels of authority.

_____ 9. Our biggest rival had twenty levels of authority.

_____ 10. But our biggest worry was a new organization in the industry made up of liaisons among several specialist firms.

Short Answer Questions

Fill-in the missing word(s).

1. Formalization is a particular problem for _______________ workers who must deal directly with outsiders.

2. As a rule, size is associated with _______________ complexity.

3. The essential characteristic of complexity is _______________ .

4. Flatness versus tallness is an index of the _______________ division of labor.

5. The goals of marketing managers must be _______________ to the organization and oriented toward the marketplace.

6. An organization with Pacific, Prairie, Central and Atlantic regions is probably using geographic ___________.

7. Strict specialization and strong formalization are often _______________ with human needs for growth and achievement.

8. Matrix departmentation provides a good _______________ between product and functional demands.

9. The larger the span of control, the less _______________ there is for coordination by direct supervision.

10. In a network organization, various functions are often coordinated by _______________ mechanisms.

ANSWER SHEET FOR CHAPTER 15

PRE-TESTING YOUR UNDERSTANDING OF THE CHAPTER

Key Concepts Matching

1. S	2. E	3. I	4. T	5. J	6. D	7. K	8. C	9. L	10. N
11. W	12. M	13. U	14. G	15. V	16. N	17. A	18. B	19. F	20. P
21. R	22. O	23. Q							

True/False Questions

1. T	2. T	3. F	4. F	5. F	6. T	7. T	8. F	9. F	10. F
11. T	12. F	13. T	14. T	15. F	16. T	17. F	18. F	19. F	20. F

Multiple-Choice Questions

1. B	2. D	3. C	4. D	5. B	6. A	7. C	8. D	9. B	10. A

POST-TESTING FOR EXAMS

True/False Questions

1. T	2. F	3. T	4. T	5. T	6. F	7. F	8. T	9. F	10. F

Multiple-Choice Questions

1. B	2. D	3. A	4. B	5. D	6. A	7. C	8. B	9. A	10. C
11. B	12. C	13. C	14. B	15. D	16. B	17. A	18. B	19. A	20. B

Application Situations Exercise

1. T	2. D	3. F	4. C	5. N	6. R	7. U	8. G	9. V	10. Q

Short Answer Questions

1. boundary role	2. increased	3. variety	4. vertical	5. external
6. departmentation	7. incompatible	8. balance	9. potential	10. market

EXERCISE FOR CHAPTER 15

ORGANIZING XYZ PAPER COMPANY

Advanced preparation: To be completed before class.

XYZ does not have an organization chart. Below is a list of its management titles. On a non-book page, departmentalize (using the letters A-U) the firm by assigning tasks to be accomplished by forming a division of labor and grouping related activities. Afterward, write out the organization chart on the next page placing both the title and letter in each box.

A. sales manager
B. accountants
C. engineering department
D. vice president-personnel
E. president
F. credit manager
G. product A manager (facial tissue, paper towels, etc.)
H. product B supervisor
I. vice president-finance
J. advertising manager
K. vice president-manufacturing
L. quality control manager
M. product A supervisor
N. sales supervisor product B
O. purchasing manager
P. training manager
Q. data processing manager
R. vice president-marketing
S. product B manager (writing paper, envelopes, etc.)
T. sales supervisor product B
U. assistant to the president

After completing your organization chart, answer the following questions.

1. Which type of departmentation is used?
2. Does there appear to be standardization of work processes, outputs, and skills at XYZ?
3. What type of coordination methods would you recommend to XYZ management?
4. Determine the span of control for the each manager.
5. Is your structure flat or tall?
6. Do you think XYZ uses formalization? How?
7. Discuss the vertical and horizontal complexity of XYZ.

XYZ's Organization Chart

Draw your organization chart below

Copyright 1988, Robert N. Lussier, reprinted by permission

CHAPTER 16

ENVIRONMENT, STRATEGY, AND TECHNOLOGY

LEARNING OBJECTIVES

- DISCUSS THE COMPONENTS OF AN ORGANIZATION'S EXTERNAL ENVIRONMENT.
- EXPLAIN HOW ENVIRONMENTAL UNCERTAINTY AND RESOURCE DEPENDENCE AFFECT WHAT HAPPENS IN ORGANIZATIONS.
- UNDERSTAND HOW ORGANIZATIONAL STRUCTURE CAN SERVE AS A STRATEGIC RESPONSE TO ENVIRONMENTAL DEMANDS.
- EXPLAIN HOW VERTICAL INTEGRATION, MERGERS, ACQUISITIONS, STRATEGIC ALLIANCES, INTERLOCKING DIRECTORATES, AND THE ESTABLISHMENT OF LEGITIMACY REFLECT STRATEGIC RESPONSES.
- DESCRIBE THE BASIC DIMENSIONS OF ORGANIZATIONAL TECHNOLOGY.
- EXPLAIN HOW ORGANIZATIONS MUST MATCH STRUCTURE TO TECHNOLOGY.
- DISCUSS THE IMPACT OF ADVANCED INFORMATION TECHNOLOGY ON JOB DESIGN AND ORGANIZATIONAL STRUCTURE.

KEY CONCEPTS

External environment

Open systems

Interest groups

Environmental uncertainty

Resource dependence

Strategy

Vertical integration

Strategic alliances

Interlocking directorates

Technology

Technological routineness

Technological interdependence

Pooled interdependence

Sequential interdependence

Reciprocal interdependence

Advanced information technology

CHAPTER SUMMARY

Key concepts are identified by **bold** *faced type.*

I. The External Environment of Organizations

The **external environment** consists of conditions and events surrounding the organization that influence its activities.

The external environment has a great influence on organizations, and conditions are constantly changing.

A. Organizations As Open Systems

Open systems are systems that take inputs from the external environment, transform some of these inputs, and send them back into the external environment as outputs. This concept is important because it sensitizes us to the needs for organizations to cope with environmental demands on both the input and the output side.

B. Components of the External Environment

There are many components of the external environment:

- The general economy can affect organizations which would profit from an upturn or suffer from a downturn.
- All organizations need customers for their goods and services.
- Organizations are dependent on suppliers for labor, raw materials, equipment, and component parts.
- Successful organizations devote considerable energy to maintaining the activities of competition, while attaining resources, customers, and supplies.
- Organizations cannot ignore the social and political events that occur around then.
- The environment contains a variety of technologies that are useful for achieving organizational goals.

Another factor in an organization would be **interest groups**: parties or organizations other than direct competitors who have some vested interest in how an organization is managed.

C. The Environment of Saturn

General Motors used several technological advances in the development of Saturn. It also used strict quality control, and it forged an innovative contract with the United Auto Workers. GM felt that it could produce a new car that would compete with Japanese imports and not with its own models.

D. Environmental Uncertainty

Environmental uncertainty is a condition that exists when an environment is vague, difficult to diagnose, and unpredictable. Uncertainty depends upon a combination of the environment's *complexity* (from simple environments to complex environments) and the environment's *rate of change* (from static environments to dynamic environments).

- *Simple environments* involve relatively few important sectors, and these are fairly similar to each other.
- *Complex environments* contain a large number of dissimilar sectors to which managers must pay attention.
- *Static environments* have elements which remain fairly stable over time. Predictable cyclicality such as seasonal sales would also be seen as "stable" in a larger sense.
- *Dynamic environments* are in a constant state of change and the change is unpredictable and irregular.

E. Resource Dependence

Resource dependence refers to the dependency of organizations upon environmental inputs such as capital, raw materials, and human resources. Hence, organizations must develop strategies for managing both resource dependence and environmental uncertainty.

II. Strategic Responses to Uncertainty and Resource Dependence

Strategy is the process by which top executives seek to cope with the constraints and opportunities posed by the organization's environment. Organizations devote much time and effort to this ongoing process.

A. Organizational Structure As A Strategic Response

Studies by Lawrence and Lorsch indicate a close relationship between environment, structure, and effectiveness. In general, organizations do tailor structure to strategy in coping with the environment. In ongoing organizations, however, structure sometimes dictates strategy formulation.

B. Other Forms of Strategic Response

Among the other forms of strategic response organizations can take are:

- **Vertical integration** or the strategy of formally taking control of sources of supply and distribution.
- Mergers and acquisitions which involve the takeover or joining with other organizations.
- **Strategic alliances** which involve actively cooperative relationships between legally separate organizations.
- **Interlocking directorates** in which one person serves as a director on two or more boards.
- Establishing legitimacy by conforming to established industry practices, bringing high profile people onto the board of directors, or making visible responses to social issues

All of these are methods organizations might use to cope with environmental uncertainty. Which method is chosen will depend upon the organizations structure and its strategy.

III. The Technologies of Organizations

A. Technology

Technology can be defined as the activities, equipment, and knowledge that are necessary to turn organizational inputs into desired outputs. The concepts of technology and environment are closely related. Also, different parts of an organization rely on different technologies, just as they respond to different aspects of the environment as a whole.

B. Basic Dimensions of Technology

According to Charles Perrow, **technological routineness** refers to the extent to which exceptions and problems affect the task of converting inputs into outputs:

- *Exceptions*: An organization that uses standardized inputs to produce standardized outputs confronts few exceptions compared with one that uses varied inputs and produces varied outputs. Technology is less routine as exceptions increase.
- *Problems*: When exceptions occur, are the problems difficult to figure out? That is, can employees use programmed decision-making? Technology becomes less routine as problems become less analyzable.

These dimensions can be arranged or classified into:

- *Craft technologies* which deal with standard inputs and outputs.
- *Routine technologies* such as assembly line operations.
- *Nonroutine technologies* which deal with exceptional inputs or outputs.
- *Engineering technologies* which encounter many exceptions of input or required output, but deal with these exceptions by standardized responses.

James Thompson has worked on the concept of **technological interdependence** which is the extent to which organizational subunits depend on each other for resources, raw materials, or information.
His classifications include:

- *Mediating technologies* which operate under **pooled interdependence.** This is a condition in which organizational subunits are dependent upon the pooled resources generated by other units but are otherwise fairly independent. Example: taxi company.
- *Long-linked technologies* which operate under **sequential interdependence.** This is a condition in which organizational subunits are dependent upon the resources generated by units that precede them in a sequence of work. Example: assembly line.
- *Intensive technologies* which operate under **reciprocal interdependence.** This is a condition in which organizational subunits must engage in considerable interplay and mutual feedback to accomplish a task. Example: hospital operating room.

C. Structuring To Cope With Technology

The most famous study of the relationship between technology and structure was performed by Joan Woodward. She classified technologies as:

- *Unit* which produces small units or batches. e.g., locomotive manufacturing
- *Mass* which produces large batches or mass production. e.g., bakeries
- *Process* which continuously transforms inputs into outputs. e.g., petroleum refineries

In general, her studies indicate that organizational structures do vary with technology and that this variance is related to organizational effectiveness. Successful firms with unit and process technologies relied on organic structures, while successful firms engaged in mass production relied upon mechanistic structures.

IV. Implications of Advanced Information Technology

Advanced information technology refers to the generation, aggregation, storage, modification, and speedy transmission of information made possible by the advent of computers and related devices. Today it is widely used and is becoming steadily more important in the corporate world.

A. The Two Faces of Advanced Technology

In general, information technology gives companies choices about how to organize work. These choices may allow managers to slash jobs, de-skill and ceaselessly monitor employees or they may support improved productivity, superior decision-making and enriched jobs. Technology is never completely neutral, but much of its impact is determined by how it is used.

B. Advanced Manufacturing Technology

Companies are relying more and more on computer intelligence and memory. This technology is being used for a variety of tasks. This technology is being integrated into other advanced technologies used by the organization.

The CAD/CAM system or computer-aided-design/computer-aided-manufacturing system is an example of the applied use of advanced information technology.

This technology is also applied to organizational structure and has caused a shift to flatter, more organic structures. When applied to job design, this technology can reduce worker control and water down existing skills or provide the ability for employees to have greater input into their jobs and enrich skills.

C. Advanced Office Technology

Most office technology systems are used for text processing, communization, information storage and retrieval, analysis of information, and administrative support.

This technology has impacted organizational structure by tending to create more flatness in companies and reducing the need for supervisors and middle management personnel.

This technology can also affect job design, although the effects on the quality of working life vary with job status. Clerks and secretaries are affected the most by losing jobs or having to learn new skills.

Word processors and video display screens have caused eyestrain, muscle strain, and stress symptoms. On the whole, however, professionals and managers have taken to advanced office technology fairly well.

Research is still ongoing about the long-term effects of advanced office technology, so it may be years before we can tell whether it was a blessing or a bane to organizations.

PRE-TESTING YOUR UNDERSTANDING OF THE CHAPTER

Key Concepts Matching

Match the letter of the key concepts with the appropriate definitions.

A. Advanced information technology
B. Environmental uncertainty
C. External environment
D. Interest groups
E. Interlocking directorates
F. Open system
G. Pooled interdependence
H. Reciprocal interdependence
I. Resource dependence
J. Sequential interdependence
K. Strategic alliances
L. Strategy
M. Technological interdependence
N. Technological routineness
O. Technology
P. Vertical integration

_____ 1. Those events and conditions surrounding the organization that influence its activities.

_____ 2. Systems that take inputs from the external environment, transform some of those inputs, and send them back into the external environment as outputs.

_____ 3. Parties or organizations other than direct competitors who have some vested interest in how an organization is managed.

_____ 4. That which exists when an environment is vague, difficult to diagnose, and unpredictable.

_____ 5. Dependence upon resources that are necessary for organizational survival.

_____ 6. The process by which top executives seek to cope with the constraints and opportunities posed by the organization's environment.

_____ 7. The strategy of formally taking control of sources of supply and distribution.

_____ 8. Actively cooperative relationships between legally separate organizations.

_____ 9. A condition that exists when a person serves as a director on two or more boards.

_____ 10. The activities, equipment, and knowledge that are necessary to turn organizational inputs into desired outputs.

_____ 11. A function of exceptions and problems in the transformational task of a department or organization.

_____ 12. The extent to which organizational subunits depend on each other for resources, raw material, or information.

_____ 13. The dependence of each unit upon the pooled resources generated by other units.

_____ 14. The dependence of each unit of the technology upon the activity of the unit that preceded it in a sequence.

_____ 15. The considerable interplay and feedback that must occur between the units performing a task in order to accomplish it properly.

_____ 16. The generation, aggregation, storage, modification, and speedy transmission of information made possible by the advent of computers and related devices.

True/False Questions

Circle the letter of the correct answer.

T F 1. There is no concrete evidence that the external environment has influence on organizations.
T F 2. Open systems take inputs from within and send them out as outputs.
T F 3. Customers are not part of an organization's external environment.
T F 4. Technology refers to ways of doing things as well as to machinery.
T F 5. Saturn is a new automobile venture by Ford.
T F 6. As uncertainty increases, cause-and-effect relationships become less clear.
T F 7. The OPEC oil embargo of 1973 had no effect on Detroit auto makers.
T F 8. Strategy is a device employed by chief executives to keep their jobs.
T F 9. Organizations usually tailor structure to strategy in coping with the environment.
T F 10. Economic forecasting is useful in predicting demands for goods and services.
T F 11. Major oil companies are usually horizontally integrated.
T F 12. Mergers and acquisitions can be effective in coping with resource dependence.
T F 13. Colleges and universities have now begun merging for strategic advantage.
T F 14. Interlocking directorates are prohibited by law when the firms are direct competitors.
T F 15. Organizations never really choose their technology.
T F 16. Engineering technologies deal with exceptions of input and require output by using standardized responses.
T F 17. Technological routineness deals with doing the same tasks everyday.
T F 18. The most famous study of the relationship between technology and structure was performed by Joan Woodward.
T F 19. Generally, successful firms that engage in mass production rely on mechanistic structure.
T F 20. The same technology that can de-skill jobs can often be used to build skill into new jobs.

Multiple-Choice Questions

Select the correct answer.

_____ 1. As gasoline prices dropped in the 1980s, consumers became interested in all of the following qualities of automobiles *except*
A. size.
B. style.
C. fuel economy.
D. performance.

_____ 2. All of the following are inputs of open environments *except*
A. capital.
B. people.
C. energy.
D. services.

_____ 3. All of the following are components of the external environment *except*
A. suppliers.
B. competitors.
C. customers.
D. workers.

_____ 4. CAD stands for
A. computer-aided-design.
B. computer-assisted-drawing.
C. college-aid-department.
E. college-adjunct-dormitory.

_____ 5. Environmental uncertainty exists under all of the following conditions *except* when the environment is
A. vague.
B. easy to diagnose.
C. unpredictable.
D. difficult to diagnose.

_____ 6. All of the following are types of environments in companies *except*
A. simple environments.
B. static environments.
C. abstract environments.
D. complex environments.

_____ 7. Strategy formulation involves determining all of the following aspects of the organization *except*
A. mission.
B. profits.
C. goals.
D. objectives.

_____ 8. The TRIAD strategic alliance brings together
A. General Motors, UAW & Saturn.
B. Singapore, Malaysia & Taiwan.
C. Simiens, Toshiba & IBM.
D. Canada, US & Mexico.

_____ 9. The Lawrence and Lorsch study demonstrates close connections between the following *except*
A. environment.
B. structure.
C. adaptation.
D. effectiveness.

_____10. Saturn was developed by General Motors
A. as a test site for new ideas about organizing.
B. to break the UAW.
C. because Tennessee made them an offer they couldn't refuse.
D. to plug a gap in their product line-up.

POST-TESTING FOR EXAMS

True/False Questions

Circle the letter of the correct answer.

T F 1. Manufacturing technologies are now giving up reliance on computers.

T F 2. Generally, unit technologies require more organic designs than mass technologies.

T F 3. Extreme division of labor is very desirable in advanced technology.

T F 4. The impact of advanced office technology on job design usually depends upon job status.

T F 5. A taxi company is an example of pooled interdependence.

T F 6. Mass production assembly lines are examples of short-linked technologies.

T F 7. Extensive technologies operate under reciprocal interdependence.

T F 8. Technological routineness is caused by boredom and job fatigue.

T F 9. Interlocking directorates can provide an effective method of coping with environmental uncertainty and resource dependence.

T F 10. A health spa would be considered an application of engineering technology using Perrow.

Multiple-Choice Questions

Select the correct answer.

_____ 1. All of the following are forms of strategic response *except*
A. vertical integration.
B. interlocking directorates.
C. hostile takeovers.
D. strategic alliances.

_____ 2. All of the following might be inputs in a hospital *except*
A. sick patients.
B. naive interns.
C. untrained nurses.
D. experienced doctors.

_____ 3. All of the following are parts of Perrow's technologies except for _________ technologies.
A. craft
B. ecological
C. engineering
D. routine

_____ 4. All of the following are part of Thompson's classification of technologies *except* for ________ technologies.
A. meditative
B. mediating
C. intensive
D. long-linked

_____ 5. All of the following are technology classifications by Woodward *except*
A. unit.
B. mass.
C. process.
D. product.

_____ 6. All of the following would be included in unit technology *except*
A. small batches to order.
B. mass produced items.
C. prototype production.
D. custom-tailored suits.

_____ 7. Information technology in the factory controls all of the following *except*
A. robots.
B. personnel.
C. automated inventory management.
D. computer-numcrically-controlled machine tools.

_____ 8. All of the following are trends in advanced manufacturing technology *except*
A. capitalization on computer intelligence and memory.
B. flexibility.
C. more jobs for workers.
D. integration with other advanced technologies.

_____ 9. All of the following are involved in advanced office technology *except*
A. text processing.
B. editing.
C. information storage and retrieval.
D. communication.

_____ 10. Which of the following is <u>not</u> a good reason to vertically integrate?
A. maintain high quality
B. reduce uncertainty about suppliers
C. increase flexibility
D. ensure access to marketing channels

_____ 11. Video display screens have provoked all of the following symptoms *except*
A. stress systems.
B. eyestrain.
C. muscular strain.
D. short attention span.

_____ 12. All of the following might be types of transformational processes *except*
A. physical processes.
B. ecological processes.
C. intellectual processes.
D. emotional processes.

_____ 13. When thrust into a foreign country, you might be faced with
A. simple environment.
B. environmental uncertainty.
C. resource dependence.
D. dynamic environment.

_____ 14. As environmental uncertainty increases several effects on organizations occur *except* that
A. cause-and-effect relationships become blurred.
B. priorities are harder to agree upon.
C. more information will be processed.
D. more people will be hired.

_____ 15. Problems faced by a newly formed small business today might include all of the following *except*
A. easily rentable office space.
B. credit-wary suppliers.
C. a lack of customers.
D. careful bank managers.

_____ 16. Lawrence and Lorsch studied all of the following industries *except*
A. plastics.
B. paper.
C. packaged food products.
D. pen and pencil manufacturing.

_____ 17. Lawrence and Lorsch examined problems faced by the following departments in each company *except*
A. sales.
B. personnel.
C. production.
D. research.

_____ 18. When a company like Nabisco is taken over by R. J. Reynolds, we have an example of
A. vertical integration.
B. mergers and acquisitions.
C. strategic alliances.
D. monopolizing.

_____ 19. Organizations can engage in strategic alliances with all of the following *except*
A. competitors.
B. suppliers.
C. unions.
D. governments.

_____ 20. In Thompson's classification of technologies an example of intensive technology might include
A. a general hospital.
B. an assembly line.
C. a bank.
D. a taxi company.

Application Situations Exercise

Match the key concept with the statements that best describe them.

A. Advanced information technology
B. Environmental uncertainty
C. External environment
D. Interest groups
E. Interlocking directorates
F. Open system
G. Pooled interdependence
H. Reciprocal interdependence
I. Resource dependence
J. Sequential interdependence
K. Strategic alliances
L. Strategy
M. Technological interdependence
N. Technological routineness
O. Technology
P. Vertical integration

____ 1. The oil company took over its sources of supply and distribution.

____ 2. It did so because it was dependent upon its natural resources which were becoming scarce.

____ 3. After gaining control of its supply sources, the company began relying more and more on computer generated data and information.

____ 4. It also sought to improve its activities and knowledge in order to turn inputs into desired outputs.

____ 5. The top executives met periodically to cope with changing environments and related problems.

____ 6. The executives first sought to cooperate with the independent companies.

____ 7. But workers and suppliers were unhappy with this arrangement.

____ 8. This uncertainty and lack of predictability made most of the executives unhappy.

____ 9. They blamed outside conditions for all of their problems.

____ 10. They felt that serving as directors of different companies might give them input into solving the oil company's problems.

Short Answer Questions

Fill-in the missing word(s).

1. All organizations must have potential ______________ for their products and services.

2. Successful organizations devote considerable energy to monitoring the activities of ______________.

3. Through the teaching process, educated individuals are returned to the community as ______________.

4. An example of social trends is the increasing public interest in ______________ .

5. Resource ______________ is recognized in a properly designed strategic alliance.

6. The concepts of technology and ______________ are closely related.

7. According to Perrow, routine technologies flourish best under ______________ structures.

8. Depending on how it is employed, a given form of advanced informational technology can have exactly ______________ effects.

9. ______________ depends upon the environment's complexity and its rate of change.

10. In general, advanced technology will cause a ______________ in the number of supervisory and middle management personnel in most organizations.

ANSWER SHEET FOR CHAPTER 16

PRE-TESTING YOUR UNDERSTANDING OF THE CHAPTER

Key Concepts Matching

1. C	2. F	3. D	4. B	5. I	6. L	7. P	8. K	9. E	10. O
11. N	12. N	13. G	14. J	15. H	16. A				

True/False Questions

1. F	2. F	3. F	4. T	5. F	6. T	7. F	8. F	9. T	10. T
11. F	12. T	13. T	14. T	15. F	16. T	17. F	18. T	19. T	20. T

Multiple-Choice Questions

1. C	2. D	3. D	4. A	5. B	6. C	7. B	8. C	9. C	10. A

POST-TESTING FOR EXAMS

True/False Questions

1. F	2. T	3. F	4. T	5. T	6. F	7. F	8. F	9. T	10. T

Multiple-Choice Questions

1. C	2. D	3. B	4. A	5. D	6. B	7. B	8. C	9. B	10. C
11. D	12. B	13. B	14. D	15. A	16. D	17. B	18. B	19. D	20. A

Application Situations Exercise

1. P	2. I	3. A	4. O	5. L	6. K	7. D	8. B	9. C	10. E

Short Answer Questions

1. customers	2. competitors	3. outputs	4. environmentalism	5. interdependence
6. environment	7. mechanistic	8. opposite	9. uncertainty	10. reduction

CASE STUDY

C&C GROCERY STORES INC.

The first C&C grocery store was started in 1947 by Doug Cummins and his brother Bob. Both were veterans who wanted to run their own business, so they used their savings to start the small grocery store in Charlotte, North Carolina. The store was immediately successful. The location was good, and Doug Cummins had a winning personality. Store employees adopted Doug's informal style and "serve the customer" attitude. C&C's increasing circle of customers enjoyed an abundance of good meats and produce.

As business grew, Doug used the store's profits to open two additional stores in the Charlotte area. Over a period of twenty years the C&C chain expanded up the East coast and through the southeastern United States. Growth was at a moderate rate, because Doug did not want to overextend the chain's resources or take chances. Giving customers good service and value were more important than rapid growth. During the 1970's new stores were opened in the South and reached as far west as Texas.

By 1984, C&C had over 200 stores. A standard physical layout was used for new stores. Company headquarters moved from Charlotte to Atlanta in 1975. The organization chart for C&C is shown in Exhibit 1. The central offices in Atlanta handled personnel, merchandising, financial, purchasing, real estate, and legal affairs for the entire chain. For management of individual stores, the organization was divided by regions. The southern, southeastern and northeastern regions each had about seventy stores. Each region was divided into districts of ten to fifteen stores each. A district director was responsible for supervision and coordination of activities for the ten to fifteen district stores.

Each district was divided into four lines of authority based upon functional specialty. Three of these lines reached into the stores. The produce department manager within each store reported directly to the produce specialist for the division, and the same was true for the meat department manager, who reported directly to the district meat specialist. The meat and produce managers were responsible for all activities associated with the acquisition and sale of perishable products. The store manager's responsibility included the grocery line, front-end departments, and store operations. The store manager was responsible for appearance of personnel, cleanliness, adequate check-out service, and price accuracy. A grocery manager reported to the store manager and maintained inventories and restocked shelves for grocery items. The district merchandising office was responsible for promotional campaigns, advertising circulars, district advertising and for attracting customers into the stores. The grocery merchandisers were expected to coordinate their activities with each store in the district.

During the recession in 1980-81, business for the C&C chain dropped off in all regions and did not increase with improved economic times in 1983-84. This caused concern among senior executives. They also were aware that other supermarket chains were adopting a trend toward one-stop shopping, which meant the emergence of super stores that included a pharmacy, dry goods and groceries - almost like a department store. Executives wondered whether C&C should move in this direction and how such changes could be assimilated into the current store organization.

Source: Case prepared by Richard L. Daft. From Daft, R.L. & Steers, R.M. (1986). *Organizations: A micro/macro approach*. Glenview, IL: Scott, Foresman.

However, the most pressing problem was how to improve business with the grocery stores they now had. A consulting team from a major university was hired to investigate store structure and operation.

Exhibit 1 Organizational Structure for C & C Grocery Stores, Inc.

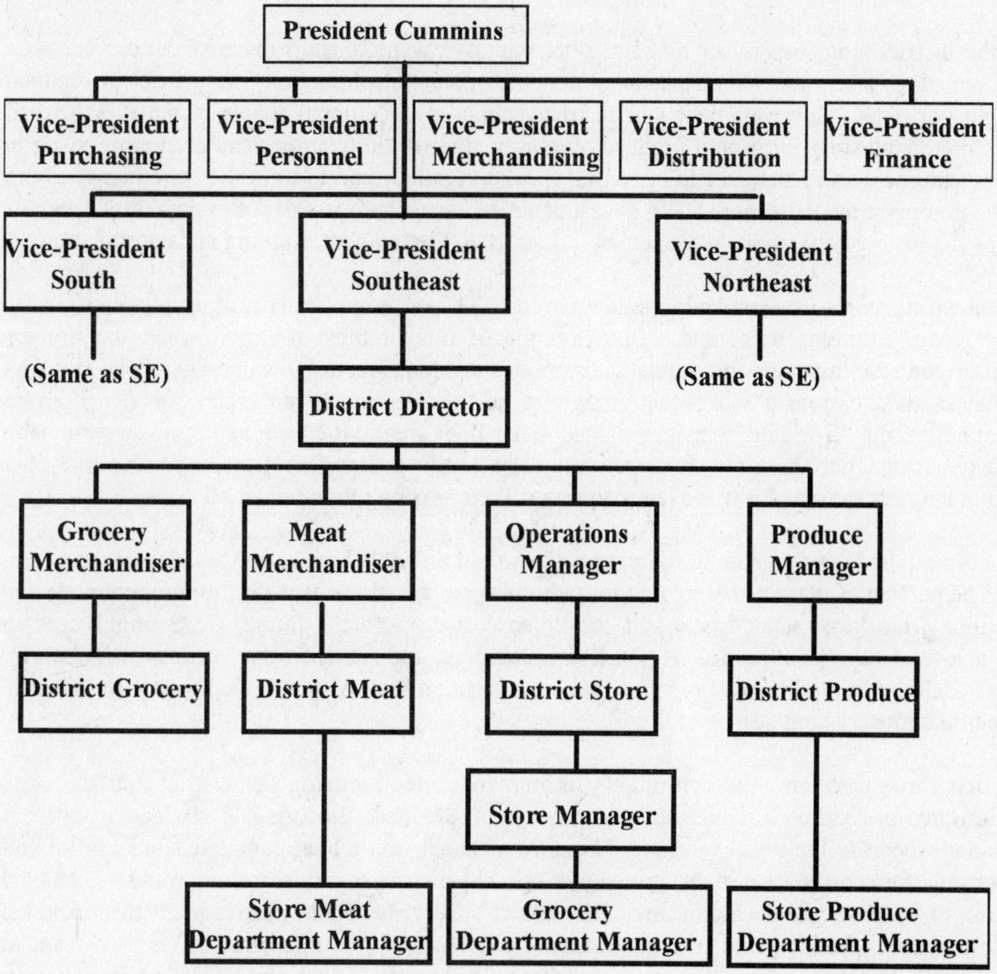

The consultants visited several stores in each region, talking to about fifty managers and employees. The consultants wrote a report that pinpointed four problem areas to be addressed by store executives.

1. The chain is slow to adapt to change. Store layout and structure were the same as had been designed fifteen years ago. Each store did things the same way even though some stores were in low-income areas and other stores in suburban areas. A new grocery management system for ordering and stocking had been developed, but after two years was only partially implemented in the stores.

2. Roles of the district store supervisor and the store manager were causing dissatisfaction. The store managers wanted to learn general management skills for potential promotion into district or regional management positions. However, their jobs restricted them to operational activities and they learned little about merchandising, meat, and produce.Moreover, district store supervisors used store visits to inspect for cleanliness and adherence to operating standards rather than to train the store manager and helpcoordinate operations with perishable departments. Close supervision on the operational details had become the focus of operations management rather than development, training and coordination.

3. Cooperation within stores was low and morale was poor. The informal, friendly atmosphere originally created by Doug Cummins was gone. One example of this problem occurred when the grocery merchandiser and store manager in a Louisiana store decided to promote Coke and Diet Coke as a loss leader. Thousands of cartons of Coke were brought in for the sale, but the stockroom was not prepared and did not have room. The store manager wanted to use floor area in the meat and produce sections to display Coke cartons, but those managers refused. The produce department manager said that Diet Coke did not help his sales and it was okay with him if there was no promotion at all.

4. Long-term growth and development of the store chain would probably require reevaluation of long-term strategy. The percent of market share going to traditional grocery stores was declining nationwide due to competition from large super stores and convenience stores. In the future, C&C might need to introduce non-food items into the stores for one-stop shopping, and add specialty sections within stores. Somestores could be limited to grocery items, but store location and marketing techniques should take advantage of the grocery emphasis.

To solve the first three problems, the consultants recommended reorganizing the district and the store structure as illustrated in Exhibit 2. Under this reorganization, the meat, grocery, and produce department managers would all report to the store manager. The store manager would have complete store control and would be responsible for coordination of all store activities. The district supervisor's role would be changed from supervision to training and development. The district supervisor would head a team that included himself and several mat, produce, and merchandise specialists who would visit area stores as a team to provide advice and help for the store managers and other employees. The team would act in a liaison capacity between district specialists and the stores.

The consultants were enthusiastic about the proposed structure. By removing one level of district operational supervision, store managers would have more freedom and responsibility. The district liaison team would establish a cooperative team approach to management that could be adopted within stores. The focus of some responsibility on a single manager would encourage coordination within stores, adaptation to local conditions, and provide a focus of responsibility for store-wide administrative changes.

The consultants also believe that the proposed structure could be expanded to accommodate non-grocery lines if enlarged stores were to be developed in the future. Within each store, a new department manager could be added for pharmacy, dry goods, or other major departments. the district team could be expanded to include specialists in these departments who would act as liaison for stores in the district.

1. Discuss the environmental components that are currently affecting C&C Grocery .

2. Apply the concepts of environmental uncertainty, resource dependence, and strategy to the C&C case.

3. In Thompson's terms, what technology does a grocery store chain use to deliver service to customers? That is, do the stores exhibit pooled interdependence (mediating technology), sequential interdependence (long-linked technology) or reciprocal interdependence (Intensive technology)? What are the implications of this technology for organizational design and coordination mechanisms?

Exhibit 2 Proposed Reorganization of C & C Grocery Stores Inc.

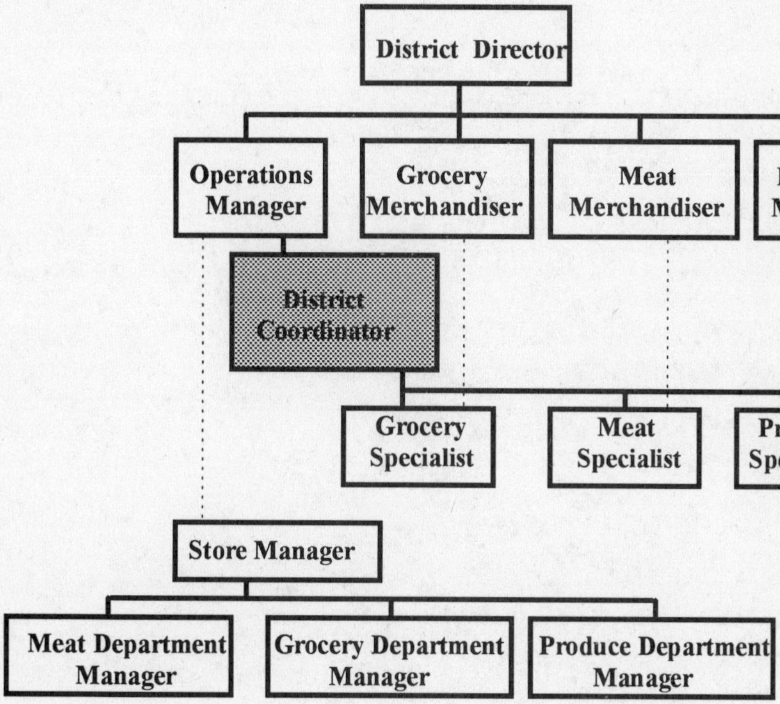

4. Using concepts from Chapter 15, compare and contrast the current organizational structure with that proposed by the consultants.

5. Evaluate the proposed structure in terms of C&C's environment, strategy, and technology. How will various personnel respond to the new structure?

CHAPTER 17

ORGANIZATIONAL CHANGE, DEVELOPMENT, AND INNOVATION

LEARNING OBJECTIVES

- EXPLAIN THE ENVIRONMENTAL FORCES THAT MOTIVATE ORGANIZATIONAL CHANGE.
- DESCRIBE THE BASIC CHANGE PROCESS AND THE ISSUES THAT REQUIRE ATTENTION AT VARIOUS STAGES OF CHANGE.
- EXPLAIN HOW ORGANIZATIONS CAN DEAL WITH RESISTANCE TO CHANGE.
- DEFINE ORGANIZATIONAL DEVELOPMENT (OD) AND DISCUSS ITS GENERAL PHILOSOPHY.
- DISCUSS TEAM BUILDING, SURVEY FEEDBACK, TOTAL QUALITY MANAGEMENT AND REENGINEERING AS OD EFFORTS.
- DISCUSS THE PROBLEMS INVOLVED IN EVALUATING OD EFFORTS.
- DEFINE INNOVATION AND DISCUSS THE FACTORS THAT CONTRIBUTE TO SUCCESSFUL ORGANIZATIONAL INNOVATION.
- UNDERSTAND THE FACTORS THAT HELP AND HURT THE DIFFUSION OF INNOVATIONS.

KEY CONCEPTS

Unfreezing

Change

Refreezing

Diagnosis

Change agents

Resistance

Organizational development (OD)

Team building

Survey feedback

Total Quality Management (TQM)

Reengineering

Organizational processes

Innovation

Creativity

Idea champions

Gatekeepers

Diffusion

CHAPTER SUMMARY

Key concepts are identified by **bold** *faced type.*

I. The Concept of Organizational Change

A. Why Organizations Must Change

All organizations are pressured to change by external sources (global economy, deregulation, changing technology) as well as by internal sources (low productivity, conflict, strikes, sabotage, high absenteeism and turnover). As environments change, organizations must keep pace and internal changes often occur in response to external pressures.

Although change is necessary, change for its own sake is not desirable, and organizations can have too much change as well as too little.

B. What Organizations Can Change

Organizations can change several aspects of their operations which include:

- Goals and strategies
- Technology
- Job design
- Structure
- People

In general, a change in one area often calls for changes in others, and changes in goals, strategies, and job design almost always require that serious attention be given to people changes.

C. The Change Process

The change process involves three basic stages:

1. **Unfreezing** which occurs when recognition exists that some current state of affairs is inadequate.
2. **Change** occurs when some program or plan is implemented to move the organization and its members to a more satisfactory state.
3. **Refreezing** occurs when the newly developed behavior, attitudes, or structures become an enduring part of the organizational system.

II. Issues in the Change Process

A. Diagnosis

Diagnosis provides information that contributes to unfreezing by showing that a problem exists, and further diagnosis can clarify a problem and suggest just what changes should be implemented.
Diagnosis can take many forms and be performed by a variety of individuals.

For serious problems, **change agents**, experts in the application of behavioral science knowledge to organizational diagnosis or change, should be consulted.

B. Resistance

Resistance occurs when people either overtly or covertly fail to support the change effort. People might resist change for many reasons which include: politics and self-interest, low individual tolerance for change, misunderstanding, lack of trust, different assessments of the situation, and a resistant organizational culture.

Resistance to change can often be reduced by involving the people who are the targets of change in the change process, ensuring good communication exists and perhaps, negotiating special incentives for change. Transformational leaders are also particularly adept at overcoming resistance to change.

C. Evaluation and Institutionalization

Evaluating change includes a consideration of reactions, learning, behavior and outcomes. Many evaluations of change initiatives never go beyond the measurement of reactions for fear of political reprisal if it is demonstrated that the change has failed.

If the change is evaluated favorably, the organization may wish to institutionalize it. That is, make whatever has changed a permanent part of the organizational system; a social fact that will persist despite possible turnover among those who actually experienced the change. But misaligned incentive systems, unrealistic expectations, improper socialization, turnover among sponsoring executives, and external pressures may all work against institutionalization.

III. Organizational Development: Planned Organizational Change

Organizational development (OD) is a planned, ongoing effort to change organizations to be more effective and more human.

OD generally recognizes that systematic attitude change must accompany changes in behavior.

IV. Some Specific Organizational Development Strategies

A. Team Building

Team building attempts to increase the effectiveness of work teams by concentrating on interpersonal processes, goal clarification, and role clarification. This process is a continuous one which involves regular diagnostic sessions, and further development exercises as needed.

B. Survey Feedback

Survey feedback involves the collection of data from organizational members and the provision of feedback about the results.

The most typical survey method is the anonymous questionnaire. The feedback is most effective when it is presented to natural working units in face-to-face meetings.

C. Total Quality Management (TQM)

Total Quality Management (TQM) is a systematic attempt to achieve continuous improvement in the quality of an organization's products and/or services. Typical characteristics of TQM programs include an obsession with customer satisfaction; a concern for good relations with suppliers; continuous improvement of work processes; the prevention of quality errors; frequent measurement and assessment; extensive training; and high employee involvement and teamwork.

Prominent names associated with the quality movement are W. Edward Deming, Joseph Juran, and Philip Crosby. TQM is mainly about achieving small gains over a long period of time. A continuum of continuous improvement exists which extends from such reactive strategies as responding to errors to more proactive strategies such as preventing errors, upgrading performance, and creating new products and services.

TQM is particularly known for specialized tools that empower employees to diagnose and solve quality problems themselves on an on-going basis:

- Flowcharts of work processes
- Pareto analysis
- Fishbone diagrams
- Statistical process control

D. Reengineering

Reengineering is the radical redesign of organizational processes to achieve major improvements in factors such as time, cost, quality, or service. **Organizational processes** are activities of work that have to be accomplished to create outputs that internal or external customers value.

Reengineering is most extensive in industries where a) much creeping bureaucracy has set in, b) large gains are available with advanced technology and c) competition has increased due to deregulation.

Because reengineering has the goal of radical change, it requires strong CEO support (transformational leader qualities help) and a clear strategy. Also, research demonstrates that reengineering must be both broad and deep to have long-lasting bottom-line results.

V. Does Organizational Development Work?

In general, most OD techniques have a positive impact on productivity and job satisfaction. OD seems to work better for managers or supervisors than for blue-collar workers. Also, changes that use more than one technique sees to have more impact. There are, however, great differences across sites in the success of OD interventions

VI. The Innovation Process

A. What Is Innovation?

Innovation is the process of developing and implementing new ideas in an organization. This can cover many different situations, although innovations are usually classified as product innovations or process innovations. Product innovations have a direct impact on the cost, quality, style, or availability of a product or service (VCR's, fax machines, 24 hour automated banking). Process innovations are new ways of designing products, making products, or delivering services (CAD/CAM, distance education).

B. Generating and Implementing Innovation Ideas

Innovation usually involves **creativity** which is the production of novel but potentially useful ideas. As a rule, creative people have an excellent technical understanding of their domain and additional *creativity-relevant* skills such as the ability to tolerate ambiguity, withhold early judgment, see things in new ways, and be open to new and diverse experiences. Creative people are not necessarily lacking in social skills, but do tend to be lower than average in their need for social approval.

People can be trained in creativity through the use of electronic brainstorming, nominal group techniques, and Delphi techniques.

Idea champions are people who recognize an innovative idea and guide it to implementation. The role of idea champion (or product champion or intrapreneur) is often an informal or emergent role and "guiding" the idea might involve talking it up to peers, selling it to management, garnering resources for its development, or protecting it from political attack by guardians of the status quo.

Effective communication both with the internal and external environments is also necessary for innovation. In some organizations, **gatekeepers** are people who span organizational boundaries to import new information, translate it for local use, and disseminate it.

Generally, decentralization, informality and a lack of bureaucracy tend to foster the information exchange that innovation requires. Also, abundant funds greatly enhance the chances of successful innovation, and both money and time are important spurs to the success of this process.

C. Diffusing Innovative Ideas

Diffusion is the process by which innovations move across an organization. Factors such as union resistance, lack of support by top management, conflict between the pilot project and the bureaucracy, among others, can hamper effective diffusion.

The rate of diffusion is often determined by factors that include the relative advantage of the new idea over the old, compatibility with the values and current practices of potential adopters, complexity - ability to comprehend the innovation, trialability - ability to give the innovation a limited trial run and observability - the visibility of consequences of use.

Despite its importance to the long term health of organizations, innovation is a political process, so it is necessary to find strong supporters at all company levels in order to ensure its success.

PRE-TESTING YOUR UNDERSTANDING OF THE CHAPTER

PRE-TESTING YOUR UNDERSTANDING OF THE CHAPTER

Key Concepts Matching

Match the letter of the key concepts with the appropriate definitions.

A. Change
B. Change agents
C. Creativity
D. Diagnosis
E. Diffusion
F. Gatekeepers
G. Idea champions
H. Innovation
I. Organizational development
J. Organizational processes
K. Reengineering
L. Refreezing
M. Resistance
N. Survey feedback
O. Team building
P. Total Quality Management
Q. Unfreezing

_____ 1. That which occurs when recognition exists that some current state of affairs is inadequate.

_____ 2. The process by which newly developed changes in behavior, attitude, or structure become an enduring part of the organizational system.

_____ 3. That which provides information that contributes to unfreezing by showing that a problem exists.

_____ 4. Experts in the application of behavioral science knowledge to organizational diagnosis and change.

_____ 5. That which occurs when people either overtly or covertly fail to support the change effort.

_____ 6. A planned, ongoing effort to change organizations, to be more effective and more human which uses the knowledge of behavioral science to foster a culture of self examination and a readiness for change.

_____ 7. An attempt to increase the effectiveness of work teams by concentrating on interpersonal processes, goal clarification, and role clarification.

_____ 8. The implementation of a program or plan to move an organization and/or its members to a more satisfactory state.

_____ 9. Collecting data from organizational members and feeding it back to them in a series of meetings in which the data is explored and discussed.

_____ 10. Activities or work that have to be accomplished to create outputs that internal or external customers value.

_____ 11. The radical redesign of organizational processes to achieve major improvements in factors such as time, cost, quality, or service.

_____ 12. The process of developing and implementing new ideas in an organization.

_____ 13. The production of novel but potentially useful ideas.

_____ 14. People who recognize an innovative idea and guide it to implementation.

_____ 15. People who span the boundary between the organization and the environment, imparting new information, translating it for local use, and disseminating it to project members.

_____ 16. The process by which innovations move across an organization.

_____ 17. A systematic attempt to achieve continuous improvement in the quality of an organization's products and/or services.

True/False Questions

Circle the letter of the correct answer.

T F 1. Unfreezing occurs when retired executives return to the corporation.
T F 2. A change in one area very often calls for changes in other areas.
T F 3. Diagnosis can usually be performed only by an expert.
T F 4. Change agents handle tolls on super highways.
T F 5. Good communication can often overcome resistance to change.
T F 6. Involving the targets of a change process can also help overcome resistance to change.
T F 7. Transformational leaders are usually unable to deal with resistance to change.
T F 8. OD usually stands for Office Donations.
T F 9. Team building is focused mainly on improving organized sports.
T F 10. Reengineering proposes a more radical change agenda than TQM.
T F 11. TQM is primarily concerned with "soft" skills and uses littl e real measurement.
T F 12. Feedback is most effective when presented to natural work units in face-to-face meetings.
T F 13. Because reengineering focuses on organizational processes, there is little need for upper management involvement or leadership.
T F 14. Creative people tend to be socially skilled but lower than average in need for social approval.
T F 15. Most OD techniques have negative effects on productivity and work attitudes.
T F 16. Most organizations prefer not to encourage innovation.
T F 17. Research shows that creative people have an excellent technical understanding of their domain.
T F 18. Idea champions are people paid to espouse a particular new idea.
T F 19. Effective communication is necessary for successful innovation.
T F 20. Gatekeepers let people into buildings after regular office hours.

Multiple-Choice Questions

Select the correct answer.

_____ 1. All of the following factors might call for organizational change *except*
A. strikes.
B. high profits.
C. high turnover.
D. poor morale.

_____ 2. Organizations can usually change all of the following *except*
A. job design.
B. technology.
C. structure.
D. corporate identity.

_____ 3. All of the following sequences take place during change *except*
A. thawing.
B. unfreezing.
C. change.
D. refreezing.

_____ 4. All of the following are possible reasons for resisting change *except*
A. lack of trust.
B. politics and self-interest.
C. low tolerance for change.
D. flexibility.

_____ 5. All of the following are variables involved in evaluating change *except*
A. reactions.
B. learning.
C. compensation.
D. outcomes.

_____ 6. The city of _______________ has made extensive use of team building.
A. Chicago
B. Tacoma
C. Philadelphia
D. New York

_____ 7. TQM uses all of the following tools *except*
A. chicken-bone analysis.
B. flowcharts of work processes.
C. pareto analysis.
D. statistical process control.

_____ 8. Part of the survey feedback involves
A. polling customers about products.
B. checking on competition.
C. collecting data from organizational members.
D. surveying the latest federal laws.

_____ 9. All of the following are aspects of reengineering *except*
A. there is an emphasis on incremental change.
B. jobs are redesigned and usually enriched.
C. a strong emphasis is placed on teamwork.
D. advanced technology is exploited.

_____ 10. Which of the following is not a strategy on the continuous improvement continuum?
A. prevent errors
B. upgrade performance
C. provide service
D. create a new product or service

POST-TESTING FOR EXAMS

True/False Questions

Circle the letter of the correct answer.

T F 1. Money and time are usually necessary to develop innovation.

T F 2. Freedom and autonomy are the most cited organizational factors leading to creativity.

T F 3. Diffusion refers to the factors that weaken the development of innovative ideas.

T F 4. Despite lack of support from top management, good new ideas will be accepted by most corporations.

T F 5. The Chicago Marriott's experience with bathroom tv's and ironing boards is a good illustration of the value of pareto analysis.

T F 6. Harley-Davidson is a good example of how successful change can bring a firm back from the edge of disaster.

T F 7. Unscrupulous firms use reengineering to work around patents and create knock-off products.

T F 8. OD is usually a spontaneous effort which is seldom planned.

T F 9. Change occurs when some program or plan is adopted to move the organization to a more adequate state.

T F 10. As a rule, people in failing organizations will not resist change.

Multiple-Choice Questions

Select the correct answer.

_____ 1. Causes of resistance to change include all of the following *except*
A. politics and self-interest.
B. weak socialization.
C. different assessments of the situation.
D. lack of trust.

_____ 2. All of the following conclusions are true about OD *except* that
A. most OD techniques have positive impacts on productivity and job satisfaction.
B. OD seems to work better for supervisors than for blue-collar workers.
C. changes that use more than one technique have more impact.
D. most OD techniques are a costly waste of time and effort.

_____ 3. Process innovations involve all of the following *except*
A. new product designs.
B. new ways of delivering services.
C. new ways of compensating workers.
D. new ways of making products.

_____ 4. Which of the following is a model of how innovation usually works?
A. idea generation > idea implementation > idea diffusion
B. idea generation > idea diffusion
C. idea creativity > idea diffusion
D. idea creativity > idea generation > idea implementation

_____ 5. All of the following are creativity-relevant skills *except*
A, ability to tolerate uncertainty.
B. being open to new experiences.
C. being prone to snap judgments.
D. seeing things in new ways.

_____ 6. People who help guide new ideas through to implementation are called
A. mentors.
B. gate keepers.
C. idea champions.
D. change agents.

_____ 7. When seeking new ideas, successfully innovative firms go directly to all of the following groups *except*
A. competitors.
B. customers.
C. workers.
D. clients.

_____ 8. All of the following might hinder diffusion *except*
A. lack of support by top management.
B. union support.
C. union resistance.
D. conflict with bureaucracies.

_____ 9. All of the following factors are determinants of the rate of diffusion *except*
A. compatibility.
B. complexity.
C. observability.
D. profitability.

_____ 10. All of the following are apt to foster innovation *except*
A. informality.
B. centralization.
C. lack of bureaucracy.
D. decentralization.

_____ 11. The early project design team for the Mazda RX-7 had members from many departments, but <u>not</u> from
A. sales marketing.
B. production.
C. cost accounting.
D. service.

_____ 12. Post-its are a product developed at
A. IBM.
B. 3M.
C. Apple.
D. Digital Equipment.

_____ 13. The technical expertise "Willie G." Davidson brings to Harley Davidson was acquired at
A. The Cranbrook Institute.
B. MIT.
C. The Pasadena Art Center College of Design.
D. MacPherson Junior High School.

_____ 14. The essential idea for Federal Express (FedEx) was first set down
A. on the back of an envelope.
B. on a co-op work assignment.
C. by a marketing research firm.
D. in an economics term paper.

_____ 15. The most typical data gathering approach in organizations involves
A. oral questions.
B. anonymous questionnaires.
C. computer surveys.
D. small, selected samples.

_____ 16. The limited influence of the Saturn project on General Motors is best explained by
A. poor product appeal.
B. difficulties in moving from a non-union to a unionized environment.
C. barriers to diffusion.
D. poor diagnosis.

_____ 17. All of the following are possible methods of organizational development *except*
A. team building.
B. quality circles.
C. survey feedback.
D. mergers and alliances.

_____ 18. Resistance to change can often be reduced by
A. firing those who resist.
B. offering rewards to those who support change.
C. involving the targets of change in the change process.
D. pressuring the resistors.

_____ 19. All of the following are issues in the change process *except*
A. diagnosis.
B. restructuring.
C. resistance.
D. evaluation and institutionalization.

_____ 20. As a result of reading this chapter, you should realize that
A. successful organizations do not need to change.
B. modern technology has eliminated the need to change.
C. all organizations must change.
D. change is usually a costly, wasteful and useless process.

Application Situations exercise

Match the key concepts with the statements that best describe them.

A. Change
B. Change agents
C. Creativity
D. Diagnosis
E. Diffusion
F. Gatekeepers
G. Idea champions
H. Innovation
I. Organizational development
J. Organizational processes
K. Reengineering
L. Refreezing
M. Resistance
N. Survey feedback
O. Team building
P. Total Quality Management
Q. Unfreezing

_____ 1. Our managers recognized the need for change when they discovered that our profits were falling.

_____ 2. They brought in experts in behavioral science to find out what the problems were and how to correct them.

_____ 3. These experts suggested a radical redesign of organizational processes.

_____ 4. The experts also suggested that the organization encourage the process of developing and implementing new ideas.

_____ 5. These experts even suggested the production of novel but potentially useful ideas.

_____ 6. Our managers hoped that new ideas and innovations would move across the organization.

_____ 7. But some people failed to support the change effort.

_____ 8. The managers tried using people who recognize the value of new ideas and help guide them through to implementation.

_____ 9. When this didn't work, the managers tried collecting data from all concerned personnel and feeding it back to them for discussion.

_____ 10. As time passed, some of the new ideas and changes in behavior and structures became an enduring part of the organizational system.

Short Answer Questions

Fill-in the missing word(s).

1. Common experience indicates that organizations are far from ________________.

2. In theory, organizations can change any aspect of their ________________ they wish.

3. Low tolerance for change is mainly an ________________ matter.

4. Reengineering focuses a great deal of attention on ________________.

5. Once we get beyond subnormal intelligence, there is no ________________ between level of intelligence and creativity.

6. Championing an innovation is usually a(n) ________________ role.

7. A list of the "quality gurus" of TQM fame would include ________________.

8. Placing more emphasis on "soft" process skills like managing change and innovation and less on acquiring "hard" factual knowledge is a hallmark of ________________.

9. ________________ are particularly adept at overcoming resistance to change.

10. The process by which a change becomes a permanent part of the organizational system is called ________________.

ANSWER SHEET FOR CHAPTER 17

PRE-TESTING YOUR UNDERSTANDING OF THE CHAPTER

Key Concepts Matching

1. Q	2. L	3. D	4. B	5. M	6. I	7. O	8. A	9. N	10. J
11. K	12. H	13. C	14. G	15. F	16. E	17. P			

True/False Questions

1. F	2. T	3. F	4. F	5. T	6. T	7. F	8. F	9. F	10. T
11. F	12. T	13. F	14. T	15. F	16. F	17. T	18. F	19. T	20. F

Multiple-Choice Questions

1. B	2. D	3. A	4. D	5. C	6. B	7. A	8. C	9. A	10. C

POST-TESTING FOR EXAMS

True/False Questions

1. T	2. T	3. F	4. F	5. T	6. T	7. F	8. F	9. T	10. F

Multiple-Choice Questions

1. B	2. D	3. C	4. A	5. C	6. C	7. A	8. B	9. D	10. B
11. C	12. B	13. C	14. D	15. B	16. C	17. D	18. C	19. B	20. C

Application Situations Exercise

1. Q	2. B	3. K	4. H	5. C	6. E	7. M	8. G	9. N	10. L

Short Answer Questions

1. static
2. operations
3. individual
4. abandoned
5. correlation
6. informal or emergent
7. Deming or Juran or Crosby
8. organizational learning
9. transformational leaders
10. institutionalization

CASE STUDY

EREHWON MANAGEMENT CONSULTANTS, INC.

Erehwon Management Consultants, Inc. (EMC) is a general consulting firm with offices in six cities, employing about 100 full-time consultants. Until recently, it had exhibited an enviable growth record based on just two "products." The firm's President began to see a slow down due to both of these products rapidly entering the mature phases of their respective life cycles. In addition, he felt that the pace of work had become too intense and that by gradually bringing down the consultant's workload, it would be advantageous to the firm in retaining less stressed employees.

Cultural Norms Before the Change Program

EMC, like many other firms in the industry, saw its success equated to billable hours and high consultant utilization rates. In other words, the success and even continued existence of EMC depended on, at a minimum, covering the fixed expenses (salary plus overhead and fringes) for its consulting staff. As a result, everyone at EMC watched the weekly "hours billed to clients."

Consultants at all levels were encouraged, usually in indirect ways, to "keep busy" on client efforts and to sell follow-up engagements. At performance review time and at promotion time, it was made explicit that sales and hard work for clients were the keys to personnel career growth at EMC. Partners seemed to be always on the road, calling on potential and current clients, seeking to reach the sales quotas. No organized marketing was done as it implied (to the partners) an unprofessional image.

A New Strategy for EMC

The President and the six partners that headed up the offices of EMC met for two days to address his concerns of an impeding slowdown and the "quality of life" issue. Since EMC had emphasized sales during its entire existence as a firm and had seen sales success equated with capitalizing on its two existing products, no R&D or new product development efforts had been attempted to date.

To address the slowdown and at the same time, to enhance the consultant quality of work life, the following strategy was formulated by the group:

- De-emphasize sales and billable hours as a measure of consultant performance.
- Set aside approximately five percent of each consultant's time (i.e., three hours per week) for R&D time. Each consultant could use such time for self-improvement of consulting skills, new product idea generation, or researching new industries to which to market existing products.
- Try to schedule consultants so that those who spent extensive time on the road (i.e., on client work) were occasionally "rewarded" with local assignments or officially recognized new product development projects (also not requiring travel).

Source: Buchowicz, B. (1990, Summer). Culture transition and attitude change. *Journal of General Management*. 45-55.

The Change Program

The President's committee realized that this new strategy represented a substantial departure from the previous approach. However, a sense of urgency seemed to dictate that the new strategy must be put in place without delay.

The head of EMC's largest office, a partner with the firm's best sales record, was given responsibility for designing implementation of the plan. His program centered on the following steps:

- Firm-wide, each consultant would receive a memo from the President stating the new strategy and the need to change.
- In each office, the partner in charge would convene the consultants to explain the new situation and encourage each consultant to develop new product ideas.
- Each office would decide on the travel and "time off" procedures so as to cause minimal disruption to clients.

The President's one-page memo was distributed about two weeks later. It took nearly three months to schedule each of the six offices to have their staff meetings, since clients seemed to continually uncover "major" crises that required consultants on-site.

Consultants' Response

The President's memo surprised and perplexed most of EMC's consultants. In essence, it stated that EMC was evolving into an organization that was willing to invest in its future through its employees. The arguments were vague and the memo seemed to lack the feeling of urgency that had originally motivated the President to act on his concerns. Few if any of the consultants seemed to seriously accept the memo as representing a real change affecting them, at least not in the near future.

The office meetings also seemed to be missing a clear sense of urgency or rationale. In several of these sessions, the partner in charge seemed less than enthusiastic and was even heard to convey that "this is temporary - don't let it affect your *real* work!"

After the meetings were over, life at EMC seemed unchanged. Partners still hustled about, responding to any and all sales leads and consultants were promoted or let go on the basis of their "partnership potential," i.e., the ability to generate business.

Moreover as the expected sales slump began to be felt earlier than anticipated, cold calling and visiting previous clients seemed to become everyone's primary activities. Even some client work in progress was slowed in order to free more staff to make sales calls.

Sales did ultimately resume, albeit spread across a variety of products and markets which lacked any cohesive theme. Partners and consultants never really changed their focus on sales. The "new program" quickly disappeared from the scene.

1. Describe the culture of Erehwon Management Consultants before and after the change effort.

2. Discuss in detail the reasons for the failure of the change effort.

3. Account for the resistance the change effort encountered. After all, the changes seem beneficial to the consultants.

4. Discuss how the techniques of team building and quality circles might have been applied at EMC.

5. Explain the factors that appear to work against "product" innovation at EMC.

6. With hindsight, how might the president have acted differently to achieve his goals?

CHAPTER 18

CAREERS

LEARNING OBJECTIVES

- DEFINE THE MEANING OF THE TERMS CAREER, EXTERNAL CAREER, INTERNAL CAREER, AND OCCUPATIONAL IDENTITY AND EXPLAIN WHY THE STUDY OF CAREERS IS IMPORTANT IN TODAY'S ORGANIZATIONS.

- EXPLAIN HOW PEOPLE'S REACTIONS TO A JOB RESULT FROM THE INTERACTION OR FIT BETWEEN CAREER ORIENTATION AND WORK ENVIRONMENT.

- DISCUSS HOLLAND'S THEORY OF CAREER TYPES AND SCHEIN'S THEORY OF CAREER ANCHORS.

- DEFINE THE LIFE STAGES AND CAREER STAGES ADULTS GENERALLY GO THROUGH DURING THEIR WORKING LIVES AND DISCUSS KEY TASKS ASSOCIATED WITH THE EXPLORATION STAGE DURING ONE'S EARLY CAREER.

- DISCUSS THE CAREER AND PSYCHOSOCIAL FUNCTIONS OFTEN ACCOMPLISHED THROUGH A MENTORING RELATIONSHIP AND IDENTIFY SPECIAL PROBLEMS THAT WOMEN AND MINORITIES FACE IN ESTABLISHING THIS RELATIONSHIP.

- DEFINE CAREER RESILIENCE AND DISCUSS CAREER STRATEGIES FOR DEVELOPING A RESILIENT CAREER.

- EXPLAIN DIFFERENT INITIATIVES ORGANIZATIONS CAN USE TO ENCOURAGE AND SUPPORT EMPLOYEES' EFFORTS TO DEVELOP RESILIENT CAREERS.

KEY CONCEPTS

Career

Age norms

External career

Career stages

Internal career

Social network

Career orientation

Mentor

Theory of career types (Holland)

Apprentice

Theory of career anchors (Schein)

Reality shock

Biosocial life stages

Career skills portfolio

Skill benchmarking

CHAPTER SUMMARY

Key concepts are identified by **bold** *faced type heading.*

I. Why Study Careers?

In recent years, organizations have changed dramatically. Downsizing or rightsizing, reengineering, and restructuring have resulted in flatter hierarchies, broader and more complex jobs, and the outsourcing of work to consultants and other firms. The career landscape has changed accordingly.

II. The Changing Career Landscape

A **career** is an evolving sequence of work activities and positions that individuals experience over time as well as the associated attitudes, knowledge, and competencies that develop throughout one's life. An **external career** is the sequence of positions that comprise one's career. An **internal career** is the individual's interpretation of objective work experiences known only from a person's own subjective sense of external events.

In addition to describing how an individual moves over a path through time, the concept of career also captures the interaction of individual and organizational factors as well as how careers provide occupational identity.

III. Individual Differences In Career Orientation

Career orientation is defined in terms of the preferred activities, talents, and attitudes that people have, and there are several ways of describing them.

A. Holland's Theory of Career Types

Holland's theory of career types: John Holland's theory identifying six distinct patterns of career orientation: conventional, artistic, realistic, social, enterprising, and investigative.

- The *conventional* type prefers rule-regulated orderly activities that generally include organizing written or numerical information. These people perform well in accounting and finance jobs and represent the most dominant career type in business occupations.

- The *artistic* career types prefer ambiguous and unsystematic activities that entail creative expression in written, spoken, or visual forms.

- The *realistic* career type prefers activities that require the physical manipulation of objects or tools in a well-ordered work environment.

- The *social* type prefers activities that involve informing, helping, or developing others. Nursing and teaching are occupations which typically fit the social type.

- The *enterprising* type prefers to focus their energies on leading and controlling others in order to reach specific organizational goals or obtain economic gain.

- The *investigative* person prefers activities that involve observing and analyzing phenomena in order to develop knowledge and understanding.

Holland's theory is concerned mainly with career choice, and is the basis for such vocational counseling used in schools to guide students into majors and career paths that are consistent with their interests.

B. Schein's Theory of Career Anchors

Schein's **theory of career anchors** identifies five distinct patterns of self-perceived talents, motives, needs, and values that evolve as one faces early work experiences: technical/functional competence, managerial competence, security, autonomy, and creativity.

- *Technical/functional competence* describes people for whom the primary factor in their career choices and decisions is the actual content of work.

- *Managerial competence* describes people whose ultimate goal is to rise to positions of managerial responsibility.

- *Security* describes people whose main goal in career planning and decision making is the development of long-term life stability and security.

- *Autonomy* describes those who greatly desire independence and freedom in an organizational setting and are willing to give up advancement to maintain it.

- *Creativity* minded people desire greatly to create something that is entirely of their own making.

C. Managerial Implications of Career Orientation

In general, people who run organizations should take into account individual orientation differences when managing human resources. Thus, all people cannot be treated the same, and managers should take steps to understand and identify key individual differences.

IV. Career and Adult Life Stages

A. Adult Life Stages

Biosocial life stages are the alternating periods of stability and transition, with predictable themes that are based in psychological and biological factors and patterns of social expectations. **Age norms** are the widely accepted expectations in society about appropriate behavior for a person at a given age.

One popular theory about adult life stages starts with *early adult transition* (ages 17-22), moves through *entering adulthood* (22-28), *Age 30 transition* (28-33), *settling down* (33-40), *mid-life transition* (40-45) and the *middle adulthood era* (45-60) until it reaches the *late adult transition & late adult era* (60+). Much of what individuals go through as they move through these stages has to do with measuring choices and incorporating new values, interests, and behaviors into an altered lifestyle. It is important for organizations to be aware of such potential differences in how their employees are experiencing their workplace obligations.

B. Career Stages

Career stages are general patterns of developmental issues, key tasks, and changes in work role activities such as those in exploration, establishment, advancement and maintenance, and late career.

Exploration is a time of discovery and choice. During this stage, people explore various occupational roles (including part-time work and summer jobs) and test out an initial occupational identity. Success at this stage is often helped if an individual is able to establish a social network of relationships, get a job that challenges their skills and abilities, and cope with the emotional side of work.

A **social network** consists of a group of one's peers, subordinates, and senior people who provide general information about what is going on in the organization as well as specific advice on how to accomplish job assignments and feedback about the consequences of different career strategies.

Substantial research confirms the importance of finding a mentor early in one's career. A **mentor** is an older or more senior person in the organization who gives a junior person special attention, such as giving advice and creating opportunities. An **apprentice** is a junior person, sometimes called a protégé, who has a mentor.

A challenging first job can have a lasting impact on people's careers. Many young people entering the work force will experience **reality shock**. This is an unsettling experience caused by the disparity between unrealistic expectations that people often have and the reality that they confront in their first job.

Establishment occurs when an individual establishes himself or herself as an independent contributor in a fairly specific area of expertise.

Advancement and maintenance occur when people focus on advancing toward key career objectives. These might include desires for promotion and titles.

Late career is a time when many people have reached their highest levels of responsibility and status within the organization. At this stage, people begin to think about retirement and pensions and often withdraw energy from career pursuits and become more concerned with nonwork factors.

Individuals who voluntarily (or involuntarily) leave existing careers to start new ones will usually recycle through an abbreviated sequence of these same four stages. As economic uncertainty and rapid technological change continue, there may be many for whom "recycling" to avoid waste hits close to home.

V. Managing a Successful Career

Various issues play a role in the creation of a successful career. Individual efforts may be supplemented by organizational efforts, especially those of mentors. It is also important to carefully balance the demands of work and family, especially in the complex world of dual career families.

A. Organizational Career Management

Many organizations have adopted performance appraisal/career planning programs which include a yearly appraisal meeting between supervisors and subordinates. However, human resource programs must focus on the long-term development of "human capital" and anticipate future job transitions employees should experience to achieve payoffs useful to the organization and the employee.

To be effective, such programs should heed these guidelines:

- Link individual development to business strategy.
- Connect career development actions to other human resource practices.
- Get line managers involved and hold them accountable for career development activities.
- Give career development activities high visibility

B. The Role of the Mentor

A mentor provides a number of career enhancing benefits to an apprentice which include:

- sponsorship
- exposure and visibility
- coaching and feedback
- developmental assignments.

Mentors can also provide certain psychosocial benefits that are helpful in developing the apprentice's self-confidence, sense of identity, and ability to cope:

- role-modeling
- acceptance and confirmation
- counseling

There are also benefits that flow to the mentor which might include having the apprentice perform mundane tasks. But mentors can also gain a feeling of competence and self worth and have their "generosity" needs met by doing successful mentoring.

Women face a particular problem when dealing with mentors. As women in executive positions remain in relative short supply, there are fewer feminine role models for them to follow and most possible mentors are men. Men are often less helpful as mentors in such relationships as they have little experience with women in roles other than wife, mother, or daughter. Mixed gender mentoring relationships can also be undermined by rumors of sexual behavior and research demonstrates that the often important informal after-work social activities that normally build such relationships are much less in evidence for that reason.

Limited racial and ethnic diversity at the top of organizations similarly constrains the mentoring opportunities available to younger minority group employees.

C. Work-Family Issues and Careers

Both the continuing increase in women's labor force participation and the pattern of economic insecurity and increasing work demands fed by downsizing and restructuring are making coping with work-family issues critical to career success in the 1990's.

Work-family conflicts vary across differing family situations and career stages (e.g., compare the possibilities for conflict for a single employee without children to those of a dual career couple with children and an aging parent to care for).

Research has identified several coping strategies such as:

- reducing or modifying the demands and expectations of others (boss, spouse, etc.)
- arrange for some flexibility in the work role
- spousal support

Obviously, organizations can do their part here. First, organizations must give employees accurate information about position demands and career paths available. Second, organizations need to provide flexible work arrangements that can lessen conflicts and may even reduce organizational costs. Finally, organizations can provide support services to help employees facing these conflicts.

VI. Developing a Resilient Career

Thinking of oneself as self-employed, even if employed in a large organization, will help to build a resilient career. There are a number of career strategies that can help people anticipate problems, manage the inevitable career twists and turns and keep their "career business" on track.

- *Know yourself.* What is your occupational identity? Strengths and weaknesses?.
- *Know your business environment.* What is happening to your company and to its industry?
- *Manage your reputation.* Make your achievements and unique skills visible.
- *Stay marketable, mobile, and always developing.* Maintain current skills and develop new skills.
- *Be both specialist and generalist.* Develop a deep competency in an area to establish yourself as a clear expert, but also develop general competencies in a broader range for versatility. A **career skills portfolio** is the sum total of one's occupational skills, abilities, and knowledge.
- *Document your accomplishments.* Results achieved and identifiable accomplishments sell well.
- *Always have a contingency plan and be ready to move.* Be open to geographic mobility.
- *Keep financially and psychologically fit.* Enough money in reserve to make it through a couple of months and some stress management skills can go a long way.

VII. Promoting Career Resilience: The Organization's Role

Organizations have a lot to gain by encouraging and facilitating employee efforts to keep their career skills vital and viable. Career resilience initiatives include:

- *Career planning programs.* Help employees work through the planning process.
- *Career counseling.* Aid employees in exploring career alternatives.
- *Career information systems.* Provide computer-assisted resource and search capability.
- *Skill benchmarking and assessment.* **Skill benchmarking** is the process of identifying required competency levels for key jobs in an industry.
- *Strategic direction and business performance information.* How are we doing?
- *Extensive education and training support.* Tuition refund, in-house training, etc.
- *Workplace flexibility.* Allow flexibility and choice in the roles that employees take on over their careers.

PRE-TESTING YOUR UNDERSTANDING OF THE CHAPTER

Key Concepts Matching

Match the letter of the key concept with the appropriate definitions.

A.	Age norms	I.	Internal career
B.	Apprentice	J.	Mentor
C.	Biosocial life stages	K.	Reality shock
D.	Career	L.	Skill benchmarking
E.	Career orientation	M.	Social network
F.	Career skills portfolio	N.	Theory of career anchors (Schein)
G.	Career stages	O.	Theory of career types (Holland)
H.	External career		

_____ 1. A sequence of work activities and positions, and associated attitudes and reactions experienced over a person's life.

_____ 2. Objective paths that employees follow in a organization as seen by external observers.

_____ 3. The individual's subjective interpretation of the meaning of various work experiences which can be known only from the point of view of the actor.

_____ 4. The preferred activities, talents, and attitudes that people have.

_____ 5. A documented theory of career orientation which uses six distinct patterns to explain many people's career orientation.

_____ 6. A theory of career types involving anchors which develop well after childhood and adolescence.

_____ 7. Stages of life associated with adult aging processes and patterns of social expectations that exist in society.

_____ 8. Widely accepted expectations in society about appropriate behavior for a person's age.

_____ 9. General patterns of developmental changes in work and role activities that are distinct from life stages.

_____ 10. A senior person in an organization who gives a junior person special attention.

_____ 11. A junior person in an organization who receives the help of a mentor.

_____ 12. The disparity between unrealistic expectations that people often have and the reality that they confront in their first job.

_____ 13. The sum total of one's occupational skills, abilities, and knowledge.

_____ 14. The process of identifying required competency levels for key jobs in an industry.

_____ 15. A group of one's peers, subordinates, and senior people who provide general information about what is going on in the organization.

True/False Questions

Circle the letter of the correct answer.

T F 1. A career involves moving on a path over time.
T F 2. People in our society are often identified by their careers.
T F 3. John Holland was a pioneer in the study of motivation.
T F 4. Nursing and teaching are occupations which fit the artistic career type.
T F 5. Holland's theory is primarily concerned with financial rewards from careers.
T F 6. Career anchors refer to one's tenure in a job.
T F 7. Creativity anchored people want to manage companies.
T F 8. Treating people differently is satisfying to those involved and helps the organizations to achieve its goals.
T F 9. Between ages 33-40 people begin to settle down in careers.
T F 10. Society puts pressure on people of a certain age to act in a certain fashion.
T F 11. In the exploration career stage people travel to jobs in different areas.
T F 12. It is no longer necessary to find a mentor in one's career.
T F 13. Late career is a time of growth only for a few people.
T F 14. Human resource programs need to focus on the long-term development of "human capital".
T F 15. Being a woman is not usually a barrier to finding a mentor.
T F 16. It is in the best interest of organizations to help employees deal with work-family conflicts.
T F 17. A network of class peers can provide functions not provided by the mentor.
T F 18. Mentors receive no benefit from the function.
T F 19. Women who become executives have usually had a mentor along the way.
T F 20. Knowing about the company is more important than knowing about yourself when making career choices.

Multiple-Choice Questions

Select the correct answer.

_____ 1. All of the following are elements in the meaning of a career *except*
A. moving on a path over time.
B. the intervention between the individual and the organization.
C. the seeking of the biggest rewards.
D. providing occupational identity.

_____ 2. All of the following are some of Holland's career types *except*
A. enterprising.
B. enthusiastic.
C. social.
D. artistic.

_____ 3. All of the following are some of Schein's career anchors *except*
A. autonomy.
B. security.
C. creativity.
D. ambition.

_____ 4. Managers can treat people differently by taking all of the following steps *except*
A. develop steps to match employees to their work environments.
B. understand individual differences and employee reactions.
C. identify job factors that deal with these differences.
D. reward all employees exactly the same way.

_____ 5. Our age norms refer to
A. our loss of strength as we age.
B. our waning health.
C. social expectations of appropriate behavior.
D. our physical appearance as we age.

_____ 6. All of the following are usually involved in the exploration stage *except*
A. traveling to different countries.
B. coping with the emotional side of work.
C. getting a challenging job.
D. establishing a social network.

_____ 7. All of the following are recognized career stages *except*
A. exploration.
B. establishment.
C. advancement and maintenance.
D. retirement and pension.

_____ 8. All of the following would be involved in career planning programs *except* for
A. individual identification of goals and abilities.
B. identification of career options within the organization.
C. identification of career options within other organizations.
D. establishment of specific career goals.

_____ 9. All of the following are psychosocial functions of mentoring *except*
A. role-modeling.
B. direct supervision.
C. acceptance and confirmation.
D. counseling.

_____ 10. The career functions of mentoring might include all of the following *except*
A. sponsorship.
B. coaching and feedback.
C. aiding financially.
D. exposure and visibility.

POST-TESTING FOR EXAMS

True/False Questions

Circle the letter of the correct answer.

T F 1. In the late career stage, people work harder and harder for the company.

T F 2. Careers provide people with chances to develop and to receive financial rewards.

T F 3. Each of us differs in terms of skills, values, goals and preferred activities.

T F 4. The enterprising career type is the most common career type found in business occupations.

T F 5. People who end up in careers different from their career orientation tend to be unhappy at work.

T F 6. Career counseling advises students about the most lucrative jobs.

T F 7. Men and women generally follow the same career stages.

T F 8. As we age, we begin to realize our own mortality.

T F 9. A social network consists of one's peers and one's mentor.

T F 10. Organizations have a large stake in the effective management of people's careers.

Multiple-Choice Questions

Select the correct answer.

_____ 1. Psychosocial functions of mentoring include all of the following *except*
A. counseling.
B. castigating.
C. role modeling.
D. acceptance and confirmation.

_____ 2. You should do all of the following to develop a resilient career *except*
A. know yourself.
B. document your accomplishments.
C. be either a specialist or generalist.
D. manage your reputation.

_____ 3. A mentor is most apt to be
A. a female co-worker.
B. a subordinate.
C. an older member of upper management, usually male.
D. one's lover.

_____ 4. Skill benchmarking attempts to identify required competency levels within
A. organizations.
B. individuals.
C. industries.
D. jobs.

_____ 5. All of the following have pioneered work in career development *except*
A. Peter Drucker.
B. John Holland.
C. Edgar Schein
D. D. J. Levinson.

_____ 6. All of the following are recognized life stages *except*
A. early adult transition.
B. retirement and demise.
C. settling down.
D. mid-life transition.

_____ 7. An occupation most suitable for a realistic career type might be
A. carpenter.
B. salesperson.
C. teacher.
D. negotiator.

_____ 8. An artistic career type might be happiest as a
A. manager.
B. salesman.
C. designer.
D. manager.

_____ 9. An investigative career type might be happiest as a
A. manager.
B. scientist.
C. financier.
D. salesman.

_____ 10. Recycling in the career context refers to
A. finding a career in the fast-growing environmental sector.
B. falling back on knowledge or skills from a previous occupation.
C. repeating the sequence of career stages after changing careers.
D. the phenomenon that labor markets track the business cycle.

_____ 11. After ages 33-40, people begin to
A. become restless and fretful.
B. settle down and focus on goals.
C. seek thrilling new adventures.
D. experiment with drugs.

_____ 12. During the establishment stage of career development, people
A. seek new jobs.
B. become contributors with specific expertise.
C. experiment with drugs.
D. think about retirement.

_____ 13. In the late career stage people
A. seek new jobs.
B. think of advancement.
C. think about retirement.
D. look for mentors.

______14. All of the following are described in Schein's theory of career anchors *except*
A. Autonomy.
B. Creativity.
C. Identity.
D. Security.

_____ 15. Which of the following pairs of Holland's career types is the most unlikely combination?
A. conventional & realistic
B. artistic & social
C. realistic & investigative
D. investigative & enterprising

_____ 16. Women often have a difficult job in finding mentors because
A. most mentors are senior males.
B. the women refuse to cooperate.
C. the organization discourages them.
D. the women are too intelligent.

_____ 17. Effective career oriented human resources programs are
A. ambiguous.
B. integrated.
C. unbalanced.
D. capricious.

_____ 18. Reality shock occurs when we
A. see the reality of our first job.
B. realize that we are mortal.
C. realize that we will age.
D. see ourselves in the mirror.

_____ 19. Younger workers often look upon senior workers as
A. wise mentors.
B. experienced resources.
C. old-timers.
D. potential managers.

_____ 20. The best career choice you can make is to seek a career that
A. pays the most money.
B. offers the most perquisites.
C. meets your personal skills and needs.
D. offers the most prestige.

Application Situations Exercise

Match the key concepts with the statements that best describe them.

A. Age norms
B. Apprentice
C. Biosocial life stages
D. Career
E. Career orientation
F. Career skills portfolio
G. Career stages
H. External career
I. Internal career
J. Mentor
K. Reality shock
L. Skill benchmarking
M. Social network
N. Theory of career anchors (Schein)
O. Theory of career types (Holland)

_____ 1. After finishing college, she needed help in deciding what type of work she should do based on her talents and needs.

_____ 2. When she did go to work, she was surprised at the differences between what she expected and the reality of the workplace.

_____ 3. Her work was good and she was promoted rapidly.

_____ 4. But despite the titles, she wasn't fully satisfied with the work.

_____ 5. She finally received the help of a senior staff member who advised her about work and advancement strategies.

_____ 6. Her mentor told her to review the sum total of her occupational skills, abilities and knowledge.

_____ 7. She was then able to compare this with the required competency levels for her job in the industry.

_____ 8. As she grew older, however, her promotions stopped, and she began to think more and more of retirement.

_____ 9. Upon retirement, she decided that she generally had had a satisfactory series of work activities during her forty-year working period.

_____ 10. She then bought a motorcycle and began to behave in a way that people didn't expect in an elderly woman of 63.

Short Answer Questions

Fill-in the missing word(s).

1. The term _____________, which is borrowed from sports, is a good way to describe the necessity to manage one's own career .

2. Another name for an apprentice is a _____________ .

3. The artistic career orientation is the most dissimilar to the ____________ type.

4. Holland's theory is the basis for much ____________ counseling.

5. ____________ is the major disillusionment with one's life often suffered in the 40-45 year old period.

6. ____________ -anchored people are unique in their overarching desire to create something that is entirely of their own making.

7. Holland's ____________ career type will probably be most comfortable in semi-skilled or crafts positions.

8. If the appraisal of an external career is objective, then the experience of one's internal career is ____________ .

9. Successful careers involve a good fit between individuals and their ____________ environments.

10. In general, careers should not be left to luck, but should be ____________ .

ANSWER SHEET FOR CHAPTER 18

PRE-TESTING YOUR UNDERSTANDING OF THE CHAPTER

Key Concepts Matching

1. D	2. H	3. I	4. E	5. N	6. O	7. C	8. A	9. G	10. J
11. B	12. K	13. F	14. L	15. M					

True/False Questions

1. T	2. T	3. F	4. F	5. F	6. F	7. F	8. T	9. T	10. T
11. F	12. F	13. T	14. T	15. F	16. T	17. T	18. F	19. T	20. F

Multiple-Choice Questions

1. C	2. B	3. D	4. D	5. C	6. A	7. D	8. C	9. B	10. C

POST-TESTING FOR EXAMS

True/False Questions

1. F	2. T	3. T	4. F	5. T	6. F	7. F	8. T	9. T	10. T

Multiple-Choice Questions

1. B	2. C	3. C	4. D	5. A	6. B	7. A	8. C	9. B	10. C
11. B	12. B	13. C	14. C	15. D	16. A	17. B	18. A	19. C	20. C

Application Situations Exercise

1. E	2. K	3. H	4. I	5. J	6. F	7. L	8. G	9. D	10. A

Short Answer Questions

1. free agent	2. protégé	3. conventional	4. guidance
5. mid-life crisis	6. creativity	7. realistic	8. subjective
9. work	10. planned		

CASE STUDY

PAMELA JONES, FORMER BANKER

Pamela Jones enjoyed banking. She had taken a battery of personal aptitude and interest tests that suggested she might like and do well in either banking or librarian ship. Since the job market for librarians was poor, she applied for employment with a large chartered bank, the Bank of Winnipeg and was quickly accepted.

Her early experiences in banking were almost always challenging and rewarding. She was enrolled in the bank's management development program because of her education (a BA. in languages and some postgraduate training in business administration), her previous job experience, and her obvious intelligence and drive.

During her first year in the training program, Pamela attended classes on banking procedures and policies and worked her way through a series of low level positions in her branch. She was repeatedly told by her manager that her work was above average. Similarly, the training officer who worked out of the main office and coordinated the development of junior officers in the program frequently told Pamela that she was "among the best of three" of her cohort of twenty trainees.

Although she worked hard and frequently encountered discrimination from senior bank personnel (as well as customers) because of her sex, Pamela developed a deep seated attachment to banking in general and to her bank and branch, in particular. She was proud to be a banker and proud to be a member of the Bank of Winnipeg.

After one year in the management development program however, Pamela found she was not learning anything new about banking or the BofW. She was shuffled from one job to another at her own branch, cycling back over many positions several times to help, meet temporary problems caused by absences, overloads and turnover. Turnover - a rampant problem in banking - amazed Pamela. She couldn't understand for many months, why so many people started careers "in the service" of banking, only to leave after one or two years.

After her first year, the repeated promises of moving into her own position at another branch started to sound hollow to Pamela. The training officer claimed that there were no openings suitable for her at other branches. On two occasions when openings did occur, the manager of each of the branches in question rejected Pamela, sight unseen, presumably because she hadn't been in banking long enough.

Pamela was not the only unhappy person at her branch. Her immediate supervisor, George Burns, complained that because of the banks' economy drive, vacated customer service positions were left unfilled. As branch accountant, Burns was responsible for day-to-day customer service. As a result, he was unable to perform the duties of his own job. The manager told Burns several times that customer service was critical, but that Burns would have to improve his performance on his own job. Eventually, George Burns left the

---

Source: Pinder, C.C. (1984). *Work motivation: Theory, issues and applications.* Glenview,IL: Scott, Foresman.

bank to work for a trust company, earning seventy dollars a month more for work similar to that which he had been performing at the BofW. This left Pamela in the position of having to supervise the same tellers who had trained her, only a few months earlier. Pamela was amazed at all the mistakes the tellers made, but found it difficult to do much to correct their poor work habits. All disciplinary procedures had to be administered with the approval of Head Office.

After several calls to her training officer, Pamela was finally transferred to her first "real" position in her own branch. Still keen and dedicated, Pamela was soon to lose her enthusiasm.

At her new branch, Pamela was made "assistant accountant." Her duties included the supervision of the seven tellers, some customer service and a great deal of paper work. The same economy drive that she had witnessed at her training branch resulted in the failure to replace customer service personnel. Pamela was expected to "pick up the slack" at the front desk, neglecting her own work. Her tellers seldom balanced their own cash, so Pamela stayed late almost every night to find their errors. To save on overtime, the manager sent the tellers home while Pamela stayed late, first to correct the teller's imbalances, then to finish her own paper work. He told Pamela that as an officer of the bank, she was expected to stay until the work of her subordinates and her own work, were satisfactorily completed. Pamela realized that most of her counterparts in other BofW branches were willing to give this sort of dedication; therefore, so should she. This situation lasted six months with little sign of change in sight.

One day, Pamela learned from a phone conversation with a friend at another branch that she would be transferred to Hope, British Columbia to fill an opening that had arisen. Pamela's husband was a professional, employed by a large corporation in Vancouver. His company did not have an office in Hope; moreover, his training was very specialized, so that he could probably find employment only in large cities anyway.

Accepting transfers was expected of junior officers who wanted to get ahead. Pamela inquired at Head Office and learned that the rumor was true. Her training officer told her, however, that Pamela could decline the transfer if she wished, but couldn't say how soon her next promotion opportunity would come about.

1. Depressed, annoyed, disappointed and frustrated, Pamela quit the bank.

2. Contrast Pamela Jones' external career with her likely conception of her internal career.

3. Compare Pamela's occupational self-concept (her needs, aptitudes, and preferences) with the opportunities, constraints, and demands of the banking jobs she held. In doing this, try to describe her in terms of Holland's theory of career types and Schien's theory of career anchors.

4. In career stage terminology, Pamela was at the exploration stage and perhaps into the establishment stage during the events described in the case. In terms of career stage concepts, what were some critical events or issues that affected Pamela?

5. Imagine that you are Pamela's mentor during the period described in the case. What advice would you give her?

6. Advise the bank on how to improve its career management system.

➢ NOTES ➣

➤ NOTES ◄

➢ NOTES ➣

➢ NOTES ⮘

➢ NOTES ➣